SMOKE AND MIRRORS

A Church Deceived over Sexuality

Sarah Sedgwick

Smoke and Mirrors

Copyright© Transformed Ministries

INDEPENDENTLY PUBLISHED

ISBN: 9798880382231

1st Edition

Contents

This book is dedicated to my sister Becky. For your love, support, advice and ability to make me laugh, I am forever grateful!

With grateful thanks to all who have supported me as I have written this book. Particular thanks to Michele & Anita for their dedication to editing and to all the members of the Transformed Family who have selflessly shared their testimony.

CHAPTER 1 - INTRODUCTION

Sitting in the hair salon, colour in my hair, I was chatting to God about my next move. To put it in context, just that morning I had finally signed the contract to sell my business which had been all consuming for the past ten years. Being a software provider for sports clubs meant user support was offered seven days a week, 364 days of the year, and even when I had been able to snatch a few days away, the phone and laptop were a permanent fixture. Service level agreements being what they are, I was duty bound to check my phone for messages at least once an hour between 8am and 10pm every day (although I can't honestly say that I was always that meticulous), but I am sure you get the idea? It was a tie, a commitment that required dedication and passion.

But passion for the business was not something I had any longer. Since becoming a Christian four and a half years earlier, it had become increasingly apparent to me that my future was not in business, but in God's business, and my enthusiasm for being self-employed took a nose-dive.

Here I was, free at last, basking in that moment of freedom, understanding that this was always part of God's grand plan for my life. Now I was asking the question, what next?

Do not get me wrong, it is not that I did not have an idea where God was leading me; on the contrary, I had a good idea! It was more about homing in on His plan now that I was free to do whatever He asked of me, checking in to confirm whether I was on the right path. You see, God had already set the ball rolling over the previous few months and the future was becoming clearer every day. Indeed, as the business sale was planned and negotiated, I had been on the receiving end of several miracles and blessings which were all pointing to a niche ministry, namely talking to the Church about sexuality and faith.

Looking back, I see that God had been working from many different angles, masterminding several events that had led me to this point in time, setting the scene and catapulting me into an uncertain yet exciting future.

The first angle, and blessing number one, was the imminent publication of my first book. I had drafted this book just one year into my Christian walk but had not been successful in getting a publishing deal. Frustratingly, two publishers had provided valuable feedback very quickly after I had first written it, but neither were able to publish. One felt that their audience were "evangelical" and as such they were the wrong publisher for me, the other was concerned that the topic of the book (namely my freedom from same sex attraction (SSA)) may compromise them as a Christian publishing house.

I continued to submit the manuscript to a few of the larger, well known publishing houses, who can take up to a year to respond, but I had no success. Disheartened, particularly through recognising that writing about freedom from SSA would elicit mixed reactions, even in the Christian publishing world, I had let my book take a back seat.

A visit to the Cherish ladies conference in 2018 jolted me into action. Lisa Harper was one of the keynote speakers, and whilst I only have a few notes in my journal from her talk, underlined on that page in my journal is a reference to Psalm 68. If I am honest, I do not remember much of the talk, or the context, yet what I do remember is that immediately after having heard her speak I was inspired. I sat, surrounded by a few thousand women who were worshipping God, and I wrote the following:

> *"Nothing should stop me from trying to get this book published. The enemy would have me believe that I should delay, but that is not so. I have a ministry, I have a calling, I must speak out and use my experiences. God*

has SHAPED me, and my past is part of my shape. I am
an oak of righteousness, I am an overcomer, God chose
me specifically and as such I will not let Him down."

Without realising it I had pinpointed the issue very succinctly, the enemy (namely Satan) was lying to me, and I had been listening. Looking back, that reference to Psalm 68 was clearly more significant than I realised at the time, and I now see it is a Psalm that echoes my passion and desires for the Church to stand firmly on the Word of God and battle the lies of Satan as he seeks to destroy the Church.

May God arise, may his enemies be scattered; may his
foes flee before him. Psalm 68:1 (NIV)

Praise be to the Lord, to God our Saviour, who daily bears
our burdens. Our God is a God who saves; from the
Sovereign Lord comes escape from death. Surely God will
crush the heads of his enemies, the hairy crowns of those
who go on in their sins. Psalm 68:19-21 (NIV)

God wants to set his people free; salvation is available to all in the form of freedom from sin and death. That is our message of hope. But those who refuse to turn from their sinful ways will be crushed, trapped by the sin they love and destroyed by death; this applicable to all who fail to repent, who fail to see their actions or behaviours as sinful. God sent Jesus to die for our freedom and we can celebrate the formidable promise we have from Him of eternal life as we love Him, yet, through repentance, show reverent fear of the consequences of our sin. This was the message that I so desperately wanted to deliver to a generation through sharing my story, but equally, this a message that Satan so desperately wanted to silence.

My time at Cherish was the push I needed, and as my journal entry clearly illustrated, I finally recognised that inaction was not an option. I decided there and then that I would not return to Cherish the following year without a book contract. And that was the start of a roller coaster ride where God provided abundantly. He provided the finances as I crowd funded the book.

He boosted my confidence which had taken a nosedive after I failed to secure a publishing deal, and he provided a publisher who agreed to publish my book. I was excited that finally the truth of God's word was going to be launched into the public domain.

The words I had written in my journal were indeed prophetic. I did have a calling, and what was soon to become my longed-for ministry was drawing ever closer as blessing number two unfolded.

Journaling has played an important part in my walk with the Lord and this second blessing is also recorded in an entry in May 2019, where I wrote this bold question of God:

> *"Lord may my testimony touch one thousand lives this year."*

The very next day I received an email from the Christian Institute, asking if they could feature me in a short video encompassing the main points of my testimony and to share what my message would be to others who may be questioning their sexuality. This, the answer to my prayer journaled the day before, was as the result of an email I had sent to the Christian Institute at the start of the year and was an incredible response from God. I knew that the work of the Christian Institute supported the authority of God's word, and that through asking me to feature in this film, they were recognising my story as one that was valid in a society where voices like mine were so often ignored or silenced.

Filming this video via Skype just a few days later, I was both terrified and excited. I was aware that God had answered my prayer in such a powerful way, and I felt a weight of responsibility. I was acutely aware of the impact this video would have if I could just get my point across well. A lot of prayer went into that day, and I knew from the moment the camera went live that the Holy Spirit was indeed speaking for me, as God's word says, *'for the Holy Spirit will teach you at that time what you should say[1]*. Looking back, I

---

[1] Luke 12:12 NIV

was relaxed, I did not overthink, and I was able to articulate my feelings succinctly yet with true clarity.

At the point of writing, the Christian Institute video[2] has already been viewed over twenty thousand times (surely an answer to that original prayer to touch 1,000 lives). Even more relevant to this story is that it was shared to the Methodist Evangelicals Together (MET) Facebook page by one of those viewers, and that led to blessing number three.

At the time the video was released, the Methodist Church of Great Britain were on the verge of meeting for their annual conference, where, amongst other things, they were scheduled to talk about a proposal to affirm same sex marriage within the Church. As with any divisive topic, there were many differing opinions, and the video I had featured in was posted on a couple of unofficial Methodist Facebook pages. These postings elicited a range of comments and feedback, some of which were quite unpleasant and intensely personal. The blessing for me came from the posting on the MET page, as this resulted in the MET team, who watched the video, inviting me to speak at a fringe event at the Methodist conference. Indeed, they told me later that my testimony had been an answer to prayer, as they had fervently prayed for someone from within the Methodist church to come forward with a testimony of freedom from homosexuality.

This invitation was a significant blessing, because it gave me both a platform to share my personal story of God's transforming love, but also confirmed my feelings that my voice should be heard. The level of confusion, of hurt, of compromise, and the misinterpretation of Scripture that I witnessed via social media alone, convinced me that the church was in crisis. I realised there and then that a full-time ministry was essential, if God were to use me to shine light into the church as it battled the ultimate deception, namely the lie that homosexual acts are not sinful.

Three blessings, three pivotal moments in my life led me to this point in time. I had the confidence to sell my business yet not seek another job,

[2] https://youtu.be/b-61Buc9-ug

the confidence to set up Transformed Ministries not really knowing where that would take me, and the confidence to say, God, over to you.

My personal journey (which you can read about in my first book, Transformed by God's Love[3]), was a journey of exploration. God called to me after I had lived as a lesbian for over thirty years. From God first speaking to me, to the time I surrendered my life to Him, I spent many hours studying God's word, trying to understand what it meant for me and my relationship with Him. Having worked through argument and debate from both ends of the spectrum, I was finally convicted of the authority of God's word and the transformative love he offered me. This gave me a perspective that few have experienced, and it opened my eyes to the fact that Christianity is under significant attack from Satan, his chosen tool, gender identity and sexuality. This includes physical attack (in the form of persecution of individuals and churches), moral attack, as we are targeted for maintaining strong moral teaching related to our Biblical roots and finally intellectual attack, whereby false teachers are causing many to question their strongly held beliefs and values.

So, back to the hair salon, back to that oh so important question, what next? And as I looked up and saw the reflection of another mirror in my mirror, the words came into my head, "smoke and mirrors." That was the point where I knew what God was saying, He was calling me to highlight deception, to look at how Christianity is being attacked on several fronts via a form of smoke and mirrors, or more precisely, deceit and lies.

I saw quite clearly in that moment that Satan was using the illusion of "smoke and mirrors" and many Christians have been completely fooled by his illusion. Jesus himself said that those who believe will also be subject to Satan's deception, he references these in Matthew 24 as "the elect".

---

[3] Transformed by God's Love, Exploring issues of sexuality in the Christian faith – Sarah Sedgwick, Kingdom Publishers 2019

For false messiahs and false prophets will appear and
perform great signs and wonders to deceive, if possible,
even the elect. Matthew 24:24 (NIV).

This is just one of many references in the Bible which will be explored later in this book which stand out as a dire warning that, "in the end times Christians will be deceived."

To be clear on my theory, according to Wikipedia "smoke and mirrors" is a classic technique in magical illusions that makes an entity appear to hover in empty space. The phrase has become more widely used in our language today to describe a theory or proposal that when studied closely proves to be an illusion. It can also be described as trickery or deception and historically refers to those stage magicians who used a combination of smoke and mirrors to trick their audience into seeing something that is not there, or not seeing something that is there, in order to perform elaborate illusions.

And here we are today, in an era of smoke and mirrors, in the time which Isaiah warned us about, when we are told that people will call evil good and good evil.

Woe to those who call evil good and good evil, who put
darkness for light and light for darkness, who put bitter for
sweet and sweet for bitter.
Isaiah 5:20 (NIV).

It is certainly true that within the culture of the western world, the boundaries between good and evil are often blurred and, in some cases they are non-existent. I would go as far as to suggest that same-sex relationships, which just a few decades ago were morally unacceptable, are now openly endorsed and celebrated. On the other hand, evangelical Christianity is now seen by many as promoting a morally unacceptable stance towards homosexuality. This is a definite reversal of our Christian understanding of good and evil.

An example of this is from a recent post I made on social media on my ministry page. The post simply said:

"I'm looking for UK based Christians who have a testimony of being "Changed" (freedom from SSA) who would be interested in featuring in a book of testimony. If you or someone you know may be interested, please ask them to contact me."

The following day I received a message from a friend that someone who had seen the post on her timeline was threatening to report it as hate speech. I was horrified to say the least. Reading and re-reading the post I could see nothing in it that could be classed as hate fuelled. Yet this is the world and the times we live in; if Christians speak out against gay marriage, they potentially risk being labelled as homophobic or accused of hate speech. Unfortunately, the voices of those who talk of freedom from SSA are increasingly being targeted in an attempt to keep us silenced. But it is difficult to silence testimony which speaks the truth of our experience and relationship with God and this book will use testimony to shatter the illusion that Satan has worked so hard to achieve.

Should this turn of events surprise us? On reading the Bible, probably not, for from the beginning of time we are told that Satan was the craftiest of all the beasts.

Now the serpent was more crafty than any of the wild animals the LORD God had made. He said to the woman, "Did God really say, 'You must not eat from any tree in the garden'?" Genesis 3:1 (NIV)

The Bible is clear that Satan will continue to seek to deceive into the end times, yet despite the warnings and all that is written about Satan the deceiver, there are many church attending Christians who have come to believe the lies. Many Christians, in the UK and other parts of the western world today, do not agree with the Bible that homosexual acts are sinful. In fact, many do not agree that sex outside of marriage is an issue if the circumstances fit their own definitions of morality.

An example close to my heart is that of the Methodist Church in the UK, who in 2019 voted on a motion which consents in principle to the marriage of same sex couples on their premises, these ceremonies being overseen by Methodist ministers, probationers, or members of the Methodist church. The proposal did not just scrape through, it passed by two hundred and forty-seven votes to forty-eight votes, which is a ratio of five to one.

Other denominations have also been sucked into worldly thinking. The United Reformed Church have introduced same sex marriage, and this was passed by a vote of two hundred and forty to twenty-one. The Church of England are well on the path to this, and the Scottish Episcopal Church introduced it after a positive vote from six of their seven synods. It is not difficult to see the way that some elements of the church are moving.

And that is why I have authored this book, which seeks to explore what the Bible teaches us about Satan's deceit and how this impacts the way we live as Christians. It is written to question what impact this understanding has on how we view sexuality and faith in the twenty first century.

> Do not conform to the pattern of this world but be transformed by the renewing of your mind. Then you will be able to test and approve what God's will is-his good, pleasing, and perfect will. Romans 12:2 (NIV)

Throughout the following chapters I will look at smoke, as it relates to both the smoke of Satan and the holy smoke of God, seeking to illustrate how easily we can be swayed by persuasive arguments and subtle deception. I will also look at mirrors and how as Christians, we are to mirror God's character, with a recognition that Satan will twist that and seek to persuade us to mirror the fallen values of this world. Because of the nature of my testimony and my passion for freedom within the church, I will focus on the area of sexuality. However, lies and deceit are used extensively by Satan to pull any of us away from a walk with God. My hope is that much of what you read can be transposed to other situations that Christians may face, including the intense attack on gender identity which is having such a damaging effect on our young people today.

A question for all of us as we consider the content of this book and our own understanding and attitude towards sexual sin is this, 'at the end of time whose judgment seat will I stand before?' Will it be Stonewall, the British parliament, the BBC (or other news media), the LGBTQ+ lobbies on social media, the established church? Or will I stand before God's throne, where His truth, as expressed in his Word (our Bibles), will stand out as the truth and no longer be negotiable or open to human interpretation? This is a particularly important question for us to consider.

Finally, to conclude this introduction, it is important to me that I make it clear that God loves us all. Whatever your own situation or relationship with God, these matters need to be discussed and thought about at the point that you want to explore who God is for you. There are many people who have no desire for a relationship with God and as such, who am I to author a book to insist that His plans and designs for humanity are to be obeyed by us all? It is to those who want to know more, who desire to understand and are searching for answers, that this is written. If you want to know God then I am convinced that you (as I did) want to know everything about his nature, his character, and his plans for your life and for the lives of all His children.

Some of what you hear from God will challenge you; it may cause disbelief, tears, anger, and confusion. Satan will use these emotions to distract you and draw you away from the truth. But when you focus on God's voice, and His voice alone, you will soon move through all that and experience joy, and God's outrageous love. As you develop the gift of discernment, you will recognise that God's rules for living (based on the ten commandments) are designed for our best interest and to create an environment in which we can thrive. My prayer is that this book will help you look past the smoke and mirrors to see the truth of who God is and why he calls us to a level of holiness that the world cannot understand.

Chapter 2 – In the Beginning

"Beloved, do not believe every spirit, but test the spirits to see whether they are of God; for many false prophets have gone out into the world." The counterfeits of the adversary often exceed the believer's expectation. If the Lord's people will humble themselves by admitting that deception is quite possible to them, they will be the less deceived." Watchman Nee[4]

Are we humble enough to recognise that some deception is possible, even probable, in the church today? Without recognition of this we may as well give up because there are too many voices for all to be true, too many differences of opinion both within and between denominations. Even within an average church congregation on a Sunday morning you will find those who believe homosexual acts are wrong, those who believe that they are good and acceptable in God's sight, and those who sit on the fence. The fence sitters have either not yet made their minds up or have not had reason to even think about their opinion. It is clear to see that deception is real, alive, and active in the church today, and we know from Scripture that it has been around since the Garden of Eden.

The Old Testament provides us with some essential background. It is here that we have the account of Satan's first deception in the Garden of Eden. But more than that, we have several key passages that give us clear warnings of the deception to come. Passages which speak prophetically of a time when there will be a change in moral values which will result in generations seeing good as evil and evil as good.

What better place to start then than with Genesis and that first deception? "Did God really say that?" This is a question I am certain Satan has

---

[4] The Spiritual Man by Watchman Nee, Living Stream Ministry (1998)

whispered in the ear of every believer at some point in time. Certainly, I have been on the receiving end of that question many times as Satan seeks to muddy the water and lead me away from God. It makes sense, doesn't it? As soon as we decide to follow Jesus or start to explore what following Jesus looks like, Satan is going to do all he can to discredit our faith, to make us weak, and James was clear in how we should respond to this:

> *Do not waver, for a person with divided loyalty is as*
> *unsettled as a wave of the sea that is blown and tossed by*
> *the wind. But let him ask in faith, with no doubting, for the*
> *one who doubts is like a wave of the sea that is driven and*
> *tossed by the wind. James 1:6 (NIV)*

Here, James encourages us to ask God in faith. We can ask God for clarity and guidance on anything. Once we receive His answer, we must stick to it, no longer doubting, no longer allowing Satan to ask, "Did God really say...?"

As a young Christian I was guilty of being "blown and tossed like the wind," but I was only a baby being nurtured on the milk of God's word. Over time, as I have matured, I no longer drink the milk but eat the solid food of God's word, which has given me a firm foundation on which to stand when Satan, the accuser comes calling.

Being rooted in God's word is so important because as soon as we listen to that seed of doubt, we open the door to more prods and pokes from Satan. On many occasions I have been on the receiving end of Satan's attempt to make me feel that homosexual acts are OK with God, (even as someone who has found freedom from sexual sin). Just read this article he whispers, listen to this podcast he says, watch this video – did God really say that? Look at that couple, can their relationship really be that wrong, they love each other – did God really say that? Look at that church, they have endorsed same sex marriage, they have made the headlines – did God really say that? Listen to this leader, he used to think like you did, now he champions the cause of "gay Christians" – did God really say that?

Satan is relentless in his attacks and will continue repeatedly unless we can get to the stage in our faith where we stand tall, extend our backbone, and rebuke his lies. Strong Bible teaching leads to that confident foundation, and as the saying goes, knowledge is power. Homosexual acts are clearly spoken of in the Bible as sinful (for more background on what the Bible says you can refer to my book, Transformed by God's Love[5]), and to withstand the challenge to this truth we need to know and be confident in the Word of God. This confidence was modelled perfectly for us by Jesus himself as he used the Word to resist Satan when being tempted at his lowest point after forty days in the wilderness.

So, what did happen in the beginning? The Old Testament hits the ground running, setting the scene early on in Genesis 3.

> *…. He said to the woman, 'Did God really say, "You must not eat from any tree in the garden"?' The woman said to the snake, 'We may eat fruit from the trees in the garden, but God did say, "You must not eat fruit from the tree that is in the middle of the garden, and you must not touch it, or you will die."' 'You will not certainly die,' the snake said to the woman. 'For God knows that when you eat from it your eyes will be opened, and you will be like God, knowing good and evil.'*
> *Genesis 3:1-4 (NIV)*

The first thing that the snake (Satan) questioned was whether God had really said something, before he broadened his attack and directly contradicted God, saying "you will not certainly die." This is a challenge to God's honesty, causing Eve to question God's trustworthiness.

---

[5] Transformed by God's Love, exploring issues of sexuality in the Christian faith by Sarah Sedgwick, Kingdom Publishers 2019

Two forms of attack are on show here. The sly questioning followed by a direct attack, a clearly stated lie. I imagine Eve battling with these questions. I do not believe she caved in quickly; she struggled with an inner battle. God was close to her. We recognise that she had a personal and loving relationship with God, surely, she would have wanted to believe all He said was true. Yet Satan kept chipping away at her. What to us looks like an inexplicable moment of disobedience was quite possibly the result of a relentless attack from Satan.

What God said to Eve amounted to this. To eat of the "tree of the knowledge of good and evil" means that you will be rejecting Me as the wise and caring Father who knows what is good and right for you. God was laying it out for her, showing her that there was an order in place. God is our powerful ruler who has his throne in heaven; God is in control, and He does not need us to help him manage. He is more than capable of managing the universe! Through pointing out the tree to her, he was asking her to trust Him, to allow Him to do what was right to affect her life, to bring her joy, happiness, peace, and a sense of purpose. She was presented with a choice. Within our lives God presents us with choices, we have free will, but when we do trust Him, we too benefit from His gifts of joy, happiness etc.

When Satan came along to tempt her, he already understood what he needed to say, which angle he needed to come from to bring her down. If he could undermine God by blurring the picture, making her question God's purpose for forbidding her from eating from that tree, then he had planted the seed of doubt in her mind. Through undermining God, he sowed seeds of doubt, "Why doesn't God want me to eat the fruit?" By convincing her that by eating the fruit, she would become just a little bit more like God, he played on her human predisposition of pride, 'I want it,' and lust, 'I need it.' He was relying on our human tendency to say, 'that's not fair' and appealing to our constant appetite to want things we do not have or to be something that we are not.

Parallels can be drawn here with what we are witnessing within the LGBTQ+ community when it comes to questions of faith, or more specifically, Christianity. The objections towards what the Bible says about homosexual acts that tend to come from those who identify with the LGBTQ+ community are often driven by a sense of unfairness. What comes across is the much-held desire to live in a society where same sex relationships are accepted in the same way as opposite sex relationships. And to do this there are many who are looking to Christianity to compromise its doctrines. The pressure for Christians to change their long-held views are undoubtedly increasing; anyone speaking up and remaining faithful to the traditional biblical teaching on homosexual acts increasingly stands the risk of being shouted down. Accusations of homophobia are on the increase. Indeed, I have been on the receiving end of these types of comments, as I promote the freedom I have received, showing that even personal testimony is attacked and derided.

In one of the debates at the Methodist conference pertaining to same sex marriage, one delegate clearly intimated from the platform that anyone opposing the introduction of same sex marriage was homophobic. These accusations are so damaging when made by church members against other church members. There is a desperate need for us to come to a place where disagreement can be seen for what it is, simply a difference in interpretation, rather than being seen as hate filled opposition. Accusations of this type add fuel to Satan's fire, they play on our minds and as the quote from Watchman Nee so eloquently explains. They feed our innate desire to do it our own way, shaping Christianity into everything we want it to be rather than everything God designed it to be - *"the counterfeits of the adversary often exceed the believer's expectation[6]."*

But in reality, (and I speak more specifically to those who identify as same sex attracted) would you really want the Church to lie to you about what we believe our God says? Surely, to be treated as equals, you would want us to tell you the same things we would tell others about sin, and not soften

---

[6] The Spiritual Man by Watchman Nee, Living Stream Ministry (1998)

our beliefs to somehow appease you. Far from being homophobic, those who speak out about this sin are seeking to show God's love and bring freedom. This speech is driven by our desire that all receive salvation and our knowledge that God can help us all to receive it, no matter what our background, sexual orientation, or identity.

It is no secret that much of the LGBTQ+ identity is steeped in pride, and this leads many members of that community to the belief that they cannot change. Anyone living contrary to God's ways is failing to recognise God's supremacy and power, and His ability to guide us in ways to live our lives that maximise our opportunities to reap His promised joy, peace, and prosperity. Many Christians have bought into the concept of gay "pride" and through this are openly denying God's power to bring freedom from homosexual sin.

Psalm 63 says that God's lovingkindness is better than life itself. If we honestly believed that, then denying ourselves, sacrificing our own lives to receive God's loving kindness would result in us all being obedient to God's word. The Bible, in calling us to pick up our cross and follow, requires us to examine our lives and our responses to Scripture to truly follow the narrow path which leads to salvation. However, it is not that simple, is it, because we are hearing so many voices, which one do we listen to?

The stumbling block continues to be the deceit and lies of Satan, who it is fair to say has had a fair degree of success in causing us to question what the Bible says, as well as convincing us that homosexuality is unchangeable, for example by claiming that we are born that way. At the time of writing, a "gay gene" has not been found and I would personally argue that sexuality is more about our environment than our genetic make-up. Yet, whatever the cause of SSA, whether it is innate or inherent, we know that we are all born into sin, and it is what we choose to do with our sinful nature that matters in the eyes of God.

As the saying goes, timing is everything. Satan is happy and content when we are living our lives far from God, there is no need for him to attack us whilst we hold no threat to our own faith or the faith of others. But it is noticeable how he kicks into gear when we start to get closer to God. In considering Satan's timing, it is worth looking at Genesis 3 again. Note here that Satan picked on Eve when she was alone; doesn't that sound familiar? We know that when we are alone, we are often at our lowest, we can struggle with self-esteem and self-worth and feel unloved or not cared about. Loneliness can be a vulnerable time for each of us, a time where we may listen to unfamiliar voices and follow their leading. It is through fellowship with likeminded Christians that we can test those voices, sharing our vulnerabilities and weaknesses to find support. Sometimes we just need to chat these things through, study the Bible with another Christian or bring our concerns and temptations to God in prayer. When we are surrounded by others, we are less likely to be picked on by Satan who delights to divide and conquer. I am reminded of the saying, "If you can't beat them, join them," but suggest Satan's mantra would be the opposite, "If you can't join them, beat them." By convincing people that Christianity is phobic and unwelcoming to those who do not agree with Biblical teaching he has opened the door to the mentality, if we cannot be part of God's "club," we will bring it crashing down.

The LGBTQ+ community gives people a sense of belonging often not found elsewhere, and community is an important requirement for us all as humans. If we, the church, become organised, and learn how to love without limits, we can offer so much more to this community than we currently do. If we act in unity, we will be much better placed to counter the effects of Satan as he continues to endorse wrong choices and slur Christians as homophobes when they dare to speak out. Timing is as key for us as it is for Satan. We need to be speaking about sexuality to our children, our teenagers, and our young adults. Not only should we encourage them with God's word, but we should model how to do "inclusive" church without compromising our own beliefs, and that is something that, unfortunately, the church does not have a good record on.

Secondly, we read that Satan tempted Eve when she was close to the source, she was near the forbidden tree. That echoes loud and clear in my mind when I reflect on those Christians who have had a close friend or family member come out to them. So many of these have changed their thoughts towards same sex relationships, from one of Biblical understanding to one of liberal acceptance. This happens as a direct result of their personal relationships. Satan knows what is happening and senses their weakness. He strikes when the situation has become personal; this is a son, a daughter, a best friend - Satan senses the proximity to the source and strikes hard. Getting someone when they are close to the source of temptation is a shrewd move. Timing is everything and Satan wastes no time in doing this.

I recently had a conversation with a lay preacher who told me he was sitting on the fence, one foot in both camps and this was because in his words "my daughter is gay." He had moved to the fence once she had come out to him. He was the epitome of one who was listening to the question, did God really say that? He recognised and acknowledged the words of the Bible, but could not get his head around what that meant for his daughter, and sadly he has allowed that to cloud his judgement. This is not an isolated case, there are many other stories of those who have changed perspective because of a loved one. Indeed, my own father was reticent about my stand when I came out as "changed," saying that he was unclear as to his interpretation of Scripture. This saddens me as I question whether his viewpoint had changed simply because of my having been gay.

Whilst I recognise the difficulties of hearing that a loved one identifies as same sex attracted, I also recognise the need to keep hold of one's faith in those circumstances. It is possible (and preferable) for a Christian to be loving and supportive of that person without ever compromising what they believe. To have a friend who is confident in their faith, prepared to question and challenge in a loving way so that they can journey together with you in God's word, is a real blessing to someone who experiences

24

SSA and wants to explore God's purpose for their sexuality. It is not helpful in any exploration of faith to have people who fail to challenge you for fear of being seen as judgmental. We do not want to fall into the trap of being those talked about by Paul, who surround themselves with what their itching ears want to hear.[7]

I do not think it would it be a stretch to say that Genesis 3 is a story of "familiarity breeding contempt". Eve, intimately acquainted with God, close to Him in every way, became clouded in her view of Him as a holy God, as a God to be revered and obeyed. It is a story that we should take as a dire warning. If Satan could deceive Eve, given her closeness and relationship with God, how much more can he deceive us.

> The fear of the Lord is the beginning of wisdom, and
> knowledge of the Holy One is understanding. Proverbs
> 9:10 (NIV)

Christian discipleship requires acts of submission to God. These need to be deliberate, conscious, and continuous; they may conflict with the laws (or modern norms of societal behaviour) of the country we live in. But let us not allow anyone to tell us that we do not need to listen to God (as Satan would have us believe.) Proverbs 9 tells us that as we "fear[8]" the Lord, acting in obedience to Him, we gain wisdom and understanding.

In the beginning Satan deceived Eve; sadly we know that he continues that deceit even to this day. This quote from Smith Wigglesworth emphasises our need to remain rooted and grounded in our holy God, to recognise the deceit and unveil the mask of Satan in all circumstances.

> "To discern spirits, we must dwell with Him who is holy,
> and He will give the revelation and unveil the mask of
> Satanic power on all lines." – Smith Wigglesworth[9]

---

[7] 2 Timothy 4:3-4
[8] Proverbs 9:10
[9] From the sermon The Discerning of Spirits -
http://smithwigglesworth.com/index.php/smith-wigglesworth-sermons/ever-

25

TESTIMONY, RAVONNE, USA

Ravonne is a radical lover of Jesus, but life was not always like that for her. She came under a deep deception from Satan and lived apart from Jesus for several years. She stopped believing the truth she had grown up with, she was angry with her parents, and she wanted nothing to do with Jesus. Yet eventually the blindfold was removed from her eyes, and she recognised the deception she had been influenced by, she saw the lies for what they were.

I grew up a Pastor's kid and was deeply in love with Jesus for many years. I did not leave my Christian faith all at once, it happened subtly over a period as I grew deeper into deception. I never stopped labelling myself as a Christian, but everything I said and did was directly in contrast with the character of Christ and His word. I was living Titus 1:6: I "claimed to know God, but by my actions I denied Him." I walked away from God little by little until I was eventually not serving Him at all.

As I had been brought up in the Church, I had a good grasp of what the Bible says about homosexuality. But I began to look at those verses through a different lens now. The main Scriptures I began to question were the ones that considered homosexuality as sin. In my relationships with women, I wanted God to approve of them. As I was introduced to "new ways" of looking at the Scriptures on homosexuality, I wanted to believe them. I questioned 1 Corinthians 6:9, I began to believe that the Scripture only applied to those who were sexually promiscuous outside of God's plan before marriage. I decided to believe that if two women followed God's same plans that He has for a heterosexual couple, that the homosexual couple would also be within God's will.

Despite trying to twist the Scripture to suit my desires, deep down I knew that God meant what He said about homosexuality. In the very beginning of my deception, I recognised that God did not approve of homosexuality; but I had hoped that if I followed His guidelines with everything, except being with a woman, that He would somehow choose to overlook that one part. I thought that two women being together romantically was not as big of a deal as church people made it out to be. Once I chose to believe that God was okay with same sex relationships, if they obeyed the same rules as heterosexual ones, the lie took hold within me.

Once I accepted the lie that "God approved of homosexuality" as truth, it opened me up to a deeper level of deception. I could not read the Bible clearly. When I did read the Bible, there was a veil over my eyes, and I did not understand what I read. Eventually, I stopped reading the Bible altogether.

Galatians 6:9 in the Passion Translation explains what happened to me: "Don't you know that when you allow a little lie into your heart it permeates your entire belief system?"

Once I let the lie in, it took over my whole belief system. A veil of deception came over me and I could no longer read the Bible in clarity and truth. I wanted to believe the lie and purposely rejected what I knew to be true.

Unfortunately, I had to have a huge wake-up call in my life to see things clearly again. One night I had a near death experience where I was overdosing on drugs and was about to be taken to hell by many demons. I reached out to God and told Him I wanted to turn my life around and live for Him. Then, God showed up in the hospital and saved me from going to hell. He gave me a second chance at life! This scary experience shook me into God's truth: His design for marriage is for one man and one woman only.

After rededicating my life to Jesus and receiving the Holy Spirit, I could read the Bible clearly again! When I read the Bible without the Holy Spirit, I twisted Scripture to fit what I wanted it to say; but when I read the Bible with the Holy Spirit, He enlightened me to the truth. I could see clearly again! The veil of deception had been lifted.

This new truth has caused a paradigm shift to my reality of how I view the world. I have learned that God always means what He says in the Bible and that the Bible is the ultimate authority in the spiritual and natural realm. I have learned that I can never put any feeling or desire above God's word. Finally, I discovered that if I ever try to change God's word to fit any personal agenda, I am opening a huge door to the enemy. This will allow the devil to further deceive me and lead me down a path of destruction. Praise God that He always rescues and restores us when we cry out to Him! He is the God of truth, clarity, mercy, and love!

Chapter 3 – The Writing on the Wall

I love the book of Daniel, in particular the recounting of Belshazzar's feast, with the mysterious "writing on the wall." When Belshazzar eventually calls for Daniel to interpret the writing, it was not the message he wanted to hear. 'Mene;' God has numbered your days; 'Tekel,' you have been weighed and found wanting; 'Peres,' your kingdom will be divided and given away.

The writing was very literally on the wall, a stern warning to Belshazzar of his fate, yet the Chaldean wise men themselves were unable to interpret the writing. I find that interesting, the wisest men in that land, the learnt ones, the elite themselves, could see what was going on right in front of their eyes but had no idea what it all meant. It was only Daniel, who had God's ear, who was obedient in prayer, dedicated in his faith and unwilling to compromise, who clearly saw the warning written on that wall.

Where are today's Daniels? Where are the church leaders who are reading the signs, those who are remaining faithful to God in teaching his word and are confident enough in their faith to face the lion's den or the fiery furnace if required? Or are we sadly a nation, a church, whose days are numbered, who have been weighed and found wanting, who are facing a future where our heritage will be divided and given away? We need more leaders who have not fallen prey to Satan's deceit, whether in believing his lies or being intimidated by the consequences of taking a stance for God.

Do not get me wrong, of course I recognise that there are many churches and church leaders who are faithful to God on this topic, who have sound biblical teaching, and even those who are home to ministries which support those affected by SSA. But how I long to hear more evangelical Christians preaching on homosexuality, being bold and courageous as they speak truth and love into lives that are broken. There are still many high-profile preachers who privately speak of their take on sexual sin, yet sadly fail to preach this from their pulpit. I long to see these preachers boldly sharing their faith, where they hold no fear in talking about sexual sin of all types and have no intimidation in tackling topics of intimacy head on.

What are the barriers that prevent this from happening? My sense is that this is a direct consequence of Satan's ability to deceive us into thinking that we cannot preach on these matters for fear of upsetting the status quo. It is often because of the pressure of negative press and social media responses that church leaders have fallen to intimidation and become captivated by this highly effective tactic of Satan.

The question remains, are we the generation who are going under and relinquishing our unwavering belief in the authority of Scripture? Are we the ones who will fall to Satan's ability to deceive at the highest level of church culture?

Let us think about these questions, and where better to start than with the Old Testament as we consider deception and ask, how did we get to this place? Why have we not seen and responded to the warning signs? Are we not able to see the writing on the wall, or have we just failed to interpret it correctly?

Let us start with two of the great prophets, Isaiah and Jeremiah, in our attempt to answer these questions.

The Prophet Isaiah

One of the things that Isaiah homes in on is those who have a religion but not a faith. This is an important distinction both in his time, and now, and serves to help us answer our question.

The Merriam-Webster dictionary defines these as:

Religion

1b (1) the service and worship of God or the supernatural

1b (2) commitment or devotion to a religious faith or observance

Faith

2a (1) belief and trust in and loyalty to God

2a (2) belief in the traditional doctrines of a religion

2b (1) firm belief in something for which there is no proof

2b (2) complete trust

Looking at the definition of faith, the underpinning element is clearly "belief" and "trust." From a personal perspective, coming into a relationship with God, I had to believe what God's Word said for me in my circumstances. I needed to have an intense trust that God was calling me into a new way of life which was going to be better for me than the life I was already living. Because in truth, I could have kept attending church without changing. I had already been a regular attendee on Sundays for six months before I became a Christian. I could have continued in the service and worship of God without making one single change to my lifestyle. I could have been "religious," yet unrepentant; but that would not have afforded me the relationship I now have with Jesus, and I would not be guaranteed eternal salvation had I not put my faith and trust in Him.

The natural progression for a new believer starting out in faith is to develop knowledge in the thing that we have faith in. Through study, prayer and teaching I now have a greater knowledge of God and what he offers me. For example, I have the knowledge that I am saved by God, because I have done what he asked me to do in his Word (acknowledged Him as Lord and repented from my sins). Knowledge in this instance is power - power to rebuke Satan's lies and deceit, power to say, I not only believe in God and his Word, but I trust in God and his Word, and I know that my God keeps His promises and never lies to me. Knowledge is an essential weapon in our armoury.

The debate considering whether we profess religion or faith has been a hotly contested topic of conversation throughout the ages, and Isaiah has a lot to offer this debate as we all try and figure out our relationship with God. Isaiah tells us that "it's one thing to talk the talk, yet another to walk the walk." Saying "I am a Christian" is inconsequential if I do not repent or recognise Jesus as Lord. Members of the LGBTQ+ community, who refuse to recognise homosexual acts as sinful, are denying God's power to bring freedom from any sin. Yet there are many of us who once lived in that lifestyle who have received freedom in full and are benefiting from lives that are changed beyond our wildest dreams. Indeed, Paul speaks of this saying – "and such were some of you[10]."

If we are to say we are "Christians" we must understand what that means, including the sacrifices we might need to make, alongside the tremendous benefits we are going to receive. Calling ourselves Christians is meaningless if we are not living the life of a Christian and being obedient to God's laws.

Becoming a Christian requires trust; it is a vital component of our faith. Trusting that what God offers is greater than anything we could ever envisage, greater than our current life, greater than our identity and yes, greater than sex.

This is why religion is the target for Isaiah in chapter 29, as he condemns religious formality, pointing out that empty and meaningless religion will not stop God's judgment. Consider those who say that they are Christians yet continue to live their life as if nothing has changed. The words "empty" and "meaningless" do not sit out of place in these situations as they seek to take from God, without sacrificing for Him. God loves us with all His heart, mind, and soul, and that is why he asks us to love Him in the same way. Loving God in that way requires a degree of soul searching and a great deal of personal sacrifice. It is a lifelong process but one that starts with a simple recognition of our need of Him and a desire to be obedient to Him.

---

[10] 1 Corinthians 6:11

God will change us. We do not know what that change will look like in this world; we do know what it will look like in the next.

Isaiah speaks of Jerusalem becoming "as Ariel," which is a place that is described as "the hearth of God" or "the place where God's altar burns continually." In effect, what he is saying is that God will turn Jerusalem into a place of burnt sacrifice, a place of religious ceremony which holds no interest or attraction for God. And when you burn sacrifices, you get smoke, and as we see clearly from Isaiah, this is not what God desires from us. God wants His people to have their hearts set on Him just as His heart is set on us. Meaningless and empty sacrifice, the smoke of our platitudes is not for God. He wants the sacrifice of a broken and contrite heart.[11]

> These people come near to me with their mouth and
> honour me with their lips, but their hearts are far from me.
> Their worship of me is based on merely human rules they
> have been taught. Isaiah 29:13 (NIV).

Isaiah condemns the people for honouring God with their "mouth" and "lips" but not their "heart." He understands that man's worship of God can be driven by fear of the consequences of not worshipping Him or a misplaced reverence that is a learnt behaviour (one that has been taught by man, to man). This an intellectual response rather than a relational response which is driven from within. True worship (as we see in Proverbs 9:10) begins with proper reverence, a respectful fear for God and His Word.

In considering how Satan has managed to deceive us to such an extent, the analogy of the place of burnt sacrifice is helpful. Can you imagine the smoke rising as the continual religious sacrifice took place, devoid of meaning or passion? Likewise, as our generation seek ways to become all-encompassing and inclusive, to the extent of overlooking sinful behaviours, it is as if we are sacrificing the truth of God's Word. This heretical sacrifice causes the smoke to rise and makes the way less clear for those who

---

[11] Psalm 51:17

follow behind. I believe that it is no coincidence that the established Church in the UK, the more formal, "religious" establishments, are the ones who are distancing themselves from the authority of the Bible when it comes to homosexuality. The lines have been blurred over many years; each generation walks into another layer of smoke that is causing spiritual blindness, allowing Satan to further infiltrate with his lies.

Isaiah 29:11 brings a message that distinguishes between the ignorance of the educated and the uneducated. Those who are educated or learnt say, "I can't read it for it is sealed," and those who are uneducated say, "Sorry I can't read it." As educated Christians (and to become further educated), we should approach our study of the Bible with a simple heart and a teachable spirit. By doing this, doors open (the seals break), and we learn the will of God and develop a deep understanding of His word. It is possible, and common, for the educated to remain in their ignorance if they fail to study God's word with a humble and seeking heart. It is only through studying His word, with the help of the Holy Spirit, that we recognise that to worship God is to have a heart full of love and fear. What we think, do, and say, should all flow from the abundance of our hearts. If our hearts are full of love and fear for God, our obedience and desire to please Him will flow from within us.

Those who are "religious" do not have the same connection with God's word. They seek only to comply with customs, rules or rituals that are self-serving. Those who receive the Holy Spirit are given access to God's word as is made clear in 1 Corinthians 2:6-16.

> *The person without the Spirit does not accept the things*
> *that come from the Spirit of God but considers them*
> *foolishness and cannot understand them because they*
> *are discerned only through the Spirit. The person with the*
> *Spirit makes judgments about all things, but such a*
> *person is not subject to merely human judgments, for,*
> *"Who has known the mind of the Lord so as to instruct*

him?" But we have the mind of Christ. 1 Corinthians 2:14-16 (NIV)

My experience of coming to faith was one of a personal conviction that God's word meant what it said. A bit like the advert for a well-known decorating product, I came to the point where I believed the Bible simply "does what it says on the tin." It says homosexuality is a sin[12], it says man shall leave his parents and be joined to his wife[13], it says homosexuals will not inherit the Kingdom of God[14]. I did not need a degree and I did not need a theologian to explain it. When you have the mind of Christ you understand His word and the Holy Spirit instructs you in His ways.

I am reminded that Matthew's gospel tells us of our need to be childlike in our faith.

> *He called a little child to him and placed the child among them. And he said: "Truly I tell you, unless you change and become like little children, you will never enter the kingdom of heaven. Therefore, whoever takes the lowly position of this child is the greatest in the kingdom of heaven. Matthew 18:2-4 (NIV)*

As we pause and read Scripture once more, how important it is to block out the pervading voices of society, to get alone with God, and read with childlike enthusiasm and trust. How important it is to take the word of God from its most reliable source and ask our loving heavenly Father himself, what does this really mean?

One of the main arguments we hear from those affirming same sex relationships, relates to the interpretation of key passages of Scripture (which I do not propose to go into here, but you can read them in my book, Transformed by God's Love[15].) My advice to anyone who is seeking to

---

[12] Leviticus 18:22
[13] Genesis 2:24
[14] 1 Corinthians 6:9.
[15] Transformed by God's Love, exploring issues of sexuality in the Christian faith

understand what God says about same sex relationships is that they revisit the Bible with the mind of a child. Look at what God says about marriage, about relationships, about what is good and right for us (the ten commandments are a reliable source of guidance). The key to success is to try to do this without bringing 'baggage' to the task, our preconceived ideas, or attitudes, and see how a fresh approach may help you to view things differently.

Isaiah shows us that we have not seen and responded to the warning signs because we have turned from God. This does not necessarily mean just those who no longer attend church or affiliate to a certain denomination. Sadly, this relates to the many in our churches today who are religious yet have no faith, those who do not receive from God with a childlike faith but who seek to reinvent God in line with the ways of the world. These people's hearts are often far from God, although they praise Him with their lips. Faith is knowing God, walking in his ways, talking with Him, hearing from Him, and wanting nothing more than to honour Him and bring Him the glory. Faith is an attitude of heart that says I will pick up my cross and follow you. Faith is an attitude that says I want to know everything I can about my God, I want to meditate on His word day and night and have His word living in my heart. Faith is being obedient, not because the word tells us to, but because the Spirit within us convicts us of our unworthiness and failings, yet offers us unconditional love and forgiveness.

The Prophet Jeremiah

Whilst Isaiah has a warning for all people whose hearts are not set on God, Jeremiah has some important advice for leaders, which can be found in Jeremiah 23. If you are in a position of leadership or influence, then you will be held accountable to God for what you teach. That is a major responsibility and one that we must not take lightly. We are responsible for making the way as clear as possible, to present Scripture in its purest sense and not cause any to stumble.

> *If anyone causes one of these little ones—those who*
> *believe in me—to stumble, it would be better for them if a*
> *large millstone were hung around their neck, and they*
> *were thrown into the sea. Mark 9:42 (NIV).*

The warning is not just for church leaders and should be heeded by us all. As Christians we are in a privileged position and have a sphere of influence on those around us, both other Christians and those who do not yet know God. We have an awesome responsibility to ensure that our leadership and influence accurately reflects God's teachings and His heart.

When I consider the verse in Mark about causing others to stumble, my heart breaks because I recognise that many openly inclusive churches/Christians are causing the LGBTQ+ community to stumble and fall. In my opinion their influence is three-fold:

1. **They convince those in the LGBTQ+ community that they can continue in their lifestyle without repentance**. However, the Bible tells us there are clear consequences for all who fail to repent. They are causing those whom they are trying to "love without boundaries" to stumble by leading them into a false hope and failing to hold them accountable to God for their choices.

2. **They shut down hope for those who want to repent from their homosexual activity**. There are often situations where false teachers cause those who are on the path to repentance from homosexual behaviours, to question their need to repent, causing them to query whether change is really required. In effect, they blow smoke in their eyes, causing them to lose their way. I saw this happen before my own eyes as the Methodist Church debated same sex marriage. Because of the constant and conflicting arguments raging around whether SSA is acceptable in God's sight, some who were living celibate lives started

to question whether this really was God's will for their lives and became vulnerable and open to Satan's lies.

3. **They marginalise those who have repented and turned away from homosexual activity.** Through trivialising their choices, they cause pain; they cause many to feel persecuted for responding to God's call. This can often be an obstacle for those in this minority group as they walk into freedom. As someone who falls into this category myself, I can witness to the pain that is felt when Christians marginalise my obedience and suggest that I was mistaken to repent of acting on my SSA. Whilst I have a staunch support group around me and can weather these storms, I do fear for 'young' Christians who are in the early days of their walk. It is easy to become incredibly hurt and confused by some of the attitudes expressed by factions of Christian community towards "ex gays."

Jeremiah 23 is a chapter packed full of wise advice and it is worth taking time to study it in greater detail. It opens with a clear warning to leaders (shepherds):

> *"Woe to the shepherds who are destroying and scattering the sheep of my pasture!" declares the Lord. Therefore, this is what the Lord, the God of Israel, says to the shepherds who tend my people: "Because you have scattered my flock and driven them away and have not bestowed care on them, I will bestow punishment on you for the evil you have done," declares the Lord. Jeremiah 23:1-2 (NIV)*

It is also important that those Christians who remain faithful to the traditional interpretation of Scripture on homosexuality heed this warning. The church has not been good at "loving" our LGBTQ+ brothers and sisters, and it is not unusual to hear of pastors and street preachers using the Bible in a non-loving and abusive way to condemn their lifestyle. This is not helpful; many of the words and attitudes they purvey are hate filled.

Some social media feeds make me cringe, as supposed Christians write words that are frankly shocking, and this behaviour can equally be said to cause many to stumble. Members of the LGBTQ+ community who may have been open to attending church or listening to their Christian friends will be angered, hurt, and bemused by some of the Christian responses to their lifestyle. This in turn alienates them from the very faith that could bring them freedom.

In fact, I believe verses 3 & 4 echo God's loving heart for the LGBTQ+ community and was a prophetic declaration of what we are starting to see today. Despite what some would tell you, God absolutely loves the gay community and is moving powerfully within their ranks. There is a sense of progress as God is calling out to his prodigals, and many lives are being changed as freedom is found from homosexual sin. The phrase, God loves the sinner but not the sin, is too often used in a trite manner, but it is a truth that cannot be denied. Do not let anyone tell you that God does not love you, whatever your sin. He is just not able to tolerate any sin that keeps holding you back from his plans for your life.

> *I myself will gather the remnant of my flock out of all the countries where I have driven them and will bring them back to their pasture, where they will be fruitful and increase in number. I will place shepherds over them who will tend them, and they will no longer be afraid or terrified, nor will any be missing," declares the Lord. Jeremiah 23:3-4 (NIV)*

God is calling his children out of homosexual behaviour. My story stands alongside thousands of others from all over the world. God, in his compassion and love, is causing a revival within the LGBTQ+ community; he is gathering the remnant of his flock. In fact, we are starting to see the fulfilment of several prophecies which have spoken about a revival within this community. One of the inspirations for me comes from an article by Lou Engle[16], which talks about some of these prophecies. The one that has really inspired me is this one:

"Several years ago, I was in Nashville with a prophet friend of mine. While there he had an astounding dream. He saw a wailing wall, and on the top, it read, "100,000 LGBTQ Saved and Transformed." On the wall were names of individuals experiencing confusion in their sexuality and gender. Then people began coming to the wall, laying their hands on the names, and weeping over each individual. Suddenly, one after another, the names leapt off the wailing wall over to a testimony wall because they had been freed."

I could not help but be moved by this vision and rejoice as I recognise that my name was one of those that had already leapt on to the testimony wall. But more than that, not only are we seeing converts but we are seeing leaders being raised up from amongst them. Movements such as Equipped to Love[17], from which the "Changed Movement[18]" was birthed, are examples of shepherds who now tend those of God's children who have left homosexuality behind. This movement is growing, and other similar ones can be found around the world. Through their ministry, their peer led support (social media led) and the Rainbow Revival Freedom marches[19], you can see how this prophecy is being fulfilled. In the UK there are other shepherds, Transformed Ministries[20] being an example of a group, who offer pastoral support to a growing community of worshippers, not only in the UK, but internationally through the reach of the internet. Belonging to these groups provides individuals with a sense of security and a place where Christians have no need to fear. It is a place where nurture happens, and a place where God is restoring the years that the locust has eaten[21].

---

[16] https://louengle.com/day-26-from-stone-wall-to-wailing-wall/
[17] www.equippedtolove.com
[18] https://changemovement.com
[19] https://www.freedomtomarch.com
[20] transformedbygodslove.com
[21] Joel 2:25

For me the most exciting part of this prophecy from Jeremiah is the part that says, *they will be fruitful and increase in number.* I see this as such a wonderful promise and something that is already starting to happen. As more Christians who have left homosexuality are making a stand and sharing their stories, an atmosphere of hope and belief is being created for others who have remained silent. A considerable number of Christians who once battled SSA are now blazing a trail in which many others are following. Their numbers are growing, and their work is fruitful. Another prophecy is being fulfilled.

This passage in Jeremiah then moves on to a section (from verse 9) entitled "Lying Prophets," where Jeremiah writes of godless and wicked prophets that follow an evil course. He says, "even within the temple there will be wickedness." His prophecy talks of the time when prophets will openly lie in our churches and from our pulpits. These lies will strengthen the hands of the evildoers (and the ultimate evildoer is of course, Satan). Jeremiah is clear of the outcome of these lies for those who hear them, "not one of them turns from their wickedness."

One of the reasons that false prophets are popular is because they make people believe that everything is fine. They lead people away from the difficult and challenging requirements of being obedient to God's law and they offer an alternative and easy route. We are warned that the path to heaven is the narrow path, not the wide and easy way; let us use that to test the messages we receive, is this the way of the world, or is this God's way?

The message that says, "you are far from God, you need to repent and change," is unpopular as prophets such as Jonah knew extremely well. Jonah ran from God to avoid having to give such a message, until God gently corrected him in the stomach of a large fish!

How can we tell who is a false prophet or teacher? It is not always easy for us to know at first glance. Jesus himself said:

Watch out for false prophets. They come to you in sheep's clothing, but inwardly they are ferocious wolves. By their fruit you will recognise them. Do people pick grapes from thorn bushes, or figs from thistles? Likewise, every good tree bears good fruit, but a bad tree bears bad fruit. A good tree cannot bear bad fruit, and a bad tree cannot bear good fruit. Every tree that does not bear good fruit is cut down and thrown into the fire. Thus, by their fruit you will recognise them. Matthew 7:15-20 (NIV)

There are some clues in this passage for us to notice. False prophets/teachers are preaching God's message but they themselves do not live according to his ways (they may look like a sheep, but their lifestyle choices may be more likened to the wolf).

False teachers' water down God's message to make it more acceptable, to make it palatable to the masses. Preaching the message of God's love without talking about the "wrath of God" is much easier than telling people that God will come down hard on their sins on the day of judgment. Teachings that encompass "free grace" are clearly going to attract a greater following than teaching of the need for repentance and obedience to God's word. Sometimes these teachings are more overtly watered down, other times the tweaks are very subtle. I regularly see the subtle approach with those who teach that Bible references to homosexual acts do not apply to loving, consensual relationships. The argument revolves around interpretation of the words used (and how they have been translated from the original text), yet these teachers often fail to consider other very pertinent Bible references, for example those that pertain to marriage and sexual immorality.

These interpretations, and others like them, pamper to those who have hardened their hearts, those who will not accept the will of God for their lives. As much as God loves them and wants to set them free, they choose to harden their hearts by their own will.

But because of your stubbornness and your unrepentant heart, you are storing up wrath against yourself for the day of God's wrath, when his righteous judgment will be revealed. Romans 2:5 (NIV)

Their hearts are hardened because of deceit, whether it is a form of self-deceit or succumbing to the false teaching of others. Sadly, they have stopped listening because their hearts are set on the more palatable gospel that tells them to continue in their sin.

How then does this passage from Jeremiah help to answer my original question, "Why can't we see the writing on the wall?" I believe that these passages, and many others written by these great prophets, are clear in their message. Whilst Isaiah warned of empty and meaningless religion, Jeremiah warned of false prophets, and specifically of the lies and deceit that would infiltrate the church. His warning extends to talking about how men will walk in the stubbornness of their own heart[22] and the Lord's warning that he did not send these false prophets. God says, 'If they had stood in my council, then they would have proclaimed My words to My people.'[23] This is a clear message from God that there will be false prophets who are not proclaiming His words, and if not God's words, then whose?

Whilst some of this deceit is deliberate, much has crept in as the result of a gradual decline in discernment and passion for meditating on God's word. Just like in the game of Chinese whispers, the message about homosexual acts has become distorted over the years, and many Christians have taken false teaching at face value without seeking God's guidance on Scripture. It may be that these people genuinely believe what they have been taught and that's exactly where Satan wants to keep them.

Yet make no mistake, we are all responsible for what we believe and what we teach others. We have the Holy Spirit to give us wisdom and

---

[22] Jeremiah 23:17
[23] Jeremiah 23:22

44

discernment and we are told to test the spirits[24]. This means that rather than accepting every teaching, we must be diligent in our study of the Bible, and then, knowing what God's word says, we can test all things and handle the truth well.

> *Do your best to present yourself to God as one approved,*
> *a worker who does not need to be ashamed and who*
> *correctly handles the word of truth. 2 Timothy 2:15 (NIV)*

And isn't that just how we find ourselves in this place? Many say that they are Christian yet fail to have a personal faith; many Christians agreeing with Jesus when he speaks about love (to the extent that they promote permissive love) because it fits in well to the cultural messages that they hear every day. Yet many of those same Christians fail to adhere to the moral teaching of the Bible because they have little understanding of what it honestly says.

You may read this and realise that you have been deceived; do not be ashamed, many have. Yet now that door is open and you recognise that you were taken in, you can simply choose to come out of the deception and into God's light. Repenting of our past beliefs, we receive God's forgiveness, our attitudes and actions change, and we recommit ourselves with a new vigour and passion for spreading God's truth and love.

---

[24] 1 John 4:1

TESTIMONY, MAX*, UK

Max is a young man I have had the incredible joy of meeting with, and talking to, over the past few years. He loves Jesus with a passion, but sadly, has been the victim of false teaching. His eyes have momentarily looked away from Jesus, and he has been lured by the promises of the world. I genuinely believe that Max will turn his eyes back to Jesus, his love for him goes so deep, but for now, the world is shouting louder.

As a young man, Max had a remarkable love for Jesus. When he left home to go to college, he eagerly joined the Christian Union (CU) as he wanted to deepen his faith. Max had experienced SSA since his mid-teens but was working through his feelings with a mentor. He did not want to pursue his SSA feelings; for Max, his SSA was unwanted, something he wanted to put behind him. He was eager to find Christian community to "do life" with and make friends through.

Max threw himself into university life and was intrigued when conversations in his CU turned to faith and sexuality. Having come from a traditional Christian background, he had had little exposure to the more liberal teachings. People were telling him that they were "born this way," which in itself was eye opening to him. But on top of that, they were telling him that God was OK with it and would bless him if he chose to marry another man. Initially, he was shy of sharing his own experiences, but over time he opened up about his SSA. As he became more open, people were encouraging him to explore his sexuality. When he questioned them and told them what he believed the Bible to say, they sat him down and countered every verse with a new interpretation. Their explanations seemed plausible, and he started to believe what they were saying.

One of Max's best friends was a girl who classed herself as a "gay Christian." She had a girlfriend, was sexually active, and continually belittled Max for his conservative views. The more he debated with her, the more he started to be taken in by the false teaching. It was a gradual thing, but eventually Max started to embrace his SSA, and began dating men. Shortly after he told me about this, we chatted about his attitude to sex outside of marriage. He answered that he did not believe that now applied to him. Having been sucked into one lie, he was dismissing all teaching on sexual immorality as not applicable to him, because of how he viewed his sexual identity.

Max now labels himself as a gay Christian, and has fallen further into the deceit, by calling himself non-binary. He attends a gay affirming church where he is celebrated and championed.

For this season of his life, Max has sacrificed God's word for a lie. I know that feeling, I did it myself for 30+ years. Yet, when God opens our eyes to the truth, we suddenly see clearly and the lies are exposed. I believe this will happen for Max. There are many people praying for his eyes to be opened; his family and friends will not give up until this deceit is exposed and Max returns to his first love.

*name changed to protect his identity.

Chapter 4 – The Smoke of Satan

When I think about the whole issue of deceit, I think of the smoke and mirrors effect that I spoke of earlier and the concept of smoke screens (used to mask movement in military manoeuvres). While I was writing this book, I became more convinced that our blindness to many of Satan's tactics is caused by smoke screens which he uses to distract us from what is going on in the battle.

> *For our struggle is not against flesh and blood, but against*
> *the rulers, against the authorities, against the powers of*
> *this dark world and against the spiritual forces of evil in*
> *the heavenly realms. Ephesians 6:12 (NIV)*

We do not often talk about smoke, (why would we!), but it is part of our everyday lives. There are several types of smoke; the smoke caused by fire (and different fire types give off different smoke types), smoke caused by residue, smoke caused by proteins (which can be invisible) and then smoke which we see daily emitting from exhaust pipes, cigarettes or vapes. Some smoke is deadly, some is poisonous to inhale, some is undetectable to the human eye, some is hot, some has an unpleasant odour, and some is completely odourless.

Likewise, Satan blows out a range of smoke, all designed to take us in and encourage us to move away from God's purposes for our lives. Like the smoke we encounter in our lives, some of this is more obvious and some of this is barely detectable. Satan is a thief who wants to rob you of the most valuable possession of all, your relationship with God. He delights in his deceptive practices, seeking to draw you away from the truth and from the fullness of life offered by God.

The thief comes only to steal and kill and destroy; I have come that they may have life and have it to the full. John 10:10 (NIV)

God's word warns of the spiritual war that will take place in the future. In Revelation we read:

The great dragon was hurled down—that ancient serpent called the devil, or Satan, who leads the whole world astray. He was hurled to the earth, and his angels with him. Revelation 12:9 (NIV)

Revelation tells us that Satan leads "the whole world" astray. That is a sobering thought and one that we should recognise as a tangible threat within our churches. Satan is using various forms of smoke to blind us, and it is important that we recognise the seeming credibility of his deceit. Even as I write this, headlines within the Christian press are focussing on high profile Christians who are now declaring they have no faith. As we are warned that the entire world will be led astray, we must realise that this includes Christians (let us not forget Paul's warning[25] that "*Satan himself transforms himself into an angel of light.*")

The Bible helps us to see how we can recognise truth from lies. Jesus himself prayed this for His disciples:

"Sanctify them by Your truth. Your word is truth. John 17:17 (NIV)

And the truth is simply this, the word of God, the Bible. But do not be complacent, because Satan can deceive religious people and can use counterfeit leaders who appear genuine but are full of his lies and deceit.

As with smoke, Satan's deceit takes many forms. Let us consider some of these:

1. False doctrine

---

[25] 2 Corinthians 11:14

49

Paul in his letter to Timothy encouraged him to preach God's word. He warned him of the coming times when people would no longer hold to the doctrines of the Bible and would seek out doctrine that suited their own purposes, the message they wanted to hear.

> For the time will come when people will not put up with sound doctrine. Instead, to suit their own desires, they will gather around them a great number of teachers to say what their itching ears want to hear. They will turn their ears away from the truth and turn aside to myths. 2 Timothy:3-4 (NIV)

Being a Christian means opening yourself up to God's guidance, to allow yourself to be guided and corrected by his Word. One of the most obvious smoke screens that Satan uses is false doctrine. What is important for every Christian, or those seeking out what God's word means for them, is to get alone with God, read the Bible and rely on the Holy Spirit to convict. Yes, of course reading other books and listening to sermons is important, but not at the expense of spending time with God and in God's word. For example, we need to avoid the draw to follow one specific church leader or church, gaining our doctrine from their songs or sermons alone. If we are to avoid false doctrine, we need to be comfortable with the Bible and in a place to test what we hear from the pulpit. We must be knowledgeable in its content and committed to spending quality time reading, praying, and asking God to help us understand each word that we read.

Psalm 119 is a notable example of this. The author upholds the importance of Scripture repeatedly throughout the longest chapter in the Bible. It is worth reading it through slowly a few times to gain a sense of his passion. He recognises that we are blessed when we walk in God's laws, observe His testimonies, and seek Him with all our hearts. Moreover, you can palpably feel the author's desire to be taught. He wants to meditate on the Word, to delight in it, and he boldly claims that he will not forget God's word because he recognises the reviving power and guiding qualities it presents. His insatiable hunger for God is refreshing and not something we necessarily can boast for ourselves. The simple prayer found in verse eighteen is one we could all say:

Open my eyes that I may see wonderful things in your law. Psalm 119:18 (NIV)

Jesus himself spoke on the importance of holding to his teaching (other versions say, "remain in my word.") He goes on to underline the importance of knowing the truth, that truth which can only be found when we meditate on his word regularly.

To the Jews who had believed him, Jesus said, "If you hold to my teaching, you are really my disciples. Then you will know the truth, and the truth will set you free." John 8:31-32 (NIV)

Freedom comes from the truth; the truth can be recognised only when we have a good understanding of what God Himself says. There are several false doctrines that are prevalent today. I have homed in on two which are particularly relevant to what is happening in our churches in relation to faith and sexuality:

- **Universalism** - this is the belief that all humankind will be saved, it emphasises the universal principles of most religions and is sometimes known as "inclusion." What Universalists teach runs counter to the teaching of Jesus, who taught us that all who reject Him as Saviour will be separated from Him in eternity. Inclusive church movements are growing in popularity because of their universal appeal, yet they offer an empty religion to those refusing to turn from their sins.

  There is a difference between churches that label themselves "inclusive" and those that are naturally inclusive churches. A "labelled" church, infers that all are welcome regardless of their lifestyle or beliefs and are free to remain as they are; the implication being that all will be saved regardless of their response to the Lord. A truly inclusive church says that everyone is welcome regardless of their lifestyle or beliefs, to a church where they can explore God's ways, with a view that we all eventually come to a place of repentance as we recognise God's laws. We are all sinners who God welcomes as we seek his truth. But the repentance part is essential, Jesus himself taught that we need to repent:

> From that time on Jesus began to preach, "Repent, for the kingdom of heaven has come near." Matthew 4:17 (NIV)

Jesus took our punishment on the cross in order that we would all have access to eternal life, but he did not do it to do away with the law, but to fulfil the law. We still must recognise Him as Lord and accept his free gift of eternal life through our repentance.

- **Hyper-grace** – this teaches that God's grace is so vast it negates our need to confess our sins and repent. Of course, the Bible shows us that we are saved by grace, that our sins have been forgiven, but it also shows us that we have a part to play in receiving that grace. We are called to repentance and through our repentance we receive God's forgiveness. We cannot allow ourselves to be deceived because ultimately, one day we will be held accountable by God.

> For we must all appear before the judgment seat of Christ, so that each of us may receive what is due us for the things done while in the body, whether good or bad. 2 Corinthians 5:10 (NIV)

Being saved changes us, we are transformed, and the Holy Spirit works in us to unveil the truth of His word. Those who are not saved by grace will lack discernment when it comes to reading God's word. Even more importantly, grace and truth sit hand in hand. Jesus was full of grace and truth[26] and we who are saved by grace hold fast to His truth. Those outside of God's grace do not have the benefit nor the wisdom of His truth that is clearly laid out for us to read in both the Old and New Testament.

---

[26] John 1:14

Increasingly we are seeing church leaders and prominent Christians who affirm LGBTQ+ lifestyles pushing hyper-grace, claiming that repentance is not necessary. In an article in Premier Christianity in December 2023 Jayne Ozanne[27] said:

> "Our understanding of God's unconditional love is at the heart of division in the Church over sex and sexuality, Jesus' love for us may lead us to repent of sin, but it isn't conditional on us doing so."

Not only did Jesus refer to the need to repent in Matthew 4:17 and Mark 1:15, but we also read of the importance of repentance in the Old Testament –

> This is what the Sovereign Lord, the Holy One of Israel, says: In repentance and rest is your salvation, in quietness and trust is your strength. Isaiah 30:15

2. Sexual temptation

The second smoke screen used by Satan is his desire to cloud our understanding of sexual desire and sexual design. We are living in a world where much of our identity is tied up in sex. We are seeing hyper sexualisation of children, an increase in accessible online pornography (prevalent amongst school children even in primary education), and an ever-confusing agenda around sexual fluidity, sexual orientation, gender dysphoria and transgenderism.

In the UK there are instances where sex education is introducing age-inappropriate sexual behaviours to children in infant school. Resources for junior school children often include nudity, graphic images and terms like anal intercourse and masturbation. The introduction of drag queen story time and visits to schools of organisations such as the Mermaids,

---

[27] www.premierchristianity.com/opinion/why-sex-outside-marriage-is-not-a-salvation-issue/16880.article

53

who teach young children about transgender issues, has added to the inappropriate sexualisation of young children.

I am sure you join me in asking, how has it come to this? How have we got ourselves into the situation where sex is so prevalent and destructive in our society?

It may help to back up a few steps and think about sexual desires. Sexual desires were given to us by God to be used within a marriage of one man and one woman. God's design was good, his plans for sex within marriage were specific and thought through, not least of which was the pro-creation of children to be raised in a loving environment with the nurture of both a mother and a father.

Satan comes to destroy; he looks upon that which is good and seeks to destroy it. We know that he targets marriage and family units, the breakdown of which causes misery and often hardship for those involved. It is no surprise then, that Satan is taking full advantage of our sexual desires, to either prevent us from entering marriage in the first place (through creating environments where we seek and satisfy our lusts elsewhere), or to destroy marriages through sexual infidelity. We are also seeing an increase in attacks on identity amongst our children, confusion is rife, many being forced into situations where they feel pressured to label themselves to satisfy the world.

Satan's intentions do not go unnoticed or undocumented by Paul in his letters to the early church. In these he underlines God's intention for us to either be celibate, or in a marriage between one man and one woman and emphasises the need to flee sexual immorality.

> Now for the matters you wrote about: "It is good for a man
> not to have sexual relations with a woman." But since
> sexual immorality is occurring, each man should have
> sexual relations with his own wife, and each woman with
> her own husband. 1 Corinthians 7:1-2 (NIV)

Marriage is encouraged for those whose desires are strong. What Paul is saying is this, that if you are not built for celibacy then there is another option, marriage! Marriage is the one place where sexual desires can be acted upon within God's brilliant design for humanity.

Paul cherished his lifestyle as a single man. He saw the benefits this gave him, namely time to serve God with no distractions and no added responsibilities of family life. Singleness meant that he could give 100% of himself to God, his time, his money, his love, and that was worth celebrating. In our generation, singleness is often celebrated and desired, but the same cannot be said for celibacy. We are living in a time where we are encouraged to be promiscuous, where television programmes such as Love Island promote sex as a spectator sport, and where anyone who chooses to remain celibate for life or until marriage is seen to be a prude. But celibacy is an option and a gift, one that our society would have us believe to be second rate, but which should be recognised as having equal status to marriage.

Whether married or single, when we experience sexual desires, we become more susceptible to Satan's attacks. Satan takes the desires we are feeling and uses them to justify the sin. If we place ourselves in vulnerable situations without having a firm grounding and understanding of God's desires for our sexuality, we are in the place of Eve, close to the source, near to the forbidden tree. The closer we are to the source, the greater the temptation. We are liable to fold under pressure unless we are strong enough in our faith to rebuke Satan. Keeping ourselves from the source means not putting ourselves in situations where we may be tempted. For example, many who have found freedom from homosexuality would deliberately not go to gay clubs, bars or even to neighbourhoods they used to frequent, to protect themselves from temptation. This also means not watching films or television programmes that feature sexual scenes or gay characters (becoming increasingly difficult in today's permissive culture), and not visiting certain websites, dating apps etc. Whilst this is a common-sense approach, it is important that as young

Christians (and I do not just mean young in age), we ground ourselves in God and the Bible before we put ourselves back into any situations that may trigger unhealthy responses.

Where our children are concerned, we need to guide them and teach them before they get too close to temptation. And as can be seen from what is happening in our schools, that may mean speaking to them in an appropriate manner from quite an early age. If we are not teaching them about their God given identity and sexuality, you can be sure that someone else will be, and their message may not be the one you want your child to hear. For useful resources on how to speak to your child I recommend "Lovewise," an initiative in the UK to re-establish Biblical relationships teaching.[28] For parents of teenagers there is a series of useful videos provided by Transformed Ministries, which gives you a helpful overview of how to start conversations about sexuality with our young people[29]. Equally, as parents, we need to ensure that we are fully aware of the curriculum being taught in our schools, the resources that are being used and the external organisations being invited in to speak to our children. We must be prepared to engage in conversations with teachers and governors, to challenge anything that we feel is unhelpful and misleading in instructing our children about sexuality. It is important that we recognise the difference between teaching acceptance of diversity, and a teaching which seeks to indoctrinate our children with homosexual and transgender ideals. This is essential if we are to maintain any confidence in schools playing a realistic and acceptable role in educating our children in the areas of sex and relationship education.

God gifted us sexual desires and they are meant to be used within the boundaries of God's grace and truth. This helps us to see that, for those who do not marry there is a grace available to enable them to manage their singleness and a truth to be found that sex is not to be treated as an idol. Sex is not a prerequisite to living a happy and fulfilled life. For those who

---

[28] lovewise.org.uk
[29] https://transformedministries.teachable.com

do marry, sex is a gift, one to be treasured and protected, because Satan does, and will, continue to delight in breaking up a marriage.

Satan seeks (and has been successful in many ways) to separate sexual desire from grace and truth, so it simply becomes a self-serving pleasure which can take many forms: promiscuity, adultery, pornography, prostitution, masturbation, and homosexuality to name a few. Without grace and truth, our focus becomes inward. We can quickly be overcome by the temptations that assault us and inevitably, without a focus on Jesus, we succumb.

Society has changed rapidly in the past few decades. The 1960s and 1970s saw the advent of "free love", where sexual liberation and sexual freedom resulted in many adopting a casual attitude towards sexual intercourse. This opened the doors to a more liberal attitude to all things sexual. With the arrival of the internet and the resulting ease of access to sexual content in the nineties, attitudes towards sex have become increasingly more permissive.

A study in America[30] which looked at attitudes about sex over the past forty years revealed some interesting statistics. For this study which took place over a forty-year period, a different group of 18 to 29-year-olds were asked about their attitudes towards same-sex relationships and practices. The recorded results showed significant differences in attitudes from generation to generation:

- Baby Boomer Generation (early 1970's) – 21% believed that same sex relationships and practices were not wrong at all.
- GenX'ers (early 1990's) – 26% believed that same sex relationships and practices were not wrong at all.
- Millennials (2010's) – 56% believed that same sex relationships and practices were not wrong at all.

---

[30] Jean M. Twenge; Ryne A. Sherman; Brooke E. Wells. "Changes in American Adults' Sexual Behavior and Attitudes,1972–2012," Archives of Sexual Behavior, May 2015. doi: 10.1007/s10508-015-0540-2.

The researchers concluded that:

"Overall, the results suggest that rising cultural individualism has produced an increasing rejection of traditional social rules, including those against non-marital sex[31],"

I was intrigued by what they meant by "rising cultural individualism?" Individualism can be defined as:

1a - a doctrine that the interests of the individual are or ought to be ethically paramount.

1b - a theory maintaining the political and economic independence of the individual, and stressing individual initiative, action, and interests.

Are they then inferring that the reason for our society becoming so messed up around sexual identity revolves around the shift in emphasis from group/family/community interests to the prevailing thought that it's all about me? It is my body, my life, my rights." Personal rights and interests are the main thrust of individualism, and that sentiment all stems from the third of Satan's deceptions, pride.

3. **Pride**

Another word for pride in this context is conceit (an excessive appreciation of one's own worth or virtue[32].) The Bible is quite explicit about pride, verses such as Proverbs 11:2 and Proverbs 16:18-19 speak clearly about its consequences. What is more, in 1 John we are told that pride comes from the world, that is, from Satan.

For everything in the world-the lust of the flesh, the lust of the eyes, and the pride of life-comes not from the Father but from the world. 1 John 2:16 (NIV)

---

[31] Jean M. Twenge; Ryne A. Sherman; Brooke E. Wells. "Changes in American Adults' Sexual Behavior and Attitudes,1972–2012," Archives of Sexual Behavior, May 2015. doi: 10.1007/s10508-015-0540-2.
[32] Merriam-Webster online dictionary

This verse serves as a clear warning that whilst our pride tells us we can have what we want, act on our own impulses and desires with no consequences and gives credence to our lusts, this is not God's plan for us. This prideful attitude does not come from our loving Father in heaven.

How important it is therefore, to guard our hearts from pride. We have many examples in the Bible of those who fell on their sword because of pride. King Herod[33] was eaten by worms because he would not give glory to God. King Nebuchadnezzar[34] would not repent despite being told by Daniel of his certain fate should he not humble himself. He lived like an animal for seven years, enough I am sure to make him work on his prideful attitude.

But of course, it was Satan's own pride that caused him to rebel against God. His fall is recorded in Isaiah 14, when being full of pride he challenged God himself.

> How you have fallen from heaven, morning star, son of
> the dawn! You have been cast down to the earth, you who
> once laid low the nations! You said in your heart, "I will
> ascend to the heavens; I will raise my throne above the
> stars of God; I will sit enthroned on the mount of
> assembly, on the utmost heights of Mount Zaphon. I will
> ascend above the tops of the clouds; I will make myself
> like the Most High." But you are brought down to the realm
> of the dead, to the depths of the pit. Isaiah 14:12-15 (NIV)

Satan's pride did not stop then and will not stop now; he will use it to draw as many as he can into his snare. Pride is a form of idolatry, a situation where we can make ourselves the object of our own worship. When we treat sex as something that is our right, regardless of the consequences for ourselves or others, we are acting in pride. If we have a liberal attitude towards sex, we may not fully consider the consequences of our actions.

---

[33] Acts 12:21-23
[34] Daniel 4: 25-35

For example, one of the consequences of sex outside of marriage is the high rate of abortion.

In 2021[35] there were 214,256 abortions for women resident in England and Wales, the highest number since records began. Eighty-two percent of these were for women whose marital status was single. Arguably, when a couple can simply negate the responsibility of having an unplanned child by having an abortion, they can afford to be less concerned about the potential outcome of sex and act upon their own impulses and desires without fear or worry.

Selfishness and egotism are part of our nature, and this makes us particularly susceptible to the lies that Satan will tell us. Lies that convince us that we deserve to be the centre of attention and that our ways are more important than God's ways. Pride can be in the job or position we hold, in our possessions, our looks (just think about the selfie culture), our intelligence, our relationship status, our qualifications and so much more. We are all easily flattered and even the strongest Christian needs to be aware of how easy it is to stumble, a fact that Paul was fully aware of. In his letter to Timothy, he was clear that when appointing an overseer, they were not to be a recent convert *"or he may become conceited and fall under the same judgment as the devil."* This emphasises the importance of us being mature in our faith, to keep ourselves close to the Word of God so that we too, avoid falling under the snare of conceit or pride.

Pride is a word which is synonymous with the LGBTQ+ movement. The lie that Satan has created is now so normalised that many thousands of Christians around the world happily attend "Pride" marches to endorse and celebrate the sexual freedom expressed through homosexual sin. This the biggest, and most successful deceit that Satan has pulled off; it is of our time, and it is happening right in front of our eyes. Many of these Christians

---

[35] www.gov.uk/government/statistics/abortion-statistics-for-england-and-wales-2021/abortion-statistics-england-and-wales-2021

are so convinced by this deceit that they call those who remain faithful to God's Word on sexuality, bigots or homophobes.

The writer of Psalm 119 was astute to this, and his response is one we could mirror if we choose to be committed to obeying God's laws.

> *Though the arrogant have smeared me with lies, I keep your precepts with all my heart. Psalm 119:69 (NIV)*

A close examination of what the Bible says shows us clearly that it teaches humility over pride, to love God primarily and to do nothing out of vanity or conceit.

> *Do nothing out of selfish ambition or vain conceit. Rather, in humility value others above yourselves, not looking to your own interests but each of you to the interests of the others. Philippians 2:3-4 (NIV)*

Pride teaches that we should take responsibility for our own lives, to change and shape ourselves into what we want to be, with little concern for what our behaviour and actions mean for others. I am reminded of the annoying slang term, "whatever," (which incidentally was voted the most annoying word[36] in the US for ten years up to and including 2019). Used widely by teenagers and young adults, this word is indicative of a generation that care little for what other people think about them, or their actions. Conversely, the Bible teaches humility, and in our humility, we recognise that change and transformation is only possible because of what Jesus did for us on the cross, and that true humility is obedience to the Sovereign Lord and his Word.

I believe that those who confess to being "gay Christians," those who do not believe that homosexual acts are sinful, have fallen into the trap of pride. They do not believe that they need to be a "new creation," they believe that God has given them a homosexual orientation and as such they can freely act upon it. But God's word tells us differently:

---

[36] the Marist Institute for Public Opinion

Therefore, if anyone is in Christ, the new creation has come: The old has gone, the new is here! 2 Corinthians 5:17 (NIV)

To experience change we are called to relinquish our old identity. It is no good saying I will give my life to Jesus, but I still want my identity to be as a bank robber, an adulterer or as a gambler. In the same way we cannot say I want my identity to continue to be as a homosexual. Giving our lives to Jesus means total surrender, and confident trust that he can transform us. We are told to have confidence in what we hope for. Pride creates a smokescreen that says, "I don't want to hope for a change in my sexual orientation because that's who I am." Faith creates the confidence to say, "I'm not sure how you're going to do this Lord, but I'm trusting you for total transformation. I want my identity to be in you." This identity may change quickly, or it may be a slow process, but when God is involved, it is certainly something that can, and will, happen over a lifetime of commitment to Him.

On this point I know I differ with many who have come out of the gay community and chosen to be celibate for Christ. I do not condemn them; I simply believe that freedom is available and desirable. We are called to be transformed by the renewing of our minds[37], and I have witnessed great freedom from those who have allowed the Holy Spirit free range to work, not hampering themselves with an identity God never gave them, nor expected them to walk in. That is not to say everyone has a change of sexual desires, but I believe it does mean that everyone can have a change in how those desires affect them and how they walk in freedom from temptation.

Now faith is confidence in what we hope for and assurance about what we do not see. Hebrews 11:12 (NIV)

---

[37] Romans 12:2

4. Bitterness

It does not take much to make some people bitter, bitterness is found in most families and communities, including churches. Bitterness can come on quickly, or smoulder over a longer period, and is a by-product of hurt feelings. If not corrected quickly, a slight can become a festering wound which we pick at until it turns into a grudge, filling our minds disproportionately. Soon we are thinking about how to exact revenge (even if we have no real intention of following through) and we find that instead of keeping our minds on what is good, true, and right, we are focusing too much time on making a mountain out of the molehill.

Bitterness is an attitude that Satan is very at home with and one he will encourage in those who will listen to him. When you find yourself slighted, you have been away from church for a few weeks and no one has contacted you, the lies of Satan will start. Do they care? They have not rung me; they obviously do not care about me, and so it goes on. As we start to listen to the lies, the root of bitterness forms and, before we know it, Satan has a hold on us that is out of all proportion to the root cause.

Bitterness can even cause us to sin, seeking vengeance or harbouring hate in our heart. It has the propensity to distort our view of many things. We only need to read the story of Herodias[38] to see how deep the root of bitterness burrows and the devastating results of such bitterness. Her anger at John the Baptist, who criticised her marriage to Herod, culminated in his murder at her request. That root went deep, she had taken his words to heart, and we can only imagine how she had revelled over plotting his downfall.

One area of bitterness that I experienced, before I surrendered my sexuality to God, was down to the fact that I wanted God to allow me to be gay and Christian. I felt slighted that I was second rate, my love was not equal to those of my heterosexual friends. Oh, how Satan loves to use that card, taunting us that we are not worthy of God's love, when in fact the

---

[38] Story can be found in Mark 6

63

exact opposite is true, for while we are still in our sin Jesus died for us[39]. That bitterness was something that kept me from exploring my faith for over thirty years. The lie of Satan, telling me that as a homosexual God could not love me, led to a bitterness that caused me to say, if that's the case then I don't want what you offer, when the reality was that I really did want and need that freedom. In my situation the bitterness caused a blindness; I was unwilling to look past my bitterness to find the truth.

Bitterness can be described as Satan's tear gas, smoke in our eyes. Smoke that causes us to smart, it causes tears, and it causes us to blame God for our own poor choices and lack of reverence. But the good news is, we do not have a high priest who is unable to sympathise with our weaknesses, for he himself was tempted in every way yet remained without sin[40]. We can talk to Jesus about our bitterness, and he understands. It is helpful to peel back the layers of this bitterness to fully recognise the way Satan has magnified an innocuous comment, action or misunderstanding to cause so much hurt.

5. Lack of faith

Lack of faith leaves us wide open to the deceit of Satan. When we are strong in our faith, nothing he throws at us will stick. In fact, those with strong faith will be fully clothed in the armour of God, and the burning arrows Satan throws at us will most often bounce off with ease. Take Job as an example. If any of us had suffered just one of the woes that he suffered, I am not sure how we would have fared. Yet Job had an immense faith and would not denounce his God. We read of others who suffered for God, yet would not deny Him or bow down to idols: Shadrach, Meshach, and Abednego the most well-known as they survived the fiery furnace.

As a young Christian I struggled immensely with lack of faith because of a lack of intimacy with God's word. When questions arose, most specifically around homosexuality and what the Bible said, I continued to be shaky on

---

[39] Romans 5:8
[40] Hebrews 4:15

64

the whys and wherefores of my decision to become celibate. It was because of my lack of in-depth knowledge of the Bible that Satan could so easily cause me to stumble. I would constantly revisit the question, "could I be a gay Christian," for months after I was saved. Whilst still living a celibate life, I was seeking God, longing for other answers that would make my walk "easier." I am sure Satan was trying to trip me up, taunting me to turn back to my old lifestyle, telling me that the Bible did not prohibit it, that I had misunderstood God's word.

Quite early on in my Christian journey I prayed for God to "bind his word to my heart," I recognised that this was going to be an area of attack and I knew that I needed to have a vast weapon bank to protect myself. Over time, as God has answered this prayer; my faith has strengthened immensely and I am no longer susceptible to these attacks (although do not get me wrong, I still know times when Satan will give it a go!)

As Christians we will face fears, problems, and hardships. But we face them in the knowledge that God protects us, shields us and fights for us. Building up our faith is essential to empower us to stand up to Satan and rebuke his lies.

> *Consequently, faith comes from hearing the message,*
> *and the message is heard through the word about Christ.*
> *Romans 10:17 (NIV)*

In this chapter I have sought to show you just five of the things that Satan uses to create smoke to cause us to question our faith. Whether it is him using one or more of these ways to create general questions over our faith or using just one or two to cause us to question specific areas of faith, we must be aware of his schemes.

Satan will use false teachers to change doctrine to appeal to a wider, secular audience. He will use sexual temptation, seeking to normalise behaviours which are contrary to God's word, and he will encourage us to become self-seeking, proud individuals rather than those living in humility as God desires. He will encourage us to question how we are treated by others, liberally sowing seeds of bitterness and where he sees a chink in our shield of faith, he pounces on it at speed.

There is some sound and relevant advice in Peter's first letter which exhorts us to protect ourselves in all circumstances:

> *Be alert and of sober mind. Your enemy the devil prowls*
> *around like a roaring lion looking for someone to devour. 1*
> *Peter 5:8 (NIV)*

TESTIMONY, BIANCA, USA

Bianca was sold out for Jesus as a teenager, but life caught up with her. When she finally admitted her SSA, she did what she felt was the honourable thing and left church, not wanting to be a hypocrite. She wasn't embedded in the LGBTQ+ culture but was in and out of relationships with other women for a few years before she finally surrendered her life back to Jesus. Now Bianca is a ministry leader, a passionate and effective Bible teacher and a mentor to many who have questions around issues of sexuality (not just homosexuality).

I experienced my first same-sex encounter at 19 years of age. I couldn't for the life of me grasp all that this meant or would entail in the years to follow. All I knew was that I wasn't to tell a soul, for many reasons, but mostly because I wanted to maintain a certain "reputation". Up until this point, I was what I thought to be the "perfect" Christian. I served in multiple ministries at church. I didn't do drugs, I wasn't drinking, and I wasn't having sex with anyone. I was a "good girl". I remember I used to get frustrated with my youth group. I thought, "Surely they don't love you as much as I love you God". I had everything under control, or so I thought.

Although I very much struggled with same-sex attractions, I never embraced the concept. I believed that I didn't have a problem. I certainly wanted everyone to believe that about me too. I really did think I had control of the situation. My first same-sex encounter relationship eventually ended. But the seed this sin planted in my heart, never got uprooted.

In Old Testament Hebrew, the word 'pride' is translated from many words. The interpretations of these words differ but the reservoir of meaning suggests "lifted up". To be prideful, is to lift yourself above Christ, above His ways, His truth, His divine perfect law.

After this encounter, I struggled with the thought that woman were more desirable than men. I thought I'd be happier with a woman versus a man. I'd fight the thought here and there, but eventually that became my ultimate truth. So much so, that I eventually left the church and "God" to be in a relationship with a woman and do things my way!

What started as a small seed, took 10 years to fully develop into a major stronghold in my life, so much so, that I left everything I knew to be true, for "my truth". I exalted what I wanted above God. I told all but one soul about my experience throughout this time. I didn't want anyone to think I was a failure. I had an inflated sense of self-importance and capabilities. Pride kept me from asking for help, and it kept me in denial because I really did think I could quiet this "thought" whenever I wanted to. Pride makes you think unclearly as it gives you a false sense of reality and your role in the world.

I think of the story of David and Goliath. David would have been slaughtered if he thought he could fight a giant in his own strength. Yet that is exactly what I did. I faced my giant (my unwanted SSA) alone, and completely unprepared. I exalted myself instead of the name of Jesus and His power. I failed epically because I had an incorrect/unbiblical view of myself and my capabilities. I didn't need anyone; I thought I could handle anything and everything on my own.

Not only did 'pride' contribute to my falling away, but it also kept me in my sin longer. I remember, amid my sin, praying to God to help me, and He did. I shortly thereafter was reintroduced to the church by my boyfriend at the time, and thought I was healed just like that. I took pride in the fact that I now had a boyfriend. I wasn't gay anymore, right? I had the boyfriend, I had the job, I had the title I wanted.

Me me me! I was achieving most of the goals I had set for myself. Where was God? On the backburner, because I placed my desire and wants above His will for my life. The Bible says, apart from Me you can do nothing. I eventually got fired from that job, and I ended up cheating on my now ex-boyfriend. Where did all of "my achievements get me? Nowhere.

In James 4:6, the Bible says, "God opposes the proud but shows favour to the humble". How can God help someone who doesn't want His help? Pride places confidence in ability of self, versus God's strength and mighty power. I was doomed to fail. We all will fail if we do not surrender our entire heart, soul, and mind to God's perfect will. If you don't desire God's will for your life, it is most probably because you are exalting your will for your life over God's will for your life. We either surrender completely, or we don't at all. God requires 100% of us. He is a consuming fire, a jealous God who will not share us, even with ourselves.

In 2021, I recommitted my life to Christ. Having gone through everything I went through, I had no other option. Everything I had exalted (aside from Him) failed me. I finally came to the end of myself and my false perception of self-capabilities. Despite all my years in church growing up, I never told anyone about what I was struggling with, especially my unwanted SSA. It wasn't until I was honest with myself, others, and God, that I got the help that I needed. My ways weren't better, and I was 'never' in control despite how much I thought I was. God gets ALL the glory and only Him! Now, today, and forever. His ways will always be better than anything we can imagine for ourselves.

Chapter 5 – The Smoke of God, "Holy Smoke."

A few years ago, I worked in a café; you could describe it as a bit of a greasy spoon. Every day we provided cooked breakfasts, cooking the bacon and sausages on a griddle. Whilst I could not always see the smoke that came from the cooking process, I certainly knew that I had been in a smoky environment by the smell that permeated my hair and my clothes. I know from my time working there, that being exposed to the wrong type of smoke can be unpleasant. All of us who worked at that cafe had to change our clothes and wash our hair as soon as we returned home. If we had not washed the smoke residue away, we would have carried the rather unpleasant smell of grease around with us for the rest of the day. I am yet to find someone who likes the acrid taste of smoke in the back of their throat, the pungent smell it leaves on their clothes or the stinging sensation in their eyes, which cause tears to form and roll down their cheeks!

Our dislike of being exposed to smoke should be mirrored in our attitude towards Satan and his attempts to blindside us. However, not all smoke is the same, there is a different kind of smoke that we read about in the Bible; that is the smoke of our holy God which reflects both His glory and His anger.

In the previous chapter we looked at how Satan deceives us, and I have likened this to the use of smoke screens. Having been a beloved creation of God, Satan turned away from the God who gave him life; he became proud and exalted himself. He cultivated within himself a desire to be greater than God and was successful in deceiving a third of the heavenly host into following him. Given dominion over the earth (Jesus calls him "the ruler of the world" [41]), he has a limited time to cause havoc until he

---

[41] John 12:31

eventually faces defeat, and I believe his actions as ruler of the world can be seen as a cheap imitation of the real thing. Satan's smoke is no match for the holy smoke of God that we read about in both the Old and New Testament.

The Smoke of God's Glory

The fire of God is not without smoke! Where better to start than in Revelation chapter 15, where we read that the sanctuary was filled with smoke from the glory of God and from his power? What a wonderful image that is. Take note, though, of the verses that precede this image of God's glory. In verses 3 and 4 we read the song of those who had been victorious over the beast, those who revere God in all his holiness:

> *Great and marvellous are your deeds,*
> *Lord God Almighty.*
> *Just and true are your ways,*
> *King of the nations.*
> *Who will not fear you, Lord,*
> *and bring glory to your name?*
> *For you alone are holy.*
> *All nations will come*
> *and worship before you,*
> *for your righteous acts have been revealed.*
>
> *Revelation 15:3-4 (NIV)*

We serve a God who is holy, righteous, and set apart. His words have eternal consequence, and His glory highlights our need for His amazing grace. He is a God who commands fear and reverence; He is to be honoured and respected. I feel that in many ways we have become over familiar where God is concerned. Perhaps our attitude can be partially accredited to us having departed from the Old Testament way of approaching God, which stood as a constant reminder to God's people of His holiness. Before the veil was torn in two, the regular 'man in the street' could not approach God, only the high priest could enter the holy of holies through a curtain or veil. In a sense, when the priest entered this area, he came into the very presence of God, and he recognised what this meant. This changed his demeanour and attitude as he entered God's presence.

Now, praise God, we can approach God directly without the need for sacrifice or an intercessor. The question is, has this resulted, in some cases, in a loss of our sense of reverence and awe, and our level of respect or 'fear of God'? We can look to the Bible for some insight into this. There are a couple of good examples in the Old Testament of what happens when we become over familiar with God. In these documented cases we can see tangible consequences of informality in our approach and response to God.

The ark of the covenant was built to a blueprint provided directly by God, which included detailed instructions on how it should be transported. Part of the ark was the atonement cover, also known as the mercy seat, which is spoken of in Leviticus 16.

> He is to put the incense on the fire before the Lord, and
> the smoke of the incense will conceal the atonement
> cover above the tablets of the covenant law, so that he will
> not die. Leviticus 16:13 (NIV)

This gives us a clear picture of how holy God's dwelling place was; if the priest laid eyes on it, he died (hence the incense to provide a smoke covering.) This was the place where God's glory rested, the place of residence and His throne. It was situated in the Holy of Holies, the most sacred place in the temple. To understand a bit more about the ark of the covenant, it is worth exploring the blueprint which God gave for its construction:

> Make an atonement cover of pure gold—two and a half
> cubits long and a cubit and a half wide. And make two
> cherubim out of hammered gold at the ends of the cover.
> Make one cherub on one end and the second cherub on
> the other; make the cherubim of one piece with the cover,
> at the two ends. The cherubim are to have their wings

spread upward, overshadowing the cover with them. The cherubim are to face each other, looking toward the cover. Place the cover on top of the ark and put in the ark the tablets of the covenant law that I will give you. There, above the cover between the two cherubim that are over the ark of the covenant law, I will meet with you and give you all my commands for the Israelites. Exodus 25:17-22 (NIV)

It is important for us to recognise that this was the place where God would 'meet' with His people. As a place of meeting with God, it was clearly a sacred and holy place. Because of this, God had made it clear that the ark was not to be touched[42]. In fact, God had written into the design a failsafe for this, the ark was designed with poles by which the priests would transport it, protecting them from ever needing to physically touch it. What we recognise. through our reading of the Bible, is that God's presence was in the ark of the covenant. Because of that, it was a most holy place, and it was imperative that the people showed respect and reverence towards God through the way they approached and transported the ark.

We only need read the story of Uzzah in 2 Samuel,[43] to see what happened when the Israelites disobeyed God's instructions. The Israelites were guilty of two grave errors. Firstly, they placed the ark on a cart to transport it, which was clearly contrary to God's commands; it was to be carried. And secondly, and to his cost, Uzzah touched the ark (albeit to steady it) and he was struck down by God. This a stark reminder of the importance of being obedient when God gives us clear instructions. Whilst in the 21st century we would not expect God to strike someone dead for being disobedient, we should recognise that when God asks us to do something, He is serious in that request. Our best course of action is to respond in love and obedience to God's call on our lives, no matter how hard the task. When we love someone, our natural inclination is to make

---

[42] Numbers 4:15
[43] 2 Samuel 6

them happy, and that often means doing things that they ask us to do. Is our relationship with God any different? If God asks us to give up a sinful area of our life, should not our response be one that seeks to please Him.

What happened to Uzzah is not the only example in the Bible of God acting when his commands relating to the ark were ignored. In 1 Samuel[44], we read that seventy inhabitants of Beth Shemesh were put to death because they looked inside the ark.

To give a bit of background to this story, when the ark was finally returned to Israel by the Philistines, the people of the town of Beth Shemesh received it with immense joy. In Joshua 21[45] we read that the men of Beth Shemesh were priests; we can assume therefore that they would know God's expectations and would give the ark of the covenant a place of prominence and approach it with reverence. That is why it is so bewildering for us to read that they opened the sacred ark and looked inside it.

We cannot be sure why they did it; we can only speculate. Were they checking whether the inhabitants of Philistia had removed anything from the ark, or were they simply curious? Whatever the reason, God had been clear about them not touching the ark, let alone opening it up and looking inside. This was not a mistake, a slip as perhaps it was for Uzzah, this was a deliberate unholy act. The result of their disobedience was that many of them died. It was through this unholy act that finally, the inhabitants of Beth Shemesh understood that God is holy and should be respected.

These stories to us, as 21st century citizens, may seem harsh. We may question a God who would strike someone dead for touching the ark, but this is so much bigger than just touching the ark. The more pertinent question for us to ask may be, "Who can stand in the presence of God?" For we know that in God's presence men fall to their knees and bow their heads. We read that Jesus himself recognised the glory and power of God as he fell on his face to pray to his Father[46].

---

[44] 1 Samuel 6
[45] Joshua 21:16

74

Recognising God as a holy God and recognising the need to reverence the God of the ark, rather than mishandling the glory of God, is the important lesson for us here. God was clear that "He" should be moved in a specific way, a message that convinces me of the need to do the things that God tells us to do, in the way He tells us to do them. Obedience is core to our relationship with our holy God. In the same way, if God says something is sinful, it is sinful, and we have no place arguing or bargaining with an omnipotent God, although many learnt theologians have tried to do so.

When David eventually decided to bring the ark home, his driving motivation was to restore the presence of God to the Israelites. He wanted the glory of God to return to them from captivity.

> The Glory has departed from Israel, for the ark of God has been captured." 1 Samuel 4:22(NIV)

David recognised the power of God which was upon the ark of the covenant. The ark was a resting place for God's glory and the Israelites had taken strength from its presence when fighting the Philistines, they had seen enemies cursed with its presence and Obed-Edom and his household flourish with its presence.

> The ark of God remained with the family of Obed-Edom in his house for three months, and the Lord blessed his household and everything he had. 1 Chronicles 13:14 (NIV)

David knew that restoring God's glory would bring his people peace and prosperity for as long as they continued to give God the due honour and respect, and keep Him central to their lives. It is all too easy for us to minimise the importance of God's glory, or not give it a focal point in our own lives. We forget the times when God has blessed us, or the times when all was going well, and we were flourishing in our faith. Living in the first world, it is not even a matter of having forgotten, but one of not

---

[46] Matthew 26:39

recognising God's touch on our lives. We do not count our blessings because we do not recognise them as blessings. They are simply things that we have come to see as being rightfully ours (access to education, a secure home, healthcare, church membership, clothing, food etc.) And so, we forget to thank God. We forget to invite God into our situations, and we start to lose touch with who He is and what He has done and can do in our lives. We fail to recognise that God's glory is seen in the trivial things, as well as the large things; we no longer honour Him in all circumstances.

At the time of writing this chapter, I am on lockdown in the UK because of the Coronavirus. This is an unprecedented time, a time when those Christians who have been blessed to live in a first world country are beginning to recognise the challenges of our brothers and sisters in other parts of the world. For us, this is a time to reflect on whether we are honouring God in every area of our lives, asking the question, does God reign in totality, or do we merely say that He is our God, without giving Him the respect and honour He is due?

When we fall into the trap of living our comfortable lives, failing to give God the honour and worship that his glory warrants, we are in danger of becoming complacent in other areas of our faith. We are increasingly seeing Christians who are challenging God's word, asking, "Did God really say that?" or "Did God really mean that?" I have seen this manifested, in an escalation, in the number of church goers who are interpreting what the Bible says about homosexuality in ways that were unheard of before the sexual revolution. It seems that since society adopted a more relaxed attitude towards sex in the sixties and seventies, many Christians have formed their own take on how to interpret the Bible, rather than exploring the interpretations that have stood for thousands of years.

What is equally as concerning to me is that there are arguments in some denominations over the "authority of Scripture." If we do not recognise the Bible as God's inspired word, what point is there of having it? Questioning its authority leads to fundamental questions of what do we believe and what do we not? Which laws do we obey, and which do we ignore? I know that much has been written about this by scholars and theologians. Call me old fashioned, but I like to trust what Paul says in his letter to Timothy, namely that God inspires all the Bible. I believe much of the undermining of the authority of God's word is about us wanting to make it work for our lives, rather than wanting our lives to be conformed by living in obedience to God's ways.

Do we really need to question what is at the root of people's desire to translate the Scriptures in ways that indulge their human desires? Surely it is the idol of self and of sexual identity which creates a cavalier attitude within us. That is the cause of any downplaying of the authority of Scripture and the exaggeration of the concept of free love and free grace. It is our pride which says, 'I deserve it' and our lust which says. 'I need it.'

When we act like David, when he finally brought the ark of the covenant home to Israel, we are demonstrating that, more than anything else, we desire God's glory. We are expressing for ourselves a recognition of the impact that God's glory will have on our own lives and on the spiritual life of our churches. The glory of God must be present if we are to experience spiritual growth, both personally and within our churches. Like the household of Obed-Edom, when we experience the glory of God, we will thrive.

Writing in his book "The Myth of the Dying Church[47]", Glenn Stanton lays out research that shows that biblical churches in America are holding their ground or growing in terms of membership levels. On the converse, it is the liberal churches that are haemorrhaging members. Liberal churches can be described as "mishandling the glory of God," to such an extent that the glory of God has departed from within their ranks. I write this with a certain heaviness of heart, as I see the denomination that I joined after giving my life to the Lord, fall foul to liberal theology, as same sex marriage was voted through the UK Methodist synod in 2020.

---

[47] The Myth of the Dying Church, Published by Worthy Books, 2019

The time has come to invite the glory of God back into our churches, because it is only through God's glory that the deceit of Satan can be overcome. We are in a time when we can no longer fear. We must allow God's perfect love to cast out all fear as we boldly invite His glory back into our places of worship. Here are three things that I suggest churches can do to facilitate this:

1. Godly Leaders –We need leaders whose greatest desire is for the church to be separate from the world; leaders who are wholeheartedly committed to God's word. These leaders should not be concerned with popularity, increases in their congregation numbers, social media presence or money in the bank. Their heart, soul and mind should be concerned to see the glory of God manifested within their church family and communities. This might mean preaching a message that is unpopular; this might mean people boycotting your church; this might mean being trolled on social media or worse, being accused of hate speech. But if our godly leaders are preaching the truth in love, there is nothing or no one that they should fear.

2. Kingdom Culture – There is a culture available to us all, the culture of heaven. We need to trust and believe that God's ways are higher than ours, even when it is a tough call personally. We are called to repent, through changed thinking and changed behaviours, removing all thoughts and actions that are sinful from our way of living. We have access to our God who can do immeasurably more than all we ask or imagine. So instead of doing it our way or confining God to our own capabilities, we need a cultural shift where we see and do life through God's eyes. Adopting a Kingdom culture is telling Satan that we will not be sucked in by his lies, we will not bow down to his idols, and that our God is greater than anything he could ever throw at us.

3. Preach the Gospel – Unless we know and understand the word of God, we will continue to do Christianity our way. The Bible engages with us and leads us into God's vision for humanity. Christianity is often counter cultural and that is even more reason for us to understand, and

then hold to, the truth of God's word as we stand at cross purposes with the world. Church leaders must bring sound teaching into the pulpit; that sound teaching is to be built on the authoritative word of God. Additionally, this should be done without shying away from handling sensitive topics head on. For example, when was the last time you heard a sermon being preached from the pulpit on sexuality? And it is not only down to our church leaders, but we also have a responsibility ourselves to ensure that we are grounded in God's word, which is easy to do given the number of online or paper based daily bible studies which are readily available. Churches can help by holding regular bible study and small groups and ensuring that the word is fully incorporated into Sunday services. We also have a responsibility to foster a love of God's word in our children and young people.

The church was established by God as a vehicle to display his glory. When the church remains faithful to God's word in its practices and disciplines, and is led by godly leaders who are equipping their church members to serve, the church proclaims the glory of God. If a church fails to distinguish itself from the world, its members fail to change their ways in obedience to God and the leaders fails to teach biblical truth, the church no longer displays God's glory. Our goal, as the church, is to ensure that we positively reflect God's glory through all we do and speak.

The Smoke of God's Anger

There are several references within the Bible to God's anger. It is not an area that we like to dwell on; many people struggle with the thought of God being angry. Some people are prone to say that the God of the Old Testament was different from how God is now and that he showed his anger more vehemently in those times. That does not mean God does not get angry today; God does not change (Malachi 3:6). We may think that his anger today is manifested in different ways from the past, but however it is displayed, we can be sure that God still experiences moments of righteous anger driven by the ignorance and self-centred attitude of humanity.

It is important that we do not create an impression that depicts God as angry in the way that we understand anger in our culture (violent, unreasonable, or aggressive.) Human anger is often unpredictable, can be triggered by petty things, and is most often disproportionate to the thing that caused it in the first place. Anger is something that is innate within us, but we know that God is love. His anger is not something that is within Him, it is simply a provoked response to evil. Had sin never entered the world, there would be no wrath of God; nothing would provoke His anger if we had remained sinless.

Unlike us, God is slow to anger; He is patient in holding out His hand of grace to us. One day we will be fully answerable for our actions. God through His grace does not deal with us as we fully deserve right now. Instead, He reveals His anger through giving us over to our own self-destructive behaviours. Consider Romans 1; because of the behaviour of the people who believed lies and worshipped idols, God gave the people over to their own lusts, to dishonourable passions and to a debased mind. This "giving over" was the "angry" response of God.

To counter this impression of God being a vindictive, or angry God, we can talk about God's clear guidance on how to live and what His expectations of us are. Explaining that failing to live up to these will cause sorrow for God, and that our sin will naturally provoke a reaction in a righteous and perfect God, may help others to understand the difference between our anger and the anger of God.

Some things that the Bible tells us make God angry or that he "hates" are recorded in Proverbs:

> There are six things the Lord hates, seven that are
> detestable to him: haughty eyes, a lying tongue, hands
> that shed innocent blood, a heart that devises wicked
> schemes, feet that are quick to rush into evil, a false
> witness who pours out lies and a person who stirs up
> conflict in the community. Proverbs 6:16-19 (NIV)

If we simply consider our own reaction to the above, we gain a better understanding of how God must feel towards these things. If these things make our blood boil, how much more would they make a perfect God angry? Our responses help to put God's anger into perspective. They help us to understand better that His anger may not necessarily be as bad an emotion as we initially think.

The Bible talks of righteous anger[48] and that is exactly what God's anger is. It is not misplaced or mistimed, but simply anger at man's failure to revere His glory and live just and moral lives.

In the Old Testament there are many examples of God's anger and judgment against the Israelites; for example read Deuteronomy 9:8, Joshua 7:1 or Judges 2:20. But what I want to examine in closer detail is the recounting of the ten commandments in Exodus. After the commandments have been given to Moses, the people looking on from a distance are full of fear. As you read the passage you will not see a direct reference to God's anger, but the response of the people is one that is often experienced by those who feel the anger of another, namely fear. In fact, this fear was so real that they feared for their lives.

> When the people saw the thunder and lightning and heard
> the trumpet and saw the mountain in smoke, they
> trembled with fear. They stayed at a distance and said to
> Moses, "Speak to us yourself and we will listen. But do not
> have God speak to us or we will die." Moses said to the
> people, "Do not be afraid. God has come to test you, so
> that the fear of God will be with you to keep you from
> sinning." Exodus 20:18-20 (NIV)

God had just delivered the prototype for holy living to Moses, the commandments by which the people were to live. These commandments had been carefully crafted to guide the people to loving and responsible behaviour within their communities. These commands so important, so

---

[48] Ephesians 4:26-27

central to God's desires for humanity, that their delivery was accompanied by thunder and lightning and the mountain itself was covered in smoke (the holy smoke of God's presence). We do not know God's mood when He delivered these to Moses, but it could be suggested that the need for these commandments was driven out of His exasperation and sorrow at the sinful attitudes of the Israelites who had strayed so far from Him.

God speaks in a majestic display of power designed to remind the Israelites of His authority. This was not a case of God wanting to make them fearful, (we know from the Bible that God's first reassurances in frightening situations is "do not be afraid"), but a case of wanting them to recognise His authority and power, and to realise that the same power would be available to them if they just did what He asked.

The ten commandments are as relevant today as they were on the day God delivered them to Moses. But when we hear them read aloud (and that does not happen that often!), do we receive them with the same fear and trembling as the Israelites did? Unfortunately, the ten commandments tend to no longer evoke such a response, more often seen as an irrelevant set of rules not fit for twenty first century living. Yet we can learn so much from them about our God, who is still, and always will be, a jealous God[49].

The following examples consider what seven of these commandments might mean for those who continue to place their sexual orientation ahead of God's word, through the addition of some questions God may pose.

1. **You shall have no other gods before me** – God will not take a back seat and must not take second place in our lives. God is identified as the supreme power and authority and rightly demands that we put no other in His place.

   God asks: Where does your identity lie; is your sexuality more important to you than I am?

---

[49] Deuteronomy 4:24

2. **You shall not make any idols** – God is different from our idols; He is out of our control and cannot be manipulated or bargained with. God uses this command to encourage us not to reduce Him. I am reminded of the lyrics in the song King of the World[50]:

"I try to put you in the box that I've designed, I try to pull you down, so we are eye to eye, when did I forget that you've always been the king of the world?"

God asks - Are you more concerned with fitting into my world, or do you want me to fit into yours?

3. **You shall not misuse the name of the Lord your God** – God is never to be dismissed or taken lightly; His name is to be treated with respect and honour.

God asks: - How do you think I feel when you call yourself a "Gay Christian?"

4. **Honour your father and your mother** – God wants us to show due respect and love to our earthly parents; He is our heavenly Father and our behaviours and attitudes towards Him should be mirrored in our behaviours and attitudes towards our own earthly parents. But this command also emphasises God's design for marriage, and that children should have a father and a mother.

God asks: My design was for children to be brought up by a father and a mother, why do you belittle that design as you celebrate other forms of relationship?

5. **You shall not commit adultery** – God is clear that adultery and sexual immorality are an affront to Him. God wants us to remain pure, to have no sexual idols, nor a skewed understanding of our own sexuality. God is clear that the place for sex is within a marriage between one man and one woman.

---

[50] King of the World, from the Album "Be One" (2015) by Natalie Grant

God asks: Is sex so important to you that you would break my commands?

6. **You shall not give false testimony** – Proverbs tells us that God hates lying. Lying comes from the attitude of our hearts and is toxic, often leading to the breaking up of strong relationships. Lying also causes guilt and shame, and there is no place for that in the life of a Christian.

God asks: Why do you peddle falsehood about my design for sex? Are you teaching what my word says or something different?

7. **You shall not covet** – God is all we need; He alone can satisfy our souls. God tells us that "we are enough" and what we need is Him, because without Him we can never be satisfied.

God asks: Do you not trust me with what I can give you?

Take another look at the ten commandments; it is a tough list for anyone. Is it any wonder that the people saw the smoke of God's glory and power on the mountain when these were being delivered? And let us not kid ourselves, Satan is fully aware of each of these commandments and works incessantly to trip us up or deceive us into thinking that they are not important. For each question I have added that God may ask, you can be sure that Satan will jump right in with a convincing answer, unless we open our eyes to his end game.

Look at the commandments and consider the seven questions posed. What they all boil down to is one question, do you trust God to do what is right for you? But the passage relating to the giving out of the ten commandments also reminds us that God is to be revered. The smoke that the Israelites saw on the mountain (which can be likened to the smoke that David talks of as he sees God touching the mountains in Psalm 104:32 and 144:5), serves as a reminder to us that God is not to be approached lightly. He is not to be mocked and should be treated with respect. "Holy smoke" is a good thing, a sign of God's power and authority, a sign of a God who cares for His people and wants to protect them. It is a reminder of how glorious our God is. This is in direct contrast to the smoke of Satan which we looked at in the last chapter, the smoke of deceit and lies.

We need to exchange the air that we are breathing, from the smoky atmosphere created by Satan, to the pure and holy atmosphere of God. Air exchangers are used in buildings to replace the stale air that has built up inside with fresh natural air from the outside environment. This exchange of air involves the use of filtration systems that capture dust, pollen, mould, and other pollutants, ensuring that we are living in a healthier environment. Likewise, we need to apply God's filters to our lives, to ensure that the polluting messages of Satan are filtered out as we are filled with the glory of the Spirit of God.

It is time to take stock of the air we are breathing in and become more conscious of whose voices we are listening to. For some of us, that may mean taking a step back and thinking more about the holiness of God and what that means for how we approach Him. Do we give Him due worship and respect; do we take time to listen to what He is saying, spending time in meditation and silence in His company? Do we yearn to actively receive God's breath of life as we absorb his life-giving word?

> *The Spirit of God has made me; the breath of the Almighty gives me life. Job 33:4 (NIV)*

TESTIMONY, BEA, UK

Bea journeyed through deep depression, sexual confusion, emotional co-dependency, and brokenness before she finally found her true self in Jesus. She knew Jesus, she knew his word, but somehow the smoke and mirrors of the world sucked her in. But we have a God who pursues us actively and whose authentic love and desire for us will always counter the lies of the world and leave Satan with no answers or come back. Bea is now an active leader and worship leader within the UK church and reflects the love of Jesus through her life, lived for Him.

'But you love her.'
This was a phrase I heard repeatedly from Satan whilst in a same-sex relationship. It typically surfaced when I was in a time of questioning what we were doing. Why would God want me to stop something that was... so beautiful? How can loving another woman be so wrong?

Yet it was wrong. It was very wrong, and I knew it. My partner knew it too. Often, we would go through cycles of repentance, abstaining from physical contact and sex, and focus on only being friends. We managed - rather we coped for a while - until our urges for intimacy got the better of us and we would revert back to our wanton ways. Imagine that cycle as an elastic band. Yet instead of going around the band, our limited efforts of abstinence would stretch the band until the point where neither of us could maintain the strain of physical separation and we would let it ping us back to our comfort mode where we would once again return to indulging our desires.

Yet this comfort mode had a continual irritation that meant we could never really settle as a couple. The only solution was to get rid of the irritation so that we could be free to be ourselves. The irritation in question was the word of God. What the Bible says about sexuality is clear, yet we were in the process of attempting to cloud it: the smokescreen of Satan. Were we blind to what we were doing? No. Were we unaware of what God has said about men, women, relationships, and sex? No. Did we want to ignore it?

Absolutely. Yet as much as we tried, we could not. There was never any escape from it. At the time, we were both Christians actively serving in church, whilst living the lie of a secret relationship. We had no intention of telling anyone about our commitment to each other because we knew what the response would be. Staying quiet and pretence were the only options.

'But you love her.'
'Arrgghhh!'

I did indeed love her. I loved her more than anyone and anything. Therein lay the problem. My love for her – our relationship – had been put on a pedestal. Nothing was allowed to touch it, including our Holy God. This chapter speaks about how we should take stock of the ten commandments. I was guilty of idolising my partner and keeping her ahead of God. We both knew that sex outside of marriage is wrong, as well as it being wrong for two women, but we somehow thought that because our love for each other was so right, God must be wrong. What pride!

Over time we attempted to nullify the irritation by finding flaws in Scripture. We looked at different translations that could potentially offer a glimmer of hope for us to legitimately continue. We listened to testimonies of other gay Christians who had publicly come out and started to believe them more than God. What hypocrisy!

The irritation was also God's holiness. It was irrefutable and it was convicting. God is so gracious; He is so merciful. He is also so patient. He did not come against us with fire and brimstone or anger. Rather, it was His gentle, powerful, continuous stream of love that reminded us repeatedly of who He is and who we are meant to be with Him. His grace eventually wore me down and won me over. I reached a point where I could no longer justify, nor wanted to continue, the false level of comfort we had created. There was no comfort in it. The cycle, the elastic band needed snapping once and for all. I called off our relationship. Then, some months later, I found myself flirting again with another woman, eager once more for an intimate connection. Where my behaviour had been temporarily halted, desire within me had continued. When sin continues unchallenged, it will eventually find its way out into the open again, like a plant sending out its shoots underground to then sprout upwards in the right conditions.

I needed to change inwardly, not outwardly. The Holy of Holies that Sarah spoke about in this chapter, the inner sanctum where few were permitted to enter, was, conversely, what I needed to allow God to do within me. I needed to allow Him into the most private place within me, the place where desire and idolatry were residing. This prospect was as terrifying as the fear I had had during the relationship. How could I let God into my heart of hurts? It seemed impossible, but I was reaching a point where I was more willing to let go of homosexuality, than continue the effort of trying to live as a gay Christian.

Why was God so interested in me? Why couldn't He leave me alone to do what I thought I wanted to do? Because He knew that my heart was for Him. But because of sin, I could not get as close to Him as I needed to: sin cannot be in the presence of Holiness. So, what does God do when we cannot go to Him? He comes down to us, just as He did through Jesus, walking on this earth and showing us the Way to the Father. Another illustration of this in the story of the Prodigal Son, where the father runs to greet his estranged son and embrace him back into his home and restore his status. Yet this father only ran when he saw that the son had first turned away from his previous lifestyle of choice and was walking back towards him. In the same way, the moment I decided I could no longer live in my lifestyle of choice and wanted to truly return back to the Father, He came running to me and began to restore me. His righteousness and holiness were a beautiful soothing balm that aided me in my full confession and repentance of homosexuality. What a wonderful Holy Father He is!

Chapter 6 – The Warnings of Jesus

It does not take too deep a study of our Bibles to recognise that when Jesus walked the earth, he was clear about Satan and his schemes. Jesus gave many warnings, both direct and indirect, for us to be on our guard against Satan. To live a holy life, a life of obedience to Christ, it is essential that we do not rely on what other people say, but that we recognise for ourselves what these warnings look like. Some of these warnings are found directly in the words of Jesus, and others are found through our observations of the way that Jesus reacted to situations which he found himself in. To illustrate just some of these warnings, let us spend some time looking at the gospel of Matthew, which provides rich pickings. It is here that we start to see the character of Jesus unfold as he reveals his authority as the son of God.

We first read of an encounter between Jesus and Satan in Matthew 4. In chapter 3 we learnt of the baptism of Jesus and how the Spirit of God descended on him in the form of a dove. Immediately after this account, chapter 4 talks of how Jesus was tested in the wilderness. It says that, "He was led by the Spirit into the wilderness to be tempted by Satan." Note firstly those words, "He was led by the Spirit." God allowed this to happen; he gave Satan permission to approach his Son. Indeed the Spirit which had descended on Jesus freely led Him into the situation. Why was this? I believe it was because God was aware of the need for Jesus to overcome any form of temptation, to illustrate his power and authority, both to Satan at that time and for those who were to follow Jesus in the future. Make no mistake, God had agreed for this time of testing to happen to demonstrate his supreme authority.

Warning #1 – Satan uses temptation to undermine our relationship with God and to cause us to question our choices.

90

Response #1 - God allows temptation to happen to build our faith and character.

God allows temptation, but it does not mean that He wants us to act on the temptations any more than he wanted Jesus to succumb to Satan. There were good reasons that Jesus was tempted in the wilderness and good reasons why we are subject to temptation. Hebrews 4:15 is clear about why God needed to allow Jesus to be tempted:

> *For we do not have a high priest who is unable to empathise with our weaknesses, but we have one who has been tempted in every way, just as we are—yet he did not sin. Let us then approach God's throne of grace with confidence, so that we may receive mercy and find grace to help us in our time of need. Hebrews 4:15-16 (NIV)*

God allows us to be tempted because he wants us to know that we can say no to temptation when it comes our way. He wants us to recognise the authority we have, the same authority that he gave to Jesus. He wants us to have faith to use that authority freely as we live our lives for His glory. Having authority over our own minds and thoughts is essential if we are then to exercise God's authority over situations that we find ourselves in.

> *Then Jesus came to them and said, "All authority in heaven and on earth has been given to me. Therefore, go and make disciples of all nations, baptising them in the name of the Father and of the Son and of the Holy Spirit, and teaching them to obey everything I have commanded you. And surely, I am with you always, to the very end of the age." Matthew 28:18-20 (NIV)*

In fact, being subjected to temptation is a means for God to help us to grow and mature in our faith. He wants us to be wise in different situations and to discern what is right for us. As we mature in our faith, we grow to understand what he demands of us, which requires us to understand what is both good and wrong in his sight. His goal is to refine us into people who make good choices in every situation.

When Satan tempts us, God uses our responses to gauge whether we have learnt to lean on Him. He can quickly see those who are feasting on His word, eager for knowledge and understanding, and therefore able to react quickly before the temptation overcomes them. Likewise, he sees those who are confident in the authority God has given them to rebuke Satan. He also sees those who are ill equipped for the task, with little Bible knowledge or with Bible knowledge yet little faith. He sees those who listen to what others have to say about His word, rather than reading it for themselves. He is fully aware of those who have built up strong Christian friendships and support systems to help them overcome temptation, and those who have developed a culture of accountability within their church or home group, as opposed to those who try to go it alone. If we allow God to mould us, He will use each temptation to build us into stronger and better equipped disciples.

Jesus clearly modelled how we are equipped with the tools we need. The Son of God himself quoted Scripture directly to Satan in response to his attempts to make Jesus bow down to him. If that's how Jesus responded, then how much more pertinent is it for us to respond in the same way. Jesus was fully prepared; he had heard the word of God spoken in the synagogue since he was a young boy. He had studied with zeal and passion, and fully understood the power of Scripture. His immediate response to Satan was to respond directly from the heart of God's word, which gave him confidence, despite his weakness from days of fasting, to give one final rebuke as he tells Satan with strong conviction, "away from me."

As a young Christian I struggled with self-harming and was easy picking for Satan, who spent a season pointing out my weakness and seeking to demoralise me into helplessness. It was only after time in God's word, understanding how my identity had changed, that I started to find my voice. I began to see how God saw me; I was loved, adopted, and important to

Him, cherished and he had a plan for me. Gradually, I built up enough confidence in who God told me I was, to be able to respond to Satan as he told me that 'no one was bothered,' 'I was insignificant,' 'I should be ashamed,' 'I was guilty.' Finally, as I recognised the truth of God's word, I told Satan how wrong he was and quoted verses that told him just how special I am to God. That, coupled with a decision to make myself accountable to a small group of Christians, empowered me to overcome his lies, respond positively to rebuke the temptation to self-harm, and step into a new season of my walk with the Lord.

Have I been tempted again to self-harm; of course I have. Satan knows that it was my Achilles heel and liked to use it as a weapon against me, particularly when I was low, which was when I failed to remind myself of who I was in Christ. Did I succumb to that temptation? Yes, on a couple of occasions in the first two years of my faith I listened to those lies and slipped up. Yet on both occasions I met with God's understanding and forgiveness, and I found a new inner strength to rebuke Satan the next time he came knocking with the same old lies. As I matured as a Christian, this temptation became less prominent and gradually disappeared. I put this down to my increased understanding of how I can react to Satan's jibes, responding more confidently with Scripture and with an intense trust and faith in what God says about me. I recognise that God permits us to be tempted, but also that these temptations will never be more than we can manage if we trust in God[51]. To manage them well, we remain intricately connected to the source, that is God and his word.

This closeness to God, and our faith in his promise to help us to overcome any temptation, is an important consideration for those who believe that no one can walk away from homosexual sin. For their beliefs to change, there needs to be a recognition that:

- There is such a thing as sexual sin, and this sin is clearly called out in the Bible as sinning against one's own body. [52].

---

[51] 1 Corinthians 10:13

- Sex is a gift of God given to be celebrated within a covenant union of one man and one woman[53].
- Sexual activity outside of marriage is a by-product of temptation, a reaction to our human thoughts and lusts, and a positive response to Satan as he shows us the forbidden fruit, telling us it is OK to eat it.

Fortunately for us, the Bible is clear. It tells us that sex is a gift from God, reserved for marriage. Satan counters by telling us that sex is our right in every circumstance. He may make this more palatable by tempting us with lies such as, "as long as it doesn't harm anybody it's good," "it is pleasurable, therefore it must be good," "you were born with these feelings, so they cannot be wrong." Satan's goal is to con us into believing that God did not mean that only married couples can have sex, or to believe that it does not matter what God says. Satan would point out to us that most people are having sex outside of marriage, so why not Christians? Other lies come from Satan as he questions our interpretation of biblical texts, as he says, "surely that's not what that means?" In the same way that our God is not a God of confusion and chaos, recognise that Satan's number one goal is to confuse and cause mayhem.

But what do you believe? As it is our own responsibility to read the Bible in full, that is where we should seek the answer, to see how God views sex and to recognise what sexual sin looks like. Only when we seek the truth, will we experience a shift in our mind-set. In my opinion, a comprehensive reading of the Bible gives us enough knowledge to reveal that God did not make us sexual beings simply to see us to defy his design for sex (understood as being reserved for the marriage of one man and one woman.) Of course, Satan would like to keep us confused, to undermine our relationship with God, yet fortunately for us God has given us clarity. Let us not undermine God's power and His ability to bring freedom from all sin. God can do anything he sets his mind to, and often does more than we ask or imagine!

---

[52] 1 Corinthians 6:18
[53] Genesis 2:24

94

There have been some extraordinary testimonies in the last decade, as God has brought many of his children out of the homosexual lifestyle to full freedom from SSA. We have included some of these within this book, but for more examples you can look online; the Changed Movement's website is particularly good.[54] Full freedom and a changed sexual orientation is the ultimate in transformation and, I believe a goal to be fully sought and believed for. Yet like other things, God does not always lead us to total transformation whilst here on earth.

Take for example those who have a disability or illness. One person may receive supernatural, on the spot healing, another may receive healing over time, and some do not see their healing this side of eternity. That does not mean that we do not seek the transformation or that we do not believe that our God can accomplish it. We keep our eyes on Jesus, being obedient to his word and trusting in his grace to see us through. We do not come to faith solely to focus on what God is going to do for us, but to ask ourselves the question, "What am I going to do for Him?" The answer to that question does involve sacrifice. Sadly, for some in the homosexual lifestyle, the required sacrifice appears overwhelming as they struggle with what that looks like for them personally. As SSA remains a strong temptation for some, rather than ask God, 'when are you going to take this away?' perhaps what we should be asking is as laid out in the Lord's prayer: 'And lead us not into temptation, but deliver us from the evil one[55]', trusting that God will deliver, and that deliverance will ultimately result in a changed life.

Almost immediately after we read about the incident in the wilderness, Matthew's gospel turns to the more pressing business of why Jesus came to earth. Verse 17 tells us that Jesus began to preach, and his message was, "Repent, for the kingdom of heaven has come near."

---

[54] https://changedmovement.com/stories/
[55] Matthew 6:13

Warning #2 – Satan wants us to believe that we can get to heaven without repentance.

Response #2 – Jesus clearly told us that we must repent to be saved.

The whole purpose of God sending his son to earth was to give us an opportunity to reconcile with God. Satan's mission is quite simply to prevent us from reconciling and to prevent us from having a personal relationship with God. His mission means that he will go to any measure to deceive us, as the words of Jesus found in Matthew substantiate. From His exhortation to enter through the narrow gate, to his plea to pick up your cross and follow Him, Jesus is giving us every opportunity to read between the lines and recognise the reality of our calling.

The fact that there is a narrow gate is something to consider; it indicates that being a follower of God may not be as easy as some people think. When presented with two choices, the human predisposition is to take the path of least resistance. It requires strength of character and a determined mind to defy our natural instincts and sacrifice our own ways for God's ways. God did not promise us a comfortable ride; His word was written to warn and guide us, because he understood that as Christians, we would face conflict and deceit from Satan. As a result of our discipleship, we are subjected to the onslaught of Satan's lies and deception. Yet it is not only those who follow Jesus who are subjected to Satan's lies. As people search for spiritual answers, and start to explore the Christian faith, you can be sure that Satan will be doing everything in his power to prevent them from learning the truth about God.

Jesus knew that to follow Him effectively, we must be prepared to lose our own lives. For us, in the western world, this may not seem to be relevant or that significant on a personal level, but that does not mean that it is not something that may become incredibly significant to us within our rapidly changing moral landscape. We recognise that persecution and death has been a literal truth for a many Christians throughout the ages, yet are we confident that we too, could stand up for Christ if it risked our livelihood or indeed our lives?

Losing our lives looks different to us all; in every instance becoming a Christian necessitates making some level of change to our lifestyle. In some cases, these changes in how life is lived may be small, in other cases these require momentous shifts in our actions and behaviours. Think of the alcoholic, the gang leader or the drug addict who come to faith in Christ. This newfound faith impacts their relationship with family and friends, as they turn their back on the past. It may mean that places they use to frequent are off limits; they may need to move to a new neighbourhood or town. They must die to the old self and embrace the new.

The same is true of the homosexual who repents and follows Jesus. The repercussions of stepping out of that lifestyle are considerable, and I recognised from the outset that if I were to make a commitment to God, I was in for a rough ride. If you have never battled with an addiction or with habitual sexual sin, it may be hard for you to comprehend the battle that rages in the mind of someone who does struggle with these things as they explore the Christian faith.

Consider the scenario for someone in a same sex relationship who has come to the point in their relationship with God that they desire to give their life to Jesus. For them it is not just a matter of repenting and continuing their Christian walk with the same relationship dreams and aspirations that they have always had. When I repented of homosexual sin it meant recognising that sex outside of heterosexual marriage was not appropriate. The outworking of my repentance was a change in the relationship I had with my partner, from one of a sexual and intimate nature to that of a platonic friend. My repentance resulted in the loss of a lifelong partner, the loss of my security and the loss, as I interpreted it then, of a future hope of ever having an intimate relationship. It also meant alienating myself from friends from within the gay community, as once solid friendships became fraught with difficulties and tensions. For me, and others like me, it meant a new life, stepping into unchartered waters and fully relying on our newfound friend in Jesus to navigate us through.

I hope this helps you to understand why many in the LGBTQ+ community would rather believe Satan's lies, as he tells us for instance that, "God's word doesn't condemn loving same sex relationships." How much easier it would be to believe those lies and not give up on a loving relationship. Yet believing those lies means walking the wide path; it means not surrendering all to Jesus. When we step out in faith, God promises that he will walk that narrow road with us. If Jesus can pick up his cross and follow, then surely, we can too?

Jesus laid out our options[56]. We can enter through the narrow gate and travel the narrow road of life. Here Jesus is clear in his warning, 'only a few find it.' Or we can enter through the wide gate and travel the broad road that many have entered. This, the easier route, sees us walk shoulder to shoulder with the masses to our destruction. Which road do you think Satan wants you to walk? Jesus reminded us of the road to walk when he said, "I am the way, the truth and the life, no man comes to the Father except through me[57]." Repentance is only available through Jesus; the truth is only found in Jesus, and eternal life is only obtainable through Jesus.

The issue we face today is a church that is becoming increasingly liberal, in many cases a church which fails to preach sin as sin. I am not trying to be one of those old school, Bible bashing preachers here, but this is important for the salvation of millions. If we as a church say that there is no need to repent of the sin of homosexuality, because we say that it is not a sin, we are preaching a gospel contrary to the one Jesus preached. If we do not call for repentance, we too have become those false teachers and preachers spoken about so often in both the Old and New Testament. The Bible has always been clear that homosexuality is a sin[58]. Yes, I know that

---

[56] Matthew 7:13-14
[57] John 14:6
[58] Romans 1:26-27, 1 Timothy 1:8-11, 1 Corinthians 6:9-11, 1 Corinthians 7:2,

my statement will cause controversy, that's how Satan wants it to be. Yet it is undeniable that there are many references to God's plan for our sexuality and marriage in both the Old and New Testament. The question must therefore be, "How has Satan caused God's people to so reject this word?"

The next warning in the gospel of Matthew is the most potent warning, one which many have chosen to ignore for too long. Here Jesus gives us a clear and candid statement of truth that we can ill afford to ignore:

> *Watch out for false prophets. They come to you in sheep's clothing, but inwardly they are ferocious wolves. Matthew 7:15 (NIV)*

Warning #3 - Beware of people who look like Christians but who peddle a false doctrine that will strike ferociously at the heart of the Christian faith.

Response #3 – Be on your guard, for the threat is not from the world, but from within your church.

There are few people, Christians, or non-Christians, who are not aware of the saying, 'Beware of wolves in sheep's clothing[59],' which originates from Matthew 7. Jesus is warning us to be alert in our faith, and the mere fact that Jesus declares this warning to us, is another indicator of how important it is for us to take heed. He goes on to tell us that we will recognise these people by their lack of fruit, or by their bad fruit. But how do we do this in practice; how do we recognise whether someone is fruitful? Granted, when we know someone for a period, their fruit will become much easier for us to see, but it is difficult to discern the fruit of a person in the short term. An eloquent preacher comes to your church, do you really have time to discern their position? You listen to a short article on Christian radio, do you get the full picture? That is why we are told to test everything we hear[60], and this means to read the Bible (a robust and

---

Leviticus 18:22, Leviticus 20:13.
[59] Matthew 7:15

99

recognised version), pray over the message, and ask God for wisdom and discernment. It also helps to be part of a small group where you study the word with other Christians, and can bring issues and concerns to that group setting for discussion and prayer, as you seek discernment and wisdom.

When I first became a Christian, I continued to watch a lot of YouTube videos and read articles about sexuality and faith. It was at this time that I started to discern when the Holy Spirit was telling me that what I was listening to was not of God. It is hard to explain what that discernment looked or felt like, but it was a gut feeling. God was actively telling me that what I was listening to was false teaching. The more I read the Bible, and the more I listened to faithful preachers, the quicker I was able to discern a false message.

Is Jesus talking about people from other faiths and religions, or even those of no faith at all, when he brings us this warning? A quick look at the next few verses unravels that argument and clearly indicates that, sadly, Jesus is talking about those who profess to be Christians.

> *'Many will say to me on that day, 'Lord, Lord, did we not*
> *prophesy in your name and in your name drive out*
> *demons and, in your name, perform many miracles?'*
> *Then I will tell them plainly, 'I never knew you. Away from*
> *me, you evildoers!' Matthew 7:21-23 (NIV)*

Jesus talks here very clearly about, 'those who prophesied in my name,' 'those who 'drove out demons in my name,' and those who 'performed many miracles.' We know that no other faith or religion will use the name of Jesus in their practice. He is not talking about Muslims, Sikhs, Hindus or Jews, Buddhists, atheists, or agnostics. Jesus is talking about those who use His name, a clear reference to those professing to be Christians. If we open our eyes, we will see that we are not being taken in by other faiths, or indeed those of no faith, we are being deceived from within, which is a

---

[60] 1 Thessalonians 5:21

stark warning indeed. This warning is not limited to the words of Jesus as it is echoed by Luke,[61] Peter[62], John,[63] and Paul in many of his letters.

Having warned us that there would be those amongst us who would lead us into false doctrine and teaching, Jesus gave us some insight into how we should react. In direct contrast to the warning of wolves infiltrating the church disguised as sheep, we later read that Jesus describes the disciples he sent out as being 'like sheep among the wolves,[64]' with the advice ringing in their ears, 'be shrewd as snakes and as innocent as doves.' This warning is pertinent to us as we navigate the false teaching that has become a regular fixture in many churches today.

The picture of sheep amongst wolves is one of hopelessness; the sheep are hardly able to defend themselves, so they become open to attack, even death. But Jesus advises his disciples how to manage this with two seemingly contradictory pieces of advice, 'be shrewd as snakes and as innocent as doves'[65].

Be shrewd as snakes.

A dictionary definition [66]shows us that shrewd can be understood as being 'marked by clever, discerning awareness and hard-headed acumen.'

Jesus is advising the disciples, and us, to use discernment to look at situations from different angles, so that we can quickly recognise what is happening; to be able to think on our feet. We cannot afford to let emotions affect our actions, nor can we be persuaded by compassion over our intuition. This advice suggests the need for us, and our churches, to have thought through the many potential scenarios that may expose us to false

---

[61] Acts 20:26-30
[62] 2 Peter 2:1-3
[63] 1 John 2:18-19
[64] Matthew 10:16
[65] Matthew 10:16
[66] https://www.merriam-webster.com/dictionary/

teaching. Have we thought about visiting speakers and teachers and what words they may bring?

- Is our church leadership team in regular communication over more than the day-to-day operational matters, talking about the doctrine and theology in play throughout church life?
- Do we have a clear statement of faith, and does this permeate our teaching from the youngest to the oldest?
- Are we geared up to deal with church members who are vocalising an alternative theology, particularly on subjects that may be divisive within our churches? Can we discern whether this is harmless questioning or more pointed rhetoric, aimed at undermining church teachings?
- What support do we offer those living in a lifestyle that is contrary to biblical teaching; how do we support these families in love yet in truth?

I used to be a member of the Methodist church in the UK. Methodism is well known for having a system of local preachers who work in a circuit of churches, sharing the responsibility of bringing God's word to congregations on a rotational basis. Given that the denomination itself is divided about whether homosexual acts are sinful, this causes difficulties for individual churches who wish to remain faithful to traditional biblical teaching, as they seek to 'protect' their pulpit. This is close to being an untenable situation; is it possible to manage? Church leaders should act "shrewdly," as advised by Jesus, with full awareness of the potential pressure points that can cause division. Leaders need to have a positive plan of action to ensure their own church members are immersed in truth and well versed in Scripture, equipping every member to rebuke any false teaching directly from its source.

The only way that discernment can be achieved to this level is by people who are strong in their faith, aware of God's truth and empowered to act. Shrewdness in our faith comes from spending time in God, building our spiritual strength and resilience, with an unfailing trust in Jesus to deliver us from all evil. Knowing that when Satan tries to play us, we have enough ammunition in our arsenal to overpower his pretensions and arguments.

What follows then is this paradoxical comment; we are told to be as innocent as doves. Yet what Jesus is telling us makes much sense. He is showing us the need for truth, combined with love. Being wise as a serpent reflects our need to be open with the truth, not compromising it for the sake of making someone feel good or helping them to fit in. In contrast, we are to be shrewd in what we say and how we say it, loving the person always, even if the sin or behaviour they are displaying is not something that we can condone in good faith.

Be innocent as doves.

Love is our raison d'etre, the purpose for our Christian service, to love the Lord our God with all our heart, mind, and soul and to love our neighbour as ourselves. Innocence in this sense ties in to how we manage controversial situations, particularly where our faith is questioned, where we are persecuted, criticised, or despised. When we desire to be truthful to our calling, this command to be as innocent as doves encourages us to always be of good character, filled with peace and of pure motive. It is understood that we should be prepared for false teaching, to be aware that there will be some among us who Satan will use to send us down the wrong path. This then demands an acute awareness of how we are called to react in these situations. God's word shows us that we overcome Satan's attack not by reactionary and revolutionary actions, but by love. We do this by considering each situation in isolation, ensuring that our motives are pure. Our aim or our desired outcome is not to be driven by fear or a sense of loss, but by love and a strong motivation for God's love to overcome.

In my short journey with the Lord, I admit to having reacted badly on some occasions to false teaching. I fear at times I was more serpent like, than one displaying the innocence of a dove. Jesus was so right in advising us to be balanced in our views. On each occasion where I have failed to show love, I have walked away in regret, knowing in my heart that my reaction had not helped the person understand my viewpoint; nor had they seen me as a great advocate for the truth, because my reaction had come from a place of anger. The last time this happened, I was at a meeting which had been advertised as one that would promote the inclusion of same sex marriage within the Methodist church, so I had no reason not to be prepared. My failing was that I allowed emotions to drive my attitude and response. As I grow in my knowledge and relationship with the Lord, I know that I am also growing in my ability to be shrewd as a serpent and innocent as a dove. It is hard, but it is achievable. The words I write at the top of my notepad now when I attend these events is, "respond don't react." I have written these words to remind me that I should be as shrewd as a serpent, yet also as innocent as a dove in all my responses.

Let us return to the warnings which keep coming. Jesus is clear repeatedly that not everyone who calls Him Lord will be saved.

> Not everyone who says to me, 'Lord, Lord,' will enter the
> kingdom of heaven, but only the one who does the will of
> my Father who is in heaven. Matthew 7:21 (NIV)

Warning #4 - Calling Jesus 'Lord' does not make us Christians.

Response #4 - When we hear the words of Jesus, we must put them into practice and live as he asks us, to call Him Lord.

For me this is one of the most challenging Scriptures in the Bible. As a direct quote from Jesus, it cannot be ignored, maligned, or criticised; it is there to be heeded. Yet we look around our churches today and see many who come in on Sunday, lift their hands to God calling Him Lord and spend the rest of the week living as if He does not exist. Indeed, there are many who never enter a church, yet would call themselves Christians. Paul wrote a warning about this in his second letter to the church at Corinth:

> I am afraid that when I come again my God will humble
> me before you, and I will be grieved over many who have
> sinned earlier and have not repented of the impurity,
> sexual sin, and debauchery in which they have indulged. 2
> Corinthians 12:21 (NIV)

We are all sinners, there is no getting away from it, not one of us is without fault. But what marks Christians out from others is their recognition of their sin and their desire to repent and change. We are all experienced enough to know that change is rarely instantaneous, and we are all works in progress. But if the intention is there, if the humility to recognise our faults and failings and seek God's forgiveness is there, then we have made the commitment that God requires of us. This is what Paul is referencing in his letter. He speaks of the many who have not repented of their sin, yet they still call God their Lord. Can we continue to live in a life of unrepented sin and expect to be welcomed into the Kingdom of Heaven?

There is some help for us on this in Hebrews, where we read that if we deliberately keep sinning after we have received the knowledge of truth, there is no sacrifice left for our sins[67]. If we are to qualify what we mean by sinning, I would suggest that it means disobeying clear commands that are found in Scripture. Think then about how and when we receive the knowledge of truth? I suggest that this is the point when we are exposed to the teaching of the Bible and hear and understand for ourselves what it means to follow God. If at this point, we reject what God is asking us to do, then are we purposely continuing to sin? If so, we read here that there is no sacrifice, unless of course we revisit our response in the future and choose to repent and follow God, an option that, by God's grace, is always available to us.

The question to pose therefore would be, "If I know that God says that homosexual actions are sinful, and I choose to ask Jesus into my life, yet choose to continue in a same-sex relationship, have I repented?"

When we come to faith in Christ we are challenged to submit to God in all things, including the authority of His word. Sure, we will fall into temptation from time to time, but when our hearts are fully set on Jesus, we are heartbroken at our failings, we feel remorse and sorrow, and we confess our sins in prayer. What then of the practicing homosexual who reads

---

[67] Hebrews 10:26

God's word, yet continues to have sexual relations with someone of the same sex?

Some of these people will have received their teaching and understanding from the false teachers spoken of in warning #3. It might be that they have not actually received the full knowledge of God's truth, because of the environment and culture of deceit present within their church. Yet, if they have read their Bibles, they have been exposed to God's truth. The underlying factor here is the rejection of truth (is ignorance of God's word an acceptable excuse?)

Then there are those who have read God's word, as written in the Bible, yet have chosen to ignore it or discard it as being unclear, interpreting it as only being aimed at those who have sex outside of a faithful relationship. The latter is a common argument to be found within the affirming church, whereby the belief is that the Bible only condemns same gender acts outside of a loving, committed relationship. Yet part of maturing as a Christian is looking further than just one or two verses, and recognising God's overall design and purpose for our lives. From Genesis to Revelation, we can see the parallels of marriage between man and woman, and the church becoming the bride of Christ. Not only does it celebrate marriage, but the Bible also makes many references to immorality, some directly referencing homosexuality. Interpreted as a whole, the Bible is clear about the consequences of sexual immorality and these warnings are there to be heeded.

Jesus was clear, there will be some who fully believe that they are saved, who will call Him Lord, yet they will be shocked on the day of judgment. In Matthew 15, Jesus refers to Isaiah's prophecy saying that Isaiah was right when he said, 'these people honour me with their lips, but their hearts are far from me'[68]. Furthermore just a few verses later Jesus says:

> But the things that come out of a person's mouth come
> from the heart, and these defile them. For out of the heart

---

[68] Matthew 15:8

come evil thoughts—murder, adultery, sexual immorality,
theft, false testimony, slander. Matthew 15:18-19 (NIV)

It is the heart that rules many people; this is often the reason that some people take a cut and paste approach to the Bible. When they like what it says, they use it to bolster their argument. A common example is Matthew 7:1, 'Do not judge, or you too will be judged.' Christians often use this verse to justify not challenging un-biblical behaviour amongst sisters and brothers in Christ. When a verse is something that does not sit right, or fit into their doctrine, many choose to ignore it, reinterpret it, or plain simply avoid it.

As an example, have a look at what many of the advocates for introducing same sex marriage into Churches are saying about the meaning of Leviticus 18 (or any of the other verses clearly outlining homosexuality as a sin). You will find many reasons that they use to say that this law is not relevant for today.

For example, Rev Brandon Robertson[69] says that "the cultural context of the Leviticus passage does not reference loving, consensual same-sex relationships, but relationships rooted in idolatry or exploitation, both of which should be rightly condemned."

This calls for conjecture on his behalf. He is believing that the writer of Leviticus is only referencing non-consensual sex. But the passage does not caveat the law with an "only if non-consensual," in the same way he does not caveat the laws listed before or after. For example, verse 12 says – "Do not have sexual relations with your father's sister; she is your father's close relative." Taking Brandon's argument, you could say this is only relevant if sex with the father's sister is forced. If it is consensual, it is not a sin. But we do not say that, nor do we use that logic for having sex with your brother's wife (v16) or your neighbour's wife (v20). In fact, nowhere

---

[69] www.patheos.com/blogs/faithfulprogress/2021/01/an-inclusive-interpretation-of-biblical-clobber-passages/

else in the list of sins would we use that logic, and so why would it make sense for the case of homosexuality?

Are these people using the Bible as their authority, or have they bowed the knee to cultural pressures and reworked the Bible to suit their pre-conceived ideas? Does their interpretation of the Bible result from a desire to affirm their compassionate response to those who struggle to accept Biblical teaching? By compassionate response, I am referencing those who "feel sorry" for Christians who may experience SSA, because of the resulting impact it may have on their lifestyle and relationships if they follow the teaching of the Bible. It appears that many empathising Christians, out of misplaced compassion, conclude that to expect people to deny their sexuality is "unfair."

Let us spend some time talking about compassion and the danger of allowing this emotion to govern our doctrine. In responding to God's word with an imbalanced sense of human compassion, our thoughts and emotions can become clouded, rather than looking at a specific teaching and situation in isolation, Bible open, thoughts surrendered to God. An imbalanced response affects our emotions, as our thoughts turn towards the person in question, - their life, their happiness, their "rights." I say this following many conversations with Christians, who once fully surrendered to the authority of the Bible over homosexuality until one day, a family member or close friend came out to them. That is when the balance started to change. God's word had not changed, God's thoughts had not changed, the only factor that changed was that it had become personal, and this is when Satan starts to tug at their emotional heart strings.

It is understandable that a personal experience can cause us to think more deeply about a situation, and to be honest that is a good thing. But I believe that we must proceed with caution, ensuring that we do not come at it from the starting position of seeking to justify human behaviours and responses. Our challenge is to approach this newfound knowledge of our loved one's sexuality, as someone who genuinely desires to be faithful to our long-held interpretation of God's word in the past and determine what difference, if any, the sexuality of our loved one makes to those beliefs.

One of the most persuasive arguments which Satan uses is to tell us that a person can be born gay. Christians who are personally affected by homosexuality may find this a more palatable argument than one which says that homosexuality results from our upbringing and environment. In believing that God makes people gay, the logical conclusion is that certain passages in the Bible have been misinterpreted and must be revisited and redefined to fit that conclusion. It is not hard to see how this one lie whispered in the ear, you were born this way, can spiral into a doctrinal shift, as we transfer our focus away from what God has always said, to a liberal interpretation of the Bible. The way that many Christians have responded to homosexuality (and other issues such as abortion) in the past couple of decades may be partially attributable to the ease of access to a wide range of liberal theology and teaching via the internet.

We need to honestly reflect on how we read the Bible. Is it with a mind-set of seeking ways to endorse our human emotions around difficult topics, for example abortion, sex outside marriage or homosexuality, or are we able to maintain perspective? From experience, I suggest that it is quite hard to be subjective when you have a personal interest in the outcome of your interpretation. I discovered this for myself when I first started exploring faith as an openly gay woman. Initially, I tried hard to interpret the Scriptures I was reading to help me to justify how I could be a "gay Christian." It was only through God's grace, that I was finally able to detach my personal emotions from my search and see through the smokescreen that Satan had put up. I recognised that I could no longer clutch at arguments over interpretation and authority, and needed to allow the Holy Spirit full access to my heart.

Only this week, I have been following a thread on social media where a Christian claimed that homosexuality is, 'an innate and indispensable part of an individual's personality.' Yet how can this be, when there are so many proven examples of people coming out of a homosexual lifestyle and

109

fully embracing heterosexuality? How can homosexuality be indispensable? To say it is indispensable is to believe the lie of the enemy that our God is not able to bring about change and transformation, or indeed that we are not able to function as non-sexual beings. Even members of the LGBTQ+ community recognise that sexuality is fluid, although they would be more disposed to saying it is fluid from heterosexual to homosexual and not in the other direction.

In Matthew 28, Jesus tells the disciples to go and make disciples of all nations, 'teaching them to obey everything I have commanded you'. We are told to take Jesus's message into the world, not take the world's message into the world. This message of Jesus is counter cultural, a message that flips the worldly message on its head. Timothy Keller spoke about this in his sermon "The upside-down kingdom," [70] where he contrasts what the world sees as normal (the right way up kingdom) with what Christians are taught to proclaim (the upside-down kingdom). What the world applauds, riches, abundance, recognition, and self-satisfaction, is in direct contrast to what God applauds, the poor, the peacemakers, the hungry and those who weep. Those who cannot let go of the world's values, who do not recognise the value of obedience, self-denial and humility, are those who see what the world has and think that Christians are able to live as the world without becoming tainted in some way. These are people who refuse to recognise that God calls us to a life set apart, and who fail to see the importance of God's commandments to be salt and light.

One of the saddest warnings comes in Matthew 10.

> Do not suppose that I have come to bring peace to the earth. I did not come to bring peace, but a sword. For I have come to turn a man against his father, a daughter against her mother, a daughter-in-law against her mother-

---

[70] https://youtu.be/FTZ3GfL9yQM

in-law, a man's enemies will be the members of his own household. Matthew 10:34-35 (NIV)

Warning #5 – Families will not agree over My Word.

Response #5 – Satan will use family divisions to try and cause us to compromise long held beliefs.

The pressure within families from disagreements can be extreme. When we fall out over politics, relationship issues or faith issues, the repercussions are often immense. No one likes an atmosphere; sometimes it is easier to cave in or switch sides than to hold to our convictions. Sadly, this is the response that Satan seeks. When family divisions become fractious, he will plant the seed of a thought, "perhaps I should compromise, is it really that big a deal?" As we discovered earlier, as we looked at warning #4, it is often when a family member comes out as gay that their family will adapt their Christian beliefs to keep the family together.

I have the pleasure of supporting men and women through Transformed Ministries[71], both those who have turned their back on the LGBTQ+ lifestyle as they have found faith, as well as their families, pastors, and friends. One thing that stood out for me early on in this ministry was the generational differences and disagreement over what the Bible says about homosexuality, so much so, that I have listened to numerous stories of parents and children falling out over what the Bible says. Sometimes the resulting fallout is so severe that families stop talking to each other because of their inability to reconcile their differences. I am aware of family struggles where one Christian daughter threatened to report her Christian mother to a social media outlet for hate speech following a posting referring to someone being 'changed.' In other instances, parents are reticent to be open and honest about their faith for fear of being 'shouted down' by their children or being labelled homophobic. Whilst differences of opinion are not exclusively generational, it does appear that Satan has a

---

[71] www.transformedbygodslove.com

stronger grip on the younger generation because of the prevailing change in attitudes towards sex, and is trying to leverage this to increase his influence on families. These stories of families, internally broken because of differing attitudes to homosexuality, all go to fulfil the warning that Jesus gave.

It is paramount that we recognise Satan's intentions to help us to respond appropriately to these insurmountable family differences. So often Satan uses the pervading culture to convict the younger generation of the seeming normality of things that are contrary to Scripture. Yet, the Bible warns us against the devastating effects of following the ways of the world; 'do not love the world nor the things in the world,' [72]and God's word should always be our first port of call. However, for fear of losing family relationships, I have seen parents cave into the prevailing culture as they change their mind-set on the nature of same-sex acts. Christians who once held strong convictions are now often selling out to the lies of Satan to appease their children or to try to fit into the cultural norms of an increasingly secular society.

But how should we respond to the conflicts within our families? The first piece of advice is a tough one, but clearly shows us where our starting point should be. In the following couple of verses Jesus gives us clear advice:

> *Anyone who loves their father or mother more than me is*
> *not worthy of me; anyone who loves their son or daughter*
> *more than me is not worthy of me. Matthew 10:37 (NIV)*

Jesus taught us, through this verse, that our most important relationship is with God, not with our physical family. Despite the difficulties that this presents to us at first reading, we need to recognise what God is saying to us here. This is not a matter of love me and do not love your family. On the contrary, this is a call to love God with all our strength and commitment, recognising that through doing that, we are far better placed to love our

---

[72] 1 John 2:15

children/parents/other family members. Loving God, with a commitment to honour Him and to be obedient to Him, recognising that He designed us, fully understands us, and made the rules in order that we would have life in abundance, should change our perspective on things. God does not want any of us to live life in any other way than the way He designed us to live it. Becoming in tune with God, allows us to see this clearly and focuses the mind on the need to turn away from our sins. Because of our immense love for God, we then mirror His ways as we speak in love, but with truth, to help our families to know Him too. Standing up for our beliefs presents us with opportunities to discuss our interpretation of what Jesus meant in this verse, and use this as a platform to discuss some of the other warnings written about in this book.

Through quoting Matthew 10:37, we can explain that our loyalty and love are to be offered to the Lord over all earthly connections (family and friends.) Our decisions, and the direction of our faith, should therefore always be based on what God's Word tells us. We choose to be faithful to Jesus Christ because we trust in His Word.

There are passages in the Bible that remind us not to be over-sensitive to what others say,[73] and this is essential advice. Taking umbrage and taking things personally is a step towards the downwards spiral of changing one's mind to keep the peace. Disagreeing, in itself, is not an issue. You may need to live with contradictory convictions within your own household and this can be achieved if managed sensitively and with God's love at the centre. Romans 14 is helpful in how we do this:

Accept the one whose faith is weak, without quarrelling over disputable matters. Romans 14:1 (NIV)

Regardless of where you stand on homosexuality, you will always find others in the Christian faith who have the opposite view to you. Managing these differences by not quarrelling is one answer presented to us in Romans. However, my big "If" for using the passage from Romans 14 is

---

[73] Ecclesiastes 7:21-22, 1 Corinthians 13:5

the interpretation of "disputable", hence my referring to it as only being helpful to some extent. There are things in our walk which are open to dispute, but fornication and adultery do not fall into that category. With reference to these sins, Christians are told to exhort, rebuke, and reprove each other,[74] to correct the thoughts and actions of another. Arguably this verse is not altogether relevant, but I would argue that in these instances of family dispute, the advice in Romans 14 is extremely helpful.

Please remember that our job is not to convict people of sin or to straighten out their thinking (that is done through the power of the Holy Spirit,) but to speak God's truth. We are called to love. Scripture says to love our neighbour as we love ourselves, but to love God with all our heart, mind, and soul[75]. Loving God demands obedience. Quarrelling over doctrine, when it is at odds with the prevailing secular culture, is not helpful and will often cause more harm than good. In this situation is it not better to have the conversation, listen to both viewpoints and then "back off," maintaining one's own integrity whilst being confident that the other party is fully aware of your convictions and the Biblical premise for why you hold those convictions?

As these disputes drag on, whether a clearly defined battle line has been drawn, or it is simply a lack of agreement over your respective interpretations of God's Word, you will no doubt experience levels of persecution within your own home as you stand on the truth. Jesus said, "You will be hated by everyone because of me, but the one who stands firm to the end will be saved[76]." Be encouraged today, stand firm knowing that your love for your family is strengthened because of your obedience to God in recognising sin and preaching the truth.

The final warning that I want to focus on is from the words of Jesus as recorded in Matthew's gospel, and it is one that resonates loudly with me:

---

[74] 2 Timothy 2:14
[75] Mark 12:30-31
[76] Matthew 10:22

114

Then Jesus said to his disciples, "Whoever wants to be
my disciple must deny themselves and take up their cross
and follow me. For whoever wants to save their life will
lose it, but whoever loses their life for me will find it.
Matthew 16:24-25 (NIV)

Warning #6 – If you are not prepared to leave your old life behind, you will not gain eternal life.

Response #6 – Satan likes to tell us that leaving our old life is too hard to do, convincing us that we have no need to change. Do not believe him; the devil is a liar.

The hymn 'I Surrender All'[77] is very much a favourite of mine and perfectly illustrates for me what Jesus desires of us.

1. *All to Jesus I surrender,*
   All to Him I freely give;
   I will ever love and trust Him,
   In His presence daily live.

   Refrain:
   I surrender all,
   I surrender all;
   All to Thee, my blessed Saviour,
   I surrender all.

2. *All to Jesus I surrender,*
   Humbly at His feet I bow;
   Worldly pleasures all forsaken,
   Take me, Jesus, take me now.

---

[77] J. W. Van DeVenter - *The United Methodist Hymnal*, No. 354

3. *All to Jesus I surrender,*
   Make me, Saviour, wholly Thine;
   Let me feel the Holy Spirit,
   Truly know that Thou art mine.

4. *All to Jesus I surrender,*
   Lord, I give myself to Thee;
   Fill me with Thy love and power,
   Let Thy blessing fall on me.

5. *All to Jesus I surrender,*
   Now I feel the sacred flame;
   Oh, the joy of full salvation!
   Glory, glory, to His Name!

The refrain is a commitment by those singing the song, to surrender all they are to their blessed Saviour, and the verses give us more insight into what that means. Verse 1 - calls on us to trust Jesus and live in His presence daily; verse 2 - to be humble as we bow at His feet, forsaking all worldly pleasures.

Isn't this what Jesus is talking about in Matthew, when he calls us to deny ourselves? Forsaking all worldly pleasures, no longer following our own self-interest in order that we may serve a higher authority. This command to deny ourselves does not necessitate a change of personality; it does not mean we can no longer have fun or enjoy our lives. What it does mean is that we are to renounce or disown those parts of our character and lifestyle that are centred on ourselves (the element of self-idolatry), and allow ourselves to be focussed on and shaped by God.

For some of us, this command is clear in what it asks us to do. For me, I knew that it meant that I had to walk away from an active sex life to become obedient to God's commands. But I must not get bogged down in that one element of my faith walk. I was also called to stop indulging myself in gossip, to stop lying for gain, to stop seeking affirmation and attention from the wrong sources, to start tithing, and to give freely of my spare time. More recently this capacity to surrender has led me to evaluate my work and financial situation, as I felt God drawing me to ministry. For me personally, this has resulted in the sale of my business and taking a massive step of faith in trusting God to provide for all my needs, as I follow his calling. I am different from anyone else, my sin had separated me from God in the same way that other people's sin had separated them from God. The sins may be different, but the outcome was the same, I was called to look at my life and make changes. We are all called to examine our lives and surrender them to God.

This is what surrender looks like; it is part of our journey of faith. Surrender is an ongoing process; it starts with the more obvious aspects of our lives and over time the Holy Spirit hones and shapes us as we recognise those areas that are preventing us from God's best for us. Of course, these changes do not all happen at once; it is part of a process of change that takes place as we grow in our knowledge and understanding of God. As our relationship with Him develops, we better understand His character and desire for our lives, and have a greater desire and capacity to want to please Him. The lyrics of the hymn 'I Surrender All' illustrate this perfectly, as they refer to us living in God's presence 'on a daily basis." It is this daily communion with God which changes our perspective, allowing our love for Him to grow and our experience of God's presence to deepen.

We all have different experiences of coming to faith and of how this has shaped our lives. My personal journey saw me struggle for months with the question of my sexuality. I did not give my life to Jesus until I felt I had resolved that issue and surrendered my sex life to God. But what followed was not an immediate turning away from SSA or past patterns of behaviour; surrender took time (it took over a year for me to be fully free from the temptations of SSA). Whilst I had surrendered to God in choosing not to sleep with my partner, I still needed to surrender some thoughts and attitudes to Him. This was done over time as I committed myself to a life of discipleship, and thereby grew in my Christian stature and understanding.

It is so important that we recognise that change may not be immediate and not take that as a reason to believe the lies of Satan, that change is not possible. If you struggle with SSA, it is not about immediately expecting God to change you and your thoughts (although I passionately believe that over time He will). It is about surrendering to His will, recognising that God's perfect design is for sex to be between one man and one woman, and to say, 'OK, if I cannot achieve that God, then I will remain celibate'. It is through surrendering our will that God can move into our lives, filling us with His love and power, as verse four of the hymn[78] says:

All to Jesus I surrender,
Lord, I give myself to Thee;
Fill me with Thy love and power,
Let Thy blessing fall on me.

When Jesus picked up his cross, he knew what it would lead to. He knew that he did not have to go through with it, but he surrendered to God and was obedient to God's will. He faced death; he died so that our sins would be forgiven, not his, and he was one hundred percent reliant on God to resurrect him from the dead. Isn't it the same choice for us? We do not have to do anything if we do not want to, but we too are one hundred percent reliant on God for our resurrection story.

> *We were therefore buried with him through baptism into*
> *death in order that, just as Christ was raised from the*
> *dead through the glory of the Father, we too may live a*
> *new life. Romans 6:4 (NIV)*
>
> *I have been crucified with Christ and I no longer live, but*
> *Christ lives in me. The life I now live in the body, I live by*

---

[78] I Surrender All, J. W. Van DeVenter - The United Methodist Hymnal, No. 354

faith in the Son of God, who loved me and gave himself
for me. Galatians 2:20 (NIV)

Wanting to know God and to receive our salvation requires us to re-evaluate societal norms and turn them on their head. We are called to have faith; a faith in God, that his plans for us are perfect and his designs for man are trustworthy. Rather than look at the requirements of God and his design for marriage, then picking them apart to justify our own lusts and desires, the upside-down gospel teaches us to be humble, to put ourselves last, put God first, and to walk by faith and not by sight.

These six warnings given to us by Jesus himself give us an insight into the spiritual battle that we are facing every day. When we consider sexual sin, and more specifically homosexual sin, please recognise the battle, and remember we can respond to, and rebuke, Satan and his lies as he continually seeks to engage us in his dialogue on SSA. We can respond to Satan's deceit with trust and belief in the words of Jesus.

1. When we are tempted, tell Satan - *God allows temptation to happen to build our faith and character.*
2. When Satan tells us that homosexual activity is not sinful tell him - *Jesus clearly told us that we must repent to be saved.*
3. When we hear teaching from our church that does not sit right with what the Bible clearly tells us, tell Satan to depart reminding him that Jesus told us - *Be on your guard for the threat is not from the world, but from within your church.*
4. When Satan tells us you are OK you go to church, you do not have to follow the rules, tell him that Jesus tells us - *When we hear his words, we must put them into practice and live as he asks us to call Him Lord.*
5. When family members are telling you that homosexual acts are not sinful and quote Bible passages at you, remember Jesus's warning - *Satan will use family divisions to try and cause us to compromise long held beliefs.*
6. When Satan tells you there is no such thing as ex Gay Christians, remember that Satan is a liar remind him: – *That there are many who*

have already denied themselves, picked up their cross and followed
Him out of the LGBTQ+ lifestyle, into Christ's freedom.

TESTIMONY, KATRINA, USA

Katrina is a mother and grandmother who left an abusive heterosexual marriage over 20 years ago to live with her lesbian partner, who was to become her wife. She knew about God but hadn't developed a personal relationship with Him. Through a friend inviting her to take part in a Bible study her life changed forever and she now pursues Jesus with all her heart. Katrina has overcome addiction and abuse and is passionate about helping others to find freedom from all that stops them experiencing the goodness of God.

I had been in and out of church since childhood, more recently with my wife where we had experienced some prejudice and not made to feel very welcome. So my guard was up when a friend suggested to me that I start a study called 'restoring relationships' with a lady from her church.

I wanted to do this study because I had come from a dysfunctional family where I had been abused, as well as a marriage that had been traumatic and abusive. I knew that these things had affected my mental health, and I really was interested in whether God could make a difference to how I felt. But I was very concerned this lady was going to tell me I could no longer be married to my wife who I had been with since leaving my husband 26 years before.

The first thing I said to her when I went in the room was, "My marriage is off the table. " I meant it, I was happy to talk about other things but this Christian was not going to be another one who demeaned my relationship and told me I was a sinner.

As we worked through this study this lady never brought up my marriage, it was me who first spoke about it. You see I started to see things in a new light and I felt like this was something God was nudging me to think about.

The lady from church only ever spoke in truth and love to me when answering my questions and it wasn't long before I felt like I did want to honour God with my sexuality. I told my wife that I had rededicated my life to Jesus, and moved into the spare room.

This was the hardest time of my life and I struggled to trust that God was going to come through for me. I often cried out to Him, how is this going to work, I'm stuck, I don't know what to do? For a while I tried to make sense of everything and do things my own way, it just got harder and harder.

I don't think I had any idea about how creative God is and how much he cared for me. There was so much stress because of the living arrangements in the home, I had taken the bedroom on the top floor and my wife was in the room below. Living together was extremely tense and there were a lot of challenges. I wanted a way out but didn't trust that God would provide it, how wrong I was.

God sent a hurricane. Literally, a hurricane that tore through our neighbourhood yet only our house was damaged, my bedroom was condemned. This opened a door for me to move out of the home, initially into our fifth wheel, but eventually into a friend's spare room and finally into my own apartment.

Here was my first lesson in trusting that God would do what was needed to help me. I fell for the lies of Satan, I questioned God's goodness and ability to help me, and I was tempted on occasion to throw in the towel and move back in with my wife. But each time I needed Him to come through, he did.

God worked many miracles. One time I searched the internet for some support, someone who would understand my situation, and came across a ministry who worked with Christians who had same sex attraction, and made contact. The next week I made the same internet search and nothing came up. I have tried numerous times since and still there is nothing. I know that God was in that, he led me to those who knew what I was going through and provided me with community.

122

I still question God's goodness on occasion, but I now remind myself that Satan is a liar and God is good. I have so much to look back on, I can see God's handiwork all over my life; my new apartment, my job, my new church family and my new life with Jesus.

Chapter 7 – Managing False Teaching; some Lessons from the Early Church.

The letters Paul wrote to the early churches are full of wisdom and instruction for new Christians as they were trying to make sense of what it meant to follow Christ. This was not an easy time for these pioneers of the faith; they faced conflict and persecution; many were converting from Judaism to Christianity, with the need to fully embrace what this meant for how they lived their lives. Within their midst came those who promoted various teachings, including Jewish Legalism, Gnosticism, Ascetism, Antinomianism and Docetism. These false teachings were a danger to the new church; teachings that Satan would use to try and undermine and unsettle the Church before it could become fully established.

The proponents of these teachings all brought something different to the table; like they were trying to add to Christianity, to make it fit into a doctrine with which they were comfortable.

Those who taught Jewish Legalism were not comfortable with letting go of some of the legal aspects of their faith. Their leaders would teach that Christians had to submit to certain conditions of the Jewish law. For example, we read in Acts about circumcision:

> *Certain people came down from Judea to Antioch and were teaching the believers: "Unless you are circumcised, according to the custom taught by Moses, you cannot be saved Acts 15:1 (NIV)*

Yet Paul clearly teaches that this is not the case. We are free from the law, and our salvation does not depend upon our works. Discussion and debate continued around the topic of circumcision throughout Paul's time, yet Paul remained firm in his teaching. We too must remain firm in our faith, not

124

falling foul of those who would water it down or challenge our doctrines. It is worth addressing the fact that Paul had Timothy circumcised, as some read this action as an indicator of Paul's true belief, that circumcision was necessary for salvation. The Nelson Study Bible[79] explains this well:

"Salvation was not the issue here. Instead, Timothy became circumcised so that God could use him to reach all people—even the Jews—with the message of the gospel."

Paul did not want Timothy to become a stumbling block to the Jews. He knew that whilst circumcision was not necessary for salvation, adapting to the Jewish customs would result in Timothy being accepted and respected, a necessity if he was to become effective in his teaching.

Another challenge to the early church were the Gnostics. The leaders of Gnosticism believed that God's word is false, and that truth is in fact based on a secret knowledge, a knowledge that they alone had. They felt that this made them superior in their faith to Christians. It is believed that Gnosticism is what Paul was referring to in his letter to Timothy:

Timothy, guard what has been entrusted to your care.
Turn away from godless chatter and the opposing ideas of
what is falsely called knowledge, which some have
professed and in so doing have departed from the faith. 1
Timothy 6:20-21

Then there were those who followed Ascetism, who held to a belief that sin is inherent within our bodies and as such we must practice self-denial to draw closer to God. Examples of these practices may include disciplines such as fasting, poverty or sleep deprivation. Paul is clear in his letter to the church in Colossae that this was not part of the Christian faith.

Do not let anyone who delights in false humility and the
worship of angels disqualify you. Colossians 2:18 (NIV)

---

[79] The Nelson Study Bible, published by Nelsons Bibles (1997)

There were those who followed Antinomianism which relates to the belief that Christians are freed from obeying the moral law by virtue of grace. Their teachers taught that the body and soul were separate, and as such the body was free to do whatever it wanted without affecting the purity of the soul. These are referred to in Paul's letter to the church at Rome:

> *What shall we say, then? Shall we go on sinning so that*
> *grace may increase? By no means! We are those who*
> *have died to sin; how can we live in it any longer?*
> *Romans 6:1-2 (NIV)*

Then finally, we look at the proponents of Docetism, who did not believe in the incarnation of Jesus Christ. They believed that Jesus only appeared to be human, that his human body or form was in fact an illusion. This was spoken about not by Paul, but by John, who is clear that whoever denies Jesus as Christ is a liar.

> *Who is the liar? It is whoever **denies that Jesus** is the*
> *Christ. Such a person is the antichrist-denying the Father*
> *and the Son. No one who denies the Son has the Father;*
> *whoever acknowledges the Son has the Father also.*
>
> *1 John 2:22-23 (NIV)*

It is hardly surprising that Satan was working hard to infiltrate and discredit the early church. His urgent mission had to be one of seeking to extinguish the flame of Christianity before it could blaze its way into the world. The extent of the false teaching in the early days of the church reflects Satan's desire to snuff out Christianity for the last time, and sadly it is equally as prevalent today. The names may have changed, the type of teaching may have changed, but the underlying message for us must be, beware of the false teachers who come to deceive and draw you away from your first love. As Jesus warned us, these teachers are already in our places of worship, they are "wolves in sheep's clothing."

126

The reality is that Satan will attack the church in any way he can. Whenever he has a degree of success, he will continue to chip away, seeking to gain a stronger foothold. It is my belief that Satan has systematically chipped away at the Christian family unit and family values, finding ways to undermine Biblical teaching, and setting family members one against another. In the past 50 years, we have seen incredible changes in Christian attitudes towards marriage, abortion, divorce, and sexuality. In the past twenty or so years we have seen a step-change in relationships between adults and children, even within Christian homes, with the command "honour your father and mother" becoming one that is so often overlooked. When it comes to attitudes towards sex and sexuality, the generation gap has widened, and continues to do so as each generation becomes progressively more liberal. We also find ourselves in a situation where the church regularly fails to talk about God's design and purpose for sex, sexuality, and family life. In contrast there is a growing percentage of churches who will talk openly about our "rights" as humans when it comes to sexual identity and marriage, with scant regard to what the Bible teaches.

This all paints a depressing picture, but through Paul's letters to the early church we can trust that we are fully equipped to discern false teaching. We may need to pause, take some time out to consider the message of those we are listening to, being courageous and confident to refute any teaching which we recognise as pertaining to a false gospel. Just as those in the early church tested the messages that Paul was delivering, as they were receiving them, so should we. This is the first and most important principle for us to remember; test all that you hear and all that you read, with our true source, the Bible.

> *Now the Berean Jews were of more noble character than those in Thessalonica, for they received the message with great eagerness and examined the Scriptures every day to see if what Paul said was true. Acts 17:11 (NIV)*

It is not just when we consider the Bible that we need to be careful. Any student should be able to tell you the perils of taking one piece of research, one word, or teaching out of context or in isolation from other teachings. Research is essential if we are to be confident that we have gleaned the truth. As we examine the Scriptures for truth, we look at everything within them that points us to God's true meaning. When every part of Scripture is considered, it results in us having an absolute and unwavering understanding of the truth of what God desires of us, his people. David wrote of this in the Psalms:

All your words are true; all your righteous laws are eternal.
Psalm 119:160 (NIV)

Or take the New King James Version which says:

The entirety of Your word is truth, and every one of Your
righteous judgments endures forever. Psalm 119:160
(NKJV)

As we study Paul's letters to the early church it is worth reminding ourselves that we write letters as a substitute for personal visits. Our preference, whenever possible, is to meet in person, where explanations can be made face to face, with opportunity for discussion and explanation as required. But Paul had little choice, some of his letters were written to churches he knew but could not physically visit. Others were written directly to disciples that he knew who were ministering to new churches, and yet others were to churches that he had never visited, for example the church at Colossae. His letters demonstrate that the Church was constantly on his mind and in his prayers. This is hardly surprising given that he was, in effect, mentoring and supporting a series of church plants, and was acutely aware of the pressure they were under and the obstacles they would need to overcome to succeed.

The new church was born into brutal times. The Roman Empire was the dominant political and military force; a mighty empire by anyone's measure. Rome was a decadent city, full of much immorality and heavily

128

influenced by Greek culture and mythology. Whilst the Romans were tolerant of religion, their tolerance was more toward polytheistic worship, as opposed to the monotheistic religion of Christianity, where only one God is recognised and worshipped. Paul knew that this culture would lead to extensive pressures on the early church members to adapt their faith and he therefore wrote accordingly.

Letter writing is a dying art today, and for us to fully appreciate how people communicated over distance in the first century is hard. We live in a society where communication is instant and if Paul were alive today, he would have the ability to monitor these churches closely. He could listen to their online sermons, check out their "statement of faith" on their website, and gain an insight into their activities and events via their social media presence. But Paul was solely reliant on any personal insights he had gained from meeting the members of the church or knowing their leaders; his sense of the time, his knowledge of the surrounding culture, and on the personal feedback of those who had visited each church. He had personally witnessed how the teaching of Christianity had been vehemently attacked by Satan as the church was starting to establish itself. Paul was fully aware, as one who historically had been on the attacking side, that the church was vulnerable to attack from within its ranks, as well as from the Gentiles and Jews who did not accept Jesus as Messiah. This is why his letters were so important, as tools to encourage and nurture these new bands of believers.

We may not be living under the Roman Empire, but we are living in a decadent time with much immorality running through our culture. Traditionally, Britain has been a nation that has been very tolerant of religion, but more recently that tolerance has begun to dry up. Secular influences, including humanist organisations and the LGBTQ+ lobby, are gaining ground. There are many secular voices seeking to silence Christian voices in our society (education, business, health, employment etc,) as they challenge many of the principles and much of the teaching of the Bible, treating our source of truth as a personal affront to their beliefs.

Two thousand years may have passed us by, but not much has changed in relation to the pressures on God's church.

How then, do Paul's letters encourage us to be alert for the schemes of the devil? And, as we recognise that there are Christians who have fallen for the lies of Satan and propagate a false gospel of varying degrees, how does Paul's writing help us to recognise these? Specifically, for the purposes of this book, I am looking at teachings pertaining to sexual immorality, which is a subject spoken about quite clearly in many of Paul's letters[80].

Firstly, we turn to Paul's letter to the church in Rome, where we soon get a flavour of Paul's passion for God and his recognition of the battle that rages between our flesh and our spirit. Paul clearly lays out for us what God's ultimate will is for humanity, that is, for us to worship God and to present ourselves to Him as a holy sacrifice; to be pleasing to Him.

> *Therefore, I urge you, brothers, and sisters, in view of*
> *God's mercy, to offer your bodies as a living sacrifice, holy*
> *and pleasing to God—this is your true and proper worship.*
> *Romans 12:1 (NIV)*

It is also clear, from many of his letters, that Paul's deep pastoral concern for the members of the early church, resulted in him praying earnestly for them to grow in, and to gain deep knowledge of, God's will[81]. His enthusiastic prayers relayed the urgency and importance that he placed on these new disciples understanding the will of God, gaining for themselves the knowledge they would require if they were to discern what was best to keep them pure and blameless for Christ. Through the letters he wrote, Paul shows us repeatedly God's will, that our hearts and minds should be used to express worship to Him, so that our Christian walk is one that is worthy of Him. God's will for us is not a mystery, in fact Paul's knowledge

---

[80] see for example, 1 Corinthians 6:13 and 18-19, 1 Corinthians 7:2, 1 Corinthians 10:8, Galatians 5:19, 1 Thessalonians 4:3, Ephesians 5:3, Colossians 3:5
[81] Colossians 1:9, Ephesians 1:15-17, Philippians 1:9-10

of God's will for our lives is expanded in many of his letters to the early church. He encourages us to follow God's will and that means that we are called to walk:

- Differently from the world (Ephesians 4: 17-32)
- By faith (2 Corinthians 5:7)
- In humility (Ephesians 4:1-3)
- In love (Ephesians 5:2) and in light (Ephesians 5:8)
- In purity (1 Corinthians 7)
- In wisdom (Ephesians 5:15)

It certainly sounds like we have a lot of work to do if we are to achieve all these things in our walk with God. Yet there is no pressure on us personally. The Holy Spirit, who came to live in us when we gave our lives to Christ, is there to help us to transform, to change from the old into the new[82]. And that is just the starting point; God tells us that we will be transformed by the "renewing of our minds." God encourages us and empowers us via the Holy Spirit to change our lives, and that necessitates adapting the way we think. As we grow in our faith, as the fruits of the Spirit are born within us, the way we think about our lives is radically overhauled because we have stopped trying to do things in our own power and surrendered to the will of God. This process is vitally important to us as Christians because God calls us to be "different from the world." There is no point in becoming a Christian if we continue to walk in the ways of the world; we have missed the point if we think we can do that.

- Different from the world

Jesus himself said that we do not belong to this world[83]. He expands that to say that, if we were of the world we would be loved by the world, but as it is, we have been chosen by God and for that we will not be welcomed

---

[82] Colossians 3:10
[83] John 15:19

131

(that is why the world hates you). It is no secret that what God's word teaches us about sexuality differs significantly from worldly values. Whereas the world celebrates and endorses all forms of sexual expression outside of the traditional marriage of one man and one woman, God celebrates and endorses sexual expression only within the realms of traditional marriage. God's design is plainly laid out in Genesis, but also, we see God's design clearly visible in human creation. When we look at how man and woman function sexually, we see that God's design for sexual intercourse between husband and wife is perfect.

For those who have interpreted the word of God to say that we can no longer celebrate or endorse homosexuality as a lifestyle that Christians can live, we know the feeling of being hated by the world. Also, for those, like me, who have walked away from homosexuality to live in obedience to God's will, we not only know the feeling of being hated by the world, but also of being maligned and criticised by many Christians who endorse this lifestyle. It would be easy to get angry about this if we did not hold on to Paul's advice, recognising the futility of "their" thinking and the immense rewards of living within the will of God.

In the Ephesians passage, Paul highlights that Christians are to be different through revering God's designs for us, whether we understand them or not, and through being obedient to God in even the most difficult of circumstances. If the world hates you for it, do not forget that it is the world that is being deceived by Satan (the ruler of this world), and it is you who is sticking to the truth as taught by the one sovereign ruler, God.

In the same way that Paul exhorted the church at Ephesus, we should be encouraged to no longer live as the Gentiles do, "in the futility of their thinking." Paul explains this still further, "let us not be as those Gentiles who have hardened their hearts and lost sensitivity to what is right.[84]" Paul's words urge us to go back to the way of life that we have learnt, and

---

[84] Ephesians 4:17-19

that this learning has come directly from our one and only guidebook for the Christian faith, the Bible. The Bible teaches us to put off the old, corrupt self, the self that gives in to the deceitful desires put in our paths by Satan. The Bible teaches us to say no to the ways of the world and to put on our new self, one that is full of righteousness and holiness, a life dedicated or consecrated to God, which is both morally and spiritually excellent.

- People who live by faith and not by sight.

In this passage from 2 Corinthians 5, Paul talks about us awaiting our new body (our eternal home in heaven). As we wait for our resurrection we groan, longing to be clothed with our heavenly body. What Paul makes clear in verse six is that when we feel at home in our earthly bodies, we are apart from the Lord, and this is so pertinent to us as we consider our response to questions of faith and sexuality. So many people are consumed with their rights to do what they please with their body that they fail to see that there is a higher plan. They may never have encountered the word of God for themselves. Or they may be people who have lost sight of God's take on sexuality and his call for us to live differently from the world, to follow His guide for perfect living.

Freewill lends itself towards the belief that we can do what we want, when we want, where we want, and with whomever we want. What we do before we know or walk with God is to a certain extent irrelevant; in so much as we have no connection or understanding of God, and no desire to get to know Him. Our lives are lived for ourselves; our actions driven by our own desires and thoughts. I am not saying that we should live immoral or chaotic lives just because we do not know God, because our actions still have the capacity to harm us physically, emotionally, and spiritually. What I am saying, though, is that the whole scenario changes when we come to know Jesus. Our world view changes; our life choices come under our own scrutiny as we put our faith in God for things that we cannot see or understand. Walking by faith is one of those things that gets easier the more you practice it.

When I first became a Christian, whilst I knew that I wanted to be obedient to God's call, it was exceedingly difficult in the early days to live by faith. Trying to please God in obedience, by changing my attitude towards sex, was something of a mental battle (the battle of flesh and spirit spoken of so often by Paul). But as I responded to God and learned to trust Him, to lean on him and not my own understanding, I started to change; my faith increased, my thoughts started to change, and I stopped looking through the lens of my flesh and started to look through the lens of the Spirit. It was not that long after I learned to trust God, believing that He was with me in the thick of it all, that my sexual identity started to change. (Sometimes it takes that step of faith to start to see the change within).

- People of Humility

When I think about humility, I find these two passages from the Old Testament particularly poignant:

> If my people, who are called by my name, will humble themselves and pray and seek my face and turn from their wicked ways, then I will hear from heaven, and I will forgive their sin and will heal their land. 2 Chronicles 7:14 (NIV)

> He has shown you, O mortal, what is good. And what does the LORD require of you? To act justly and to love mercy and to walk humbly with your God. Micah 6:8 (NIV)

Yet when I reflect on these two passages, my heart is saddened as I recognise how far we have strayed from God's best for us. We cannot become complacent. Surely, we are in a similar position to those in the early church (under constant attack,) and we must continue to seek to live lives worthy of our calling (as Paul clearly tells the church at Ephesus).

What is a life worthy of our calling as Christians? We can learn something from Paul on this; when he addresses how the early Christians should live, he cites the need to be humble, as well as to be people who are gentle and patient. Is he reflecting on the passage from 2 Chronicles that requires us to come before the Lord in a submissive posture, to submit ourselves to Him in prayer, seeking His will more than anything else, and of course to repent of our wicked ways? In Romans 8, Paul recognises that humility is hard for us when our minds, which are governed by the flesh, are hostile to God and do not submit to God's law. Furthermore, in his letter to the church in Colossae, in response to them submitting to worldly laws and values, he wrote:

> *Since you died with Christ to the elemental spiritual forces of this world, why, as though you still belonged to the world, do you submit to its rules? Colossians 2:20 (NIV)*

If we remain governed by the flesh and fail to be transformed by the renewing of our minds, then we are hostile to God; and if hostile to God we remain unsubmitted to his laws. A Christian who remains active within the LGBTQ+ community (and by that, I mean one who continues to identify themselves as gay, whether in a relationship or not), and who sees no need to repent of any SSA demonstrates a lack of submission, and a desire to still belong to the world, rather than keeping their mind on the things of the Spirit. They are living outside of God's will for their life and that is exactly where Satan wants to keep them through his lies and deceit.

I was in the garden earlier this week; it was a sunny day with some clouds in the sky. As the sun disappeared behind a cloud, it suddenly got cooler. I needed to go inside and fetch a jumper to be comfortable. I had a keen sense that this is what it is like when we allow sin to interfere with our relationship with God. Whilst we can still stand in His presence, it gets a little cooler, and we sense a need to cover up. Perhaps the cover we use is one of "pride," of telling ourselves that we are not the one at fault (perhaps by deflecting our sin, claiming that we were made this way; putting the "blame" squarely onto God).

Pride in one's sexuality is at odds with our Christian faith. Pride in a human label is not what God desires of us and does not reflect His teaching in Micah, to walk humbly with your God.

I find the term "gay Christian" to be a challenging concept. I see it most often used by two diverse groups of people. Those who are same sex attracted, but have committed to remain celibate because of their faith, and those who have SSA, yet believe that acting on their sexuality does not affect their faith; in essence those who say that homosexual behaviour, in a loving monogamous relationship, is OK with God.

I want to focus on those who call themselves a "gay Christian," whilst also committing themselves to a life of celibacy (having previously recognised that homosexual acts are sinful). Personally, I question why labelling ourselves in this way is necessary and I wonder what the driving force behind this self-imposed label is? I do not condemn; I walk alongside them, but I have questions. Having lived most of my adult life as a lesbian, I do understand the desire to identify with a group or a community where you feel a sense of belonging (which the gay community offers so well). I sense that for some, identifying with this community may be a difficult mind-set to shake. Yet, identifying as "gay or queer" which is at odds to God's best for us, does not speak of a "renewing of the mind." When we choose to follow God, we choose to surrender all to Him, and over time He empowers us to change. I am a strong believer in the power of the tongue as we declare God's truths over our lives, and for that reason, even in the early days of my faith, I never thought of myself or referred to myself as a gay Christian.

If an individual's reason for identifying with the gay community is because they know that they will struggle with sin or temptation (and we all do), and they want people to understand the magnitude of their struggle, there is another way. Maintaining the old identity is not the answer. Rather be transparent with those around you, explaining to pastoral carers, close Christian friends, or mentors, about specific temptations and concerns. In doing this, we may need to reiterate that we are totally committed and submitted to Christ in overcoming that area of struggle, but in a good church we should then receive appropriate nurture and discipleship without the need to "label" ourselves anymore. This could be the same for someone who struggles with pornography, drug addiction, alcoholism or even gossip. The last thing we want to do is wear a label, "drug addicted Christian," "porn watching Christian," "gossiping Christian," you get the idea? If we are to be transformed by the renewing of our minds, a good place to start is to surrender our current identity to Christ and allow Him to show us who we really are.

And of course, there are other Christians who genuinely believe that God created them gay. They choose to celebrate their "queerness," yet deny themselves from walking in that identity because of their understanding of Scripture. Whilst I can love, and walk alongside these brothers and sisters, I fundamentally disagree with their belief that God created them that way and would point to teaching such as that by Richard Cohen,[85] which highlights ten factors which contribute to a child developing SSA. I do not believe that we serve a God who would make us in a specific identity, but deny us the pleasure of walking in it.

God calls us to humility and the opposite of humility is pride. Pride stands for everything that God does not want us to be. Pride is a word that has become intricately linked to the LGBTQ+ movement and it is useful to try

---

[85] Gay Children, Straight Parents: A Plan for Family Healing, Richard Cohen, Create Space Independent Publishing Platform, 2016

and understand how the LGBTQ+ movement define "pride." Wikipedia,[86] in explaining the concept of Gay Pride states:

Gay pride or **LGBTQ+ pride** *is the promotion of the self-affirmation, dignity, equality, and increased visibility of lesbian, gay, bisexual, and transgender (LGBTQ+) people as a social group. Pride, as opposed to shame and social stigma, is the predominant outlook that bolsters most LGBTQ+ rights movement.*

This definition recognises that there has been a lot of social stigma and shame surrounding human sexuality, particularly homosexuality, and defines pride in such a way that it seeks to address an imbalance. The original writer of this definition was seeking to ensure that a specific people group are treated with dignity and with equality. However, my personal observation leads me to believe that what started off as a movement to foster dignity and equality, has been hijacked by those who are more politically motivated and is now used to champion a dangerous ideology. This ideology seeks to tell us that if we do not endorse, promote, and celebrate sexual diversity, then we are bigots or homophobes. The original adoption of the word pride was designed to help challenge social stigma, but its usage by a wide section of the LGBTQ+ movement is now more in tune with alternative dictionary definitions[87] a and c below:

1: the quality or state of being proud: such as
a: inordinate self-esteem: CONCEIT
b: a reasonable or justifiable self-respect
c: delight or elation arising from some act, possession, or relationship.

I wonder whether the adoption of the word "pride" in today's culture (and not exclusively within the context of our sexuality), speaks of a society

---

[86] https://en.wikipedia.org/wiki/Gay_pride
[87] https://www.merriam-webster.com/dictionary/pride

which has subconsciously chosen to disregard God's call for us to be a humble people?

- People who live in the light and in God's love.

Ephesians 5 starts with Paul appealing to the church to follow God's example. We are encouraged to live 'in the way of love, just as Christ loved us.' Christ's love is a pure love, a love that casts out all fear, a sacrificial love. Paul goes on to remind the Ephesians that there must not be even a hint of sexual immorality in their lives, because that would be improper for a follower of Christ. Paul's message is that yes, we were once in darkness, and at that time we did engage in activities that were impure or immoral, greedy, or idolatrous. But now that we are in the light, and as the light shines into every corner of our lives, those former things are shown up in all their grubbiness. As we start our Christian walk, it is incredible how God works to change us. Things we have done for a lifetime will gradually feel wrong; the way we speak, the thoughts we harbour in our minds, the things we do. When we submit ourselves fully to God, He guides and leads us into a changed life.

I love the fact that God changes us gradually; it is a process. He does not overwhelm us by confronting all our sinful behaviour at the same time. He gives us space and time to change at a pace that we can manage. God is patient and we know that one of the fruit of the Spirit He gives to us is patience. Patience is a fruit that allows us to walk with the Lord. whilst constantly addressing our own sin and allowing God's grace to change us. Yet for us to fully complete this process, we have a need to acknowledge what constitutes sin. Key to this is Paul's advice in Ephesians 5 verse 17, 'Therefore do not be foolish, but understand what the Lord's will is.' Once again, Paul hits the nail on the head; he speaks of the urgency and importance of understanding the will of God, so that we have the best possible life with Him, both now and in eternity.

Take for example, the member of your congregation who is same sex attracted and living with a same sex partner. The most important thing is that they recognise God's love and salvation, and that they repent and give their life to the Lord. At the point they surrender their life to the Lord, they will recognise some of the things that are sinful in their life, but may not recognise all the things that God asks them to leave behind. This understanding will come through reading the word of God; through nurture and teaching. Our role is to allow them time to grow in their faith, to read God's word and seek His will, and to encourage them to ask God to help them walk in His light. You can be sure that God will address their sexual identity as part of their transformation story, and when that happens, churches need to be equipped to help them. Once anyone recognises that homosexuality is a sin in the eyes of God, there must be an expectation that they will amend their past behaviour. There is no need for us to force this issue with anyone, yet we do need to be open and honest about God's Word when the Holy Spirit gives us that opportunity. More importantly, we need to trust God, to trust in his timing and that He will continue to transform that person until they recognise all behaviour that is sinful. In welcoming all into our churches, we need to be saying that we all struggle with sin, but we shun sinful lifestyles and aim to walk the narrow path that Jesus walks with us.

- People who are pure.

In 1 Corinthians 7, Paul speaks at length about married life. In this passage, he rightly notes that Satan's goal is to tempt us (because Satan is fully alert to our lack of self-control). Paul also talks about 'burning with passion' and the importance of controlling our sexual desires. He holds what may seem to us a quite extreme viewpoint, that we would be better to marry than to struggle with sexual lust. Yet, Paul is simply being realistic; as believers we should live obedient lives in the situation we are in, and he points out that if we are unable to contain our passions then perhaps marriage is the best solution for us. Personally, I would hesitate to recommend that course of action to anyone I was mentoring, and believe there are other ways to address how we deal with any lack of self-control in this area!

Nevertheless, each person should live as a believer in whatever situation the Lord has assigned to them, just as God has called them. 1 Corinthians 7:17 (NIV)

When we are saved, we receive the Holy Spirit and new life. However, it is rare for the other circumstances of our lives to change immediately. We may be working or unemployed; we may have money in the bank or not a penny to our name; we may be married or single. Paul is encouraging us to serve God loyally in the circumstances we are currently in (and change, if required, will come). For example, the unmarried woman, sleeping with her partner, who becomes a Christian, cannot realistically immediately marry her partner for practical and financial reasons. God calls her to be obedient, abstain from sexual relations until such time as she marries. Tough? Yes, but it is worth it to live in the will of God.

Likewise, the gay man, sleeping with his partner, who becomes a Christian is called to obedience, to no longer sleep with him. The difference is clear, the requirement here is not only to give up sleeping with his partner, but to relinquish his desires to ever sleep with him again. Tough? You bet it is, but it is living in the will of God. God says that when we become a Christian we must live as a believer, whatever situation we are in. Living in line with the Spirit means that we no longer desire the things of the flesh. This is a process and one that Satan wants us to give up on early on in our walk. He will throw everything at us to discourage us. But the good news is, as we take that step of faith and partner with the Holy Spirit to change, things start to get easier, and we start seeing the fruit of our walk. That is why it was so important that Paul was direct about immorality and the consequences of this for Christians, so that we could hold fast to the truth, and through living in truth receive the full blessing of the Lord.

- To be people of wisdom.

Be very careful, then, how you live—not as unwise but as
wise, making the most of every opportunity, because the
days are evil. Ephesians 5:15-16 (NIV)

There is no difference between the time that Paul was writing and the time that you are reading this passage; the days are evil. Satan has been given dominion over the world for an abbreviated period of time; the sooner we open our eyes to that the better. We have read earlier about Satan being a wily deceiver, a sheep in wolf's clothing, and Paul continues to encourage the early church to be fully aware of this. We read in the following chapter of Ephesians about the importance of putting on our armour daily and the significant fact that our battle is not against flesh and blood, but against Satan and his army.

To become wise in the ways of God takes time and commitment, and a recognition that this is a battle; Satan is the expert deceiver. We must therefore read God's word regularly, tuning our ears to His wisdom. Paul warns us in his letter to Timothy that in the end times people will surround themselves with what they want to hear[88]; untruths, misinterpretations, or fudged doctrine, to justify their chosen path. Tuning our ears to God's mind is important; it is a personal walk with God, and we should learn to hear Him clearly (my sheep know my voice[89]). We can ask God for wisdom; He will not withhold it and we can develop wisdom through practice. We all learn from our mistakes, and there are many times in my life when I have followed a path without seeking God's wisdom first, then hit a brick wall and needed to return to seek the right path. To receive wisdom from God we need to leave the company of fools[90] and we need to fear the Lord[91].

---

[88] 2 Timothy 4:3
[89] John 10:27
[90] Proverbs 4:14-15
[91] Proverbs 1:7

In relation to the company of fools, without being harsh, this does relate to those who are not yet Christians; those whose minds are blinded to the word of the Lord. Seeing a same-sex relationship through the eyes of a non-believer, means seeing the relationship devoid of God's plans or purpose for the lives of the couple. As such, there is no reason to question that relationship as in secular terms; it is just another couple enjoying a loving/sexual relationship. Seeing it through God's eyes, however, is different and brings a deeper love and compassion for that couple; a love that desires them to know purity, to know God's absolute best for their lives and to know how His transformational love can bring them deep into his will. Through fearing God, and by that, I mean respecting Him, we change our mind-set to one that wants to know what God thinks and speaks. We want to know what God's best is for ourselves and for others, so as we seek out His wisdom, we are seeking to gain a real understanding, not just of what God says, but of why he says it. Understanding is an essential element of our journey to wisdom.

Unfortunately, the word 'fools' also relates to some within our churches, and these are the false teachers spoken about earlier. Through being wise, being confident in God's word, and remaining close to God, we are better placed to recognise those fools and distance ourselves from them and their false teaching. I encourage you to ask yourself whether their teaching stands out from the ways of the world, sets you apart as pure and holy, and encourages you to walk in humility. If it does not, then I urge you to step away and find a church which does teach these things in line with God's word.

Considering what you are being taught, in line with the above points, should encourage you to follow God's will. As we recognise together what our walk should look like, we better understand who we are seeking to become as we mature in Christ. Paul's prayers for the church emphasise the most important thing we can and must do. To pray for God's knowledge and to recognise His will, should become standard behaviour for every Christian. We should be praying this for ourselves and for our church. We must pray for us all to be humble and submitted to authority, to be Spirit filled individuals and churches, and to be those who would suffer for our God, as those who are saved and sanctified.

When we consider sexual immorality and homosexuality, how does our response measure up against the list above? As Christians does our stance on homosexuality make us different from the world?

I conclude this chapter with a reminder of Paul's teaching in Romans 12.

> *Therefore, I urge you, brothers, and sisters, in view of*
> *God's mercy, to offer your bodies as a living sacrifice, holy*
> *and pleasing to God—this is your true and proper worship.*
> *Do not conform to the pattern of this world but be*
> *transformed by the renewing of your mind. Then you will*
> *be able to test and approve what God's will is—his good,*
> *pleasing, and perfect will. Romans 12:1-2 (NIV)*

Paul knew what his early Church were up against, as much as God knew what His Church would continue to be up against in times to come. We know that Satan comes to steal, kill, and destroy, and if we are not transformed by the renewing of our minds, he has an immediate foothold. I urge you brothers and sisters to renew your minds over God's designs for marriage and sexual purity. To recognise how Satan has muddied the water and caused you to question God's word, caused you to believe that homosexuality is something we are born with and that cannot be changed. That is a lie, a smoke screen created by Satan which appears very real. But let us not forget, God's will is also very real; it is good, is pleasing and is perfect.

TESTIMONY, SARAH, UK

Sarah is in her fifty's and had a history of yo-yoing in and out of church. Satan was playing with her mind, trying to convict her that she was not worthy to be a Christian; he came to steal her joy. But in perseverance and faith she kept pursuing God and is now living a celibate, single life, enjoying contributing to the life of her local Church community. False teaching is prevalent, but the truth is found in God's word, and the conviction of the Holy Spirit.

I was the only of my parent's children not to be baptised as a baby. I was not brought up in a Christian home, although my grandmother (my father's mum) was a staunch believer. Her parents (my great grandfather and mother) were Welsh and around when the great Welsh revival happened. I am currently trying to find out if they were involved in some way.

Despite not growing up in church, I started going to a Pentecostal church when I was sixteen with a friend and soon became a born-again believer. When I was seventeen, I was working in a restaurant and befriended a gay waiter who took me to a club, and after a while I started to embrace the gay lifestyle and turned away from the church.

You may wonder what led me to believe that I was born gay. It was a culmination of events, thoughts, and opinions. From very early on, I always heard that I should have been born a boy. My parents wanted a boy and even had a name for me, Mark Antony! But I popped out instead, so I guess I always thought I was a mistake. I never liked being put in a dress. I was a tomboy and played with boy's toys instead of dolls and the like, so I did not really fit into what society told me a girl should be. Puberty was painful. I was tall, flat chested and into sports, so boys were not interested in me and could be quite cruel, so again, I felt I didn't fit in. The only place I ever felt normal and accepted was on the gay scene.

When I came back to the church in my late twenties, it was obvious there was no support or ministry for those who struggled with SSA. I was told by a pastor that gay people could not be helped, so I walked away from the faith again. I tried to ask God why I was born this way, as it was obvious to me that since I was a toddler I had been seen as 'different.' Some family members said it was obvious due to how I looked and carried myself, so I became convinced it was in my genetics and that I just had to accept it. I felt God had dealt me this card, as if it was like a disability, so it was up to Him to heal me.

But now I no longer think that way; my opinion has changed. It started with God not initially making an issue of my sexual preference. He wanted to deal with other issues first. He prioritised my inner healing above everything else. This was confirmed by a member of the pastoral team at a healing retreat I attended. This blew my mind.

Over a year or so of partnering and surrendering to God, He peeled back the many layers to reveal the root cause which led to me making the life choices I did. It was a mixture of words spoken over me, trauma, and the fact that we are all born into sin and live in a broken world, that can lead to making wrong decisions and finding love in wrong places.

I was not born gay; no one is. We are all born naked, incontinent, and unable to walk, talk and feed ourselves, but we don't stay that way, do we?

My change of opinion came more from conviction by the Holy Spirit and a closer relationship with Christ than anything else. I knew which Scriptures condemned same sex relationships and that acted as a kind of back up. I needed the conviction of the Holy Spirit to change me within and be able to help me accept that homosexuality is not the relationship that God had intended for us. The Bible has clearly taught me that God created male and female, with no in between or exceptions to the rule. Sex was created to be enjoyed within the confines of marriage, between a man and a woman. Anything outside of that is sinful.

I recognise that we all have different opinions and that is fine, but let me share with you some encouragement.

Regardless of whether you struggle with SSA or not, change in any of our behaviours and lifestyles is only possible by a heart change, which involves a relationship with Jesus Christ. God yearns to be reconciled with His creation in a heart to heart, one to one intimate relationship. Give Him your heart; let Him love you and the rest will follow.

There is nothing to fear. What you gain from a relationship with God far exceeds what you think you will lose from this life on earth. Your perspective will change from what is now and earthly, to that which is spiritual and eternal.

Chapter 8 – Mirrors – Reflecting a Fallen World

I remember as a child loving the hall of mirrors at the fair. We laughed so much as we stood in front of each mirror and saw ourselves reflected as chubby and short, elongated and skinny, or upside down with a super large head! Of course, we recognised the fact that these were not real reflections, but simply ones that distorted the truth to make us laugh. I remember too, being disappointed when visiting the Palace of Versailles, in France, to find that the famous Hall of Mirrors was not the promised entertainment of illusion, but a decadent and extravagant room designed to show off the economic prosperity and skills of the French to rival those of any other nation! The three hundred and fifty-seven mirrors, situated on seventeen arches opposite tall windows, had been designed to create an even greater illusion of grandeur and were successful in so doing.

Mirrors reflect, but not always accurately, as the two examples above show. Mirrors used in a hall of mirrors are often referred to as distorting mirrors. Instead of being a flat mirror that perfectly reflects, they are curved in certain ways to create a distorted effect. The mirrors used in the Palace of Versailles were indeed flat mirrors, but it was the positioning of these mirrors that created the illusion of space and light. The mirrors were strategically placed to reflect the daylight from the windows, to flood the room with a fresh light.

Using mirrors as an analogy should help us as we ask ourselves the question, 'How has Satan managed to create an illusion, so that when some look at him, they see light?' Just like the hall of mirrors, he has managed to convince many that his ways are good; indeed, some are convicted that his ways are God's ways. Not only has he managed to distort our perceptions, but he has also managed to magnify his influence, as with the mirrors in Versailles, to appear as an angel of light rather than

148

the prince of darkness. Paul wrote about this to the church at Corinth, warning them that Satan would disguise himself as an angel of light[92], and we should heed that warning also.

It is important firstly, to remind ourselves of who Satan is. Satan was an angel (Lucifer), and as an angel it is worth noting that he was a created being. He was one of the highest of the angels, but for an unknown reason, he became full of pride and desired to overthrow God, wishing to take on God's sovereignty. Hence, he was thrown out of heaven and as Isaiah reminds us, he was cast down to earth.

> How you have fallen from heaven, morning star, son of
> the dawn! You have been cast down to the earth, you who
> once laid low the nations! You said in your heart, I will
> ascend to the heavens; I will raise my throne above the
> stars of God; I will sit enthroned on the mount of
> assembly, on the utmost heights of Mount Zaphon. I will
> ascend above the tops of the clouds; I will make myself
> like the Most High." Isaiah 14:12-14 (NIV)

When we are under attack it is important that we remind ourselves of this fact. Satan is only a created being; yes, he has some power, but so do we. As Christians we have the Holy Spirit and are reminded in God's word[93] that 'greater is He who is in you, than he who is in the world.' But we do need to acknowledge the fact that Satan is real and that he does hold a privileged position, whereby he can deceive this world. For those who do not know Jesus, Satan is a very real threat to them ever coming to know him. The pertinent question is, how did all this come about; how, and why does Satan hold any power over the world?

We know that Satan was cast out of heaven and down to earth. It is fair to assume that from day one he was roaming the earth looking to see how he

---

[92] 2 Corinthians 11:14
[93] 1 John 4:4

149

could gain power. In fact, we know from the account in Job that this was his modus operandi:

> The LORD said to Satan, "Where have you come from?"
> Satan answered the LORD, "From roaming throughout the
> earth, going back and forth on it." Job 1:7 (NIV)

As Satan was roaming the earth, he would either have already been aware of Adam and Eve, or he certainly would have become aware of them as God's created beings. Satan would have seen that God had given them dominion over all the earth[94] and I am sure that felt like a sharp kick in the teeth to this fallen angel. This was not a shared dominion, man with God; there is no indication at all in the Bible that God wanted any part of ruling the earth. It clearly says in Genesis 'so that they may rule;' the reference of 'they' is of course a reference to Adam and Eve.

We are also told in our Bibles[95] that when God gives us a gift, He does not rescind; that gift remains ours. Adam and Eve were gifted with full dominion over the earth and all that was in it, to look after it, as good stewards, until God returns to reclaim it. God's gift remained fully available to them for as long as they obeyed His simple commands. To cut a long story short, Satan was fully aware that Adam and Eve were given sovereignty over the earth and whilst they continued to obey God, that sovereignty remained with them. He knew that if he could deceive them into sinning, they would become his slaves and that would give him his desired position as prince of the earth. This would happen because God tells us in His word that we become slaves to what we obey.

> Don't you know that when you offer yourselves to
> someone as obedient slaves, you are slaves of the one
> you obey—whether you are slaves to sin, which leads to
> death, or to obedience, which leads to righteousness?
> Romans 6:16 (NIV)

---

[94] Genesis 1:26
[95] Romans 11:29-31

It was a straightforward opportunity for Satan; deceive Eve, and he gained the power he so longed for. And we know the outcome of his plan. Satan was successful in his scheme and gained sovereignty of the earth, until that glorious day when Jesus returns to reclaim it. Satan is fully aware that the clock is ticking; he knows his time is limited. In fact, given the level of activity and attack we are seeing in the modern era, he is clearly throwing everything at it in a final attempt to take more down with him. For that is his goal; he is using his time and authority to take as many to destruction with him as he can. Not content with knowing his own destiny, he is using his time to deceive many others so that he can snatch them from God's eternal love.

We should not be surprised about this, as the Bible is clear on who Satan is and what he plans to do. Consider the many descriptive names given to Satan in the Bible; names that give us an insight into his true intentions. In John[96] he is called 'the prince of this world'; in Revelation[97] he is called 'the accuser of our brothers and sisters'; Matthew[98] calls him 'the prince of demons' and 'the tempter,[99]'and Peter[100] warns of him saying, 'Your enemy the devil prowls around like a roaring lion looking for someone to devour'. Listen to those names again:

- Prince of the world
- The accuser
- Prince of demons
- The tempter
- A prowling lion looking for someone to devour.

What a warning this is for us, and I pose a question to you now; "Do you take Satan seriously?" Do you recognise that he is the one who accuses you in your mind, who tempts you to sin, who twists the word of the Bible to

---

[96] John 12:31
[97] Revelation 12:10
[98] Matthew 12:24
[99] Matthew 4:3
[100] 1 Peter 5:8

deceive you into believing a false gospel? Do you believe that he is prowling around searching out his next victim? Because if you do not, now is the time to get serious; this is a battle and we must be prepared. The Good News for all of us is that we can resist the devil because we know that our Saviour Jesus is not only the Light of the world, but in direct contrast to Satan He is:

- ~~Prince of the world~~ King of the world
- ~~The accuser~~ Our advocate
- ~~Prince of demons~~ Prince of Peace
- ~~The tempter~~ Our deliverer
- ~~A prowling lion looking for someone to devour.~~ The Lion of Judah

Satan is a poor reflection of God; he is a counterfeit. A counterfeit is defined as something that is 'made in imitation of something else with intent to deceive.'[101] You have no doubt seen or heard about counterfeit clothing, perfumes, or jewellery. I watched a television programme recently which featured some counterfeit jewellery, and it took experts a quite considerable amount of time to study the pieces before they could definitively recognise which were real and which were the fakes. To all intent and purposes, these items look authentic, and often it takes an expert to differentiate between the counterfeit item and the real item. But once identified, the item is seen to be false and worthless, or at best its value is less than the authentic item. And that is exactly what Satan is, a cheap and worthless copy of God, a being who has managed to deceive many into thinking that he is the real deal.

Let us look at some of the ways that Satan imitates God:

- Trinity – We know that God is part of the Holy Trinity of Father, Son, and Holy Spirit. Are you as aware that Satan is part of his own trinity; the devil, the beast, and the false prophet[102] spoken of in Revelation?

---

[101] https://www.merriam-webster.com/dictionary/counterfeit
[102] Revelation 20:10

152

- Apostles – It's a well-known fact that Jesus had twelve apostles, but we also read in Paul's letter to the church in Corinth that there are false apostles, or more accurately there are apostles of Satan.[103] This a fact that is well worth our attention; we must be aware of these things if we are to fight against them effectively.

- Seal of ownership – God marks his own children;[104] we read in Revelation that a seal is put on the heads of the children of God. Not to be outdone, the counterfeit Satan also puts a seal on the hands or foreheads of his slaves.[105]

- Children – God calls us his children;[106] He gives us the right to become His children. So, as a counterfeit we would expect Satan to also have children, and we read in Matthew[107] that the 'weeds' are the children of the evil one.

These are just four examples of how Satan seeks to be the same as God; a desire of his own heart, as referenced in Isaiah,[108] 'I will make myself like the Most High.' As with anything or anybody, the truth is that we cannot make ourselves into something we are not. A Timex watch can never become a Rolex; a homemade rose water perfume can never become Chanel No 5; a woman cannot become a man; nor can Satan become the 'Most High' God.

What Satan has managed to do though, is to portray himself as authentic, which stands up to a brief glance, but would not stand up to a fuller inspection (this is why we are told to test the spirits to see if they are from God.) As with all counterfeit products, scrutinise them more closely and you begin to see the flaws and recognise the subtle differences from the

---

[103] 2 Corinthians 11:12-14
[104] Revelation 7:3
[105] Revelation 13:16
[106] John 1:12
[107] Matthew 13:38
[108] Isaiah 14:14

153

original. In seeking to present a false Jesus and a false gospel message, Satan has cleverly played on our emotions and compassions. We become impressed by what we see, rather than following the advice of Jesus to look out for the fruit. The parable of the sower could not be clearer in warning us that Satan will twist the gospel message:

> *When anyone hears the message about the kingdom and does not understand it, the evil one comes and snatches away what was sown in their heart. Matthew 13:19 (NIV)*

Satan operates by distorting truth; when we look at him, it is like looking into that curved mirror; we see something different from reality. Satan seeks to make the world look beautiful, attractive, and desirable, to lure us away from God's truth into a promise of a wonderful life, with no strings attached, no eternal consequences.

One of Satan's ploys is to try and convince humanity that there is no God. If we do not believe in a God, then we do not have to conform to any moral standards, only being subject to governmental laws; and that means freedom to sin however we wish, without consequence. But in practice, the moral law of God lives in our hearts. Whilst we are no longer subject to the law,[109] the Holy Spirit convicts us of right from wrong. As Christians, the presence of the Holy Spirit in our lives, results in us yearning to serve God and bring Him joy. We desire to do what is right in His sight. Without Christ in our lives, we no longer have these moral convictions, and God's word becomes obsolete as the world promotes free love. Satan's desire is that we no longer care about what God says is pure and right for us, in relation to sexual intimacy.

Satan recognises that if he can draw us away from God, we will become a society more focussed on him, rather than a society which is driven by God's moral laws. Sadly, as we look around, we see that Satan is having some success in convincing humanity that God is irrelevant or non-existent. Atheism is on the increase; we are now living in a society where it

---

[109] Romans 8: 1-2

is estimated that more than half have no faith whatsoever. The British Social Attitudes survey has been completed on an annual basis since 1983 and asks questions of 3,000 people each year relating to living in Britain. These people are selected through random probability sampling, which is designed to give as accurate a representation of the views of the British public as possible. This study shows that in 1983, 66% of the population identified as Christian and by 2018 this had dropped to thirty-eight%[110]. In just thirty-five years our culture has changed from one that identified most prominently as a Christian culture to one where less than two out of five people identify with Christianity. In addition, in 2018, 52% of the respondents identified as having 'no religion' at all. We can see this clearly reflected in our society as we hear more stories of Christian voices being silenced, more cases of Christian businesses being told that their practices are discriminatory, and as Christians we feel more susceptible to persecution within our workplaces or in our leisure pursuits.

Through deceiving the world into thinking that there is no God, Satan has blinded humanity to God's image. Sadly, as they look at Creation, many people no longer see this as a reflection of the God who created it; smoke and mirrors have diverted their gaze.

Whilst people are far from God, for example those who are professing atheists, agnostics, or members of another religion, they are not on Satan's radar as a threat. When people start to explore faith or when they are living in the Christian faith, that's when Satan goes on the attack and seeks to distort God's truth. His aim is to fill your mind with skewed thinking, and he is not shy at using atheists, agnostics, members of other faiths, and more worryingly other Christians, to make his case.

Let us be clear, Satan can con any of us if we allow him a foothold in our minds. If you struggle with anxiety, Satan has undoubtedly convinced you that there is something to worry about; he has deflected your eyes from Jesus. If you struggle with addiction, Satan has convinced you that you

---

[110] https://bsa.natcen.ac.uk/latest-report/british-social-attitudes-36/religion.aspx

cannot overcome the thoughts that tell you to keep going. He has blinded you to the fact that 'we are more than conquerors,' when we invite Jesus into every situation.

But I am not talking about those Christians who simply struggle with temptation or doubt from time to time. I am referencing those Christians who are false teachers and prophets: those who stand at the front of our churches in a leadership or a teaching capacity and lead us astray; those who declare false prophecies that are not of God. I particularly like the way that Tim Challies refers to these in his article[111] 'Seven False Teachers in the Church Today.' He talks about seven distinctive types of false teacher, some of which are relevant to the teaching we are seeing today on sexual immorality.

1. The Heretic – who teaches a faith that blatantly contradicts an essential teaching of the Christian faith.
2. The Charlatan – who uses Christianity as a means of personal enrichment.
3. The Prophet – who claims to be gifted by God to speak fresh revelation outside of Scripture.
4. The Abuser – who uses his position to take advantage of other people.
5. The Divider – who uses false doctrine to disrupt or destroy a church.
6. The Tickler – who is a man pleaser, not a God pleaser.
7. The Speculator – who is obsessed with novelty, originality, or speculation.

It is time for a reality check as we consider the messages we are listening to; let us wake up to the fact that Satan has an agenda too. When we read the words of the heretic who says, 'Just because the first marriage was between a man and a woman, that doesn't mean that all marriages should be,' go straight back to the Bible. What does it say in Genesis 2?

When we look at Leviticus 18, and all it says about sexual immorality, how does it read to us when we consider it with the understanding that Satan

---

[111] https://www.challies.com/articles/7-false-teachers-in-the-church-today/

wants us to remain in our sin? Do not be deceived by the tickler who wants to please those around him. To fit the Bible into the world (as opposed to the world into the Bible) he says, 'The debate is not about what the Bible says, it's about what it means'. The tickler will then go on to justify an interpretation which has concluded that homosexual acts are not sinful, by saying that Leviticus relates to specific kinds of same sex activity. He does this because he wants to satisfy the ears of the liberal Christians; he does not want to rock the boat and challenge all instances of same sex activity.

Paul's letters are not exempt from attack. In an article on the Queer Grace website, Emma Kegler,[112] writes:

> "The books, songs, and letters of Scripture were written by faithful people who had powerful experiences of God and were inspired to record them for many generations to read. Although inspired, the people who wrote the Bible were also limited by their time, their place, and their language."

This is a common argument used by many false teachers, that is, the fallibility of human writers. But this argument negates the Scripture in Timothy which tells us that 'All Scripture is God breathed[113].' Believing that God Almighty only allowed what He ordained to be written in the book is, for me, the most natural explanation for anyone who questions the authority of Scripture. I encourage you to pause, review the argument above with the mind-set that deception may be involved; how does that read to you now?

It is often insinuated that homosexuality was not understood at the time the Bible was written and that we have a much better understanding of it today. Indeed, in the same article Emma Kegler wrote:

---

[112] Why do some Christians believe it's ok to be gay, when the Bible says it isn't? http://queergrace.com/is-it-ok-to-be-gay/
[113] 2 Timothy 3:16

"In the past two hundred years, western civilization has come to understand that there is a diversity to sexuality and sexual orientation that was not recognized in previous eras."

I find this argument quite condescending, suggesting a naivety amongst the members of two great civilisations. We would be lying to ourselves if we thought that homosexuality had only become prevalent in the past two hundred years. In fact, if you read accounts of the Roman and Greek Empires you will read of extensive same-sex activity. The key distinguisher between then and now being that the Romans and Greeks did not seem to have a specific concept of sexual orientation. They would not have labelled themselves homosexual or gay, as we do in our culture; this was simply a different form of sexual expression for them.

The past two hundred years (more extensively the past fifty years) have seen our culture develop a heightened awareness of sexual orientation, to the extent that it practically dominates secular life today. The argument that understanding of sexuality and sexual orientation is of our age has been, and will continue to be, used to bring division amongst the church. In essence, it is an attempt to say that homosexual relations between two loving and consenting adults is a relatively modern phenomenon, and as such Paul was not writing about what we understand as homosexuality. Do your own research on these great civilisations and see what you think. Investigate for yourself Greek and Roman culture; see for yourself how homosexuality in a loving, monogamous relationship is not simply a phenomenon of the 20th and 21st centuries. Again, do not forget the Biblical warnings that Satan is the deceiver, as you consider the arguments in line with God's word.

Some Christians look at God through the world's eyes, when it should be the other way around. We should look at the world through God's eyes. My prayer is that as you read this book you will understand God's will for you to look directly at Him, so that you become a perfect reflection of Him, rather than looking in the mirror that Satan throws up to distract you and seeing a distorted image; a cheap imitation of the real thing.

TESTIMONY, KATY*, UK

Katy is a Christian who has experienced SSA all her life, but never acted on her attractions because of her unwavering belief in the word of God. But Katy struggled with addictions that controlled her life for many years, before she was delivered. You could say that she was a slave to those addictions, but is now living proof of the words of Jesus in John 8:36, "Who the Son sets free, is free indeed." Katy is passionate about seeing others set free from addiction and to expose the lies of Satan who seeks to keep them trapped.

I never imagined myself as ever having addictions. I was the sensible, obedient, hard-working achiever, who was strong willed enough to cope with most things.

I had given my life to Jesus at nine years old, and despite my very young age, it was an incredibly profound spiritual moment. My faith has always been strong, albeit there have been wilderness times when I wasn't close to God. But even in those times, I always had a faith.

What I didn't understand was the effects of my damaged childhood, and how that was going to deeply affect me in many ways as an adult.

And then life threw at me circumstances where I found myself in a "perfect storm" – and combined with my numerous false self-beliefs, drove me to near destruction.

I had the situation of a very demanding job working for a narcissist, a hugely stressful legal case, and I went back to university to add to my qualifications. At the time I couldn't afford legal advice, so had to do all the legal work myself. And the academic work – well, true to my messed-up beliefs from childhood, I felt I'd be worthless unless I achieved a high distinction grade.

Consequently, the pressure I placed on myself and that from outside influences meant that for two years I worked insane hours without going on vacation or taking a break. Actually, I was just becoming more unproductive, but the drive to be successful wouldn't let me take a break. At the end of two years all three stressful areas of my life ended within the space of three weeks. I finished the university course with the grades I wanted, won the legal case, and the guy I was working with was caught stealing, and so the hugely stressful job came to an abrupt end. The relief leaving that job was incredible.

Although everything on the surface was extremely successful, internally I was a mess. The enormous stress and lack of sleep or relaxation over such a long time finally caught up with me. The desperation for a break was indescribable.

But whilst part of me was crying out for rest, another part wasn't allowing it. I wouldn't rest until I had another job and was "achieving" again. But I'd end up looking at the computer screen all day, and not even do anything. Since I wasn't "achieving", I'd get very angry with myself.

To escape from the exhaustion and huge internal conflict, I started drinking. I then felt I deserved to be punished for not achieving. And one evening I cut myself as a form of punishment, hoping it would make me get back to work. But of course, the exhaustion had the final word, and so began a cycle. The self-harming quickly turned from being a form of punishment into both an expression of internal pain and a huge relief from emotions. It felt completely necessary to feel "normal" again.

The downward spiral into a very dark depression was rapid, and within a month, I was also horribly addicted to alcohol and self-harming.

Yet I was in complete denial that I had a problem and kept both the drinking and self-harming well hidden from everyone. I thought it was just a phase – and that I could handle it. I'd stop at some point and no one ever need know.

But as with all addictions, you need to do more and more to get the same escape, high and/or relief. My self-harming got to a point where I ended up in hospital and it shook my world. It was the first time I "confronted" myself that I had a problem. I knew I'd tried so many times to stop both, but they were simply too powerful. They had become as physically necessary as breathing.

If I tried to stop, the urge just grew and grew until it got to bursting point. On one such attempt I happened to be going around a shopping mall and it was the start of day three without drinking or self-harming. I was beside myself and was so desperate to self-harm all I wanted to do was break a shop window so I could cut my arms. The only reason I didn't is because I couldn't afford to replace it and I would have felt bad for the shop owners. But the urge was overwhelming.

Although I sought prayer and begged God to free me from the addictions, nothing seemed to happen. At this point the depression was so bad I felt the only way out was to end my life. I didn't want to die, but I couldn't carry on living like I was.

Fortunately, a friend had booked me in for deliverance ministry. I didn't know what to think of it, but I was so desperate I'd try anything and was always grateful to anyone who would take the time to pray for me.

The night beforehand I was gripped with an anxiety and an agitation I can't describe. It was bizarre, and I didn't know what was happening to me or where these feelings were coming from. I couldn't sit still, I couldn't concentrate, I couldn't sleep. When I picked up my Bible my hands would either shake so I couldn't read it, or I simply couldn't see the words on the page. In hindsight all these "feelings" that I thought were mine were the enemy being extremely scared of what was going to happen the next day.

So I went, and what happened with the deliverance ministry was incredible. It's impossible to fully articulate, but Jesus completely freed me from the spiritual assignments I had attached to my life.

But what shocked me the most was seeing just how powerful the enemy can be in twisting minds and driving feelings. I was amazed at how all those "needs" to drink or self-harm that I thought were coming from me, actually were coming from the enemy.

They were distinct from the emotional side, because having been freed from the spiritual influences, for the first time I had clarity, and I could also identify the thoughts and emotions as being mine. But most of all I was able to make choices again. If I did have the occasional weak moment after that and briefly drank or self-harmed, it was behaviour driven from an emotional trigger and familiarity. It didn't result in needing to do more or becoming addicted again.

To this day I am free from addiction. Completely free. It's a lie that once you are an alcoholic you will always be an alcoholic. As long as you have a God that sets you free from the spiritual influences and brings emotional healing you will be free. It's the same with the self-harm. I simply have no need for either and have no battle with them. Jesus has completely set me free.

*name changed to protect identity

Chapter 9 – Mirrors – Reflecting God's Holiness

Earlier on today I was listening to a modern worship set on YouTube and I heard the reworked words of a classic hymn sung beautifully, 'Oh how I love Jesus, because He first loved me.'[114] For me, those words illustrate so perfectly the 'mirror effect' that knowing Jesus has on us. Jesus, by his great mercy and grace, looked at me, a sinner, and loved me. As I received that love from Him, I looked back and loved Him in return; my love growing towards Him daily. And that is exactly what God wants for us and from us; for us to reflect His holiness; for us to be transformed into His likeness, so that as we look at Him, we become a reflection of Him to those around us. But He seeks us to look at Him, not through the eyes of the world, but through the eyes of a child, as wide-eyed, we take in His beauty and His holiness.

As I think about His love, I am reminded of that beautiful passage in 1 Corinthians 13 on how love is indispensable. For five years, from when I was an eleven-year-old, until I left school as a sixteen-year-old, I heard this Bible passage at every end of term assembly. Not that it meant much to me at the time, but the truth of this message remained deep within me and impacted me in more ways than I realised. What we learn from this chapter is that anything we do is worthless unless it is done in love. The passage goes on to describe what love is and says that: love is patient, kind, does not envy, does not boast, is not proud, does not dishonour others, is not self-seeking, is not easily angered, it keeps no record of wrongs, it does not delight in evil, it rejoices in truth, it protects, trusts, hopes and perseveres, it never fails[115].

---

[114] Oh, How I Love Jesus, Fredrick Whitfield, 1855

[115] Life Application Study Bible, Corinthians 13:4-8

164

Love here is expressed as a reflection of God's holiness; a holiness that ticks every box of perfection; a holiness that we can aspire towards, yet will never achieve ourselves. Perhaps part of the problem with achieving holiness is our mind-set. The passage from Corinthians goes on to talk about how we think:

> *When I was a child, I talked like a child, I thought like a child, I reasoned like a child. When I became a man, I put the ways of childhood behind me. 1 Corinthians 13:11 (NIV)*

I suggest that many of the issues we have as we reach physical maturity are based around changes in how our minds work. Part of that change sees us becoming less free in our thinking, as our experiences and the voices of the world around us taint our viewpoint. The mind of a child is a wonderful thing! There is a great YouTube clip[116] currently doing the rounds, of a toddler encountering a mirror in a department store for the first time. As he looks at the mirror in wonder, you can almost see the cogs whirling in his mind. He toddles around to the back to see what is going on, comes back and looks again; we see curiosity and a thirst for understanding. He does not just look like an adult would, glancing at his reflection and moving on, or using the mirror to check out his clothes or hair. He looks at it with a child's mind; he is visibly thinking, 'There's someone in the mirror who looks like me; they must be behind the mirror; oops no, where have they gone!'

We need to become more like that child when we look at God; dropping our pre-conceived, worldly views, to look at God through fresh eyes, with curiosity, with excitement and even with a smile on our face and joy in our heart! And within that, when we look at God, we must stop looking through the lens of the fallen world and change our lens to one that zooms in on God's holiness. Then, and only then, can our hearts be fully open to who God is, and our minds be fully prepared to receive what He is saying to us

---

[116] https://youtu.be/Xe2pQUsCUcw

and who He wants us to become. Paul describes our current experience like this:

For now, we see only a reflection as in a mirror; then we shall see face to face. Now I know in part; then I shall know fully, even as I am fully known. 1 Corinthians 13:12 (NIV)

This conjures up a picture for me of this same toddler, standing where the mirror used to be, gazing directly into God's loving face. God did not move; He is still standing in the same place, but the child now sees Him because the physical mirror has moved. How much we too, desire to see God's face without any encumbrance or barrier, to sit in His presence and ask so many questions; to gain real clarity on the big issues, including the issue of SSA. But I believe that God has already given us that clarity through His word. I will explore that through some Bible references to mirrors, the reflection of God's love, and those verses that tell us that we are made in God's image.

MIRRORS

Anyone who listens to the word but does not do what it says is like someone who looks at his face in a mirror and, after looking at himself, goes away and immediately forgets what he looks like. But whoever looks intently into the perfect law that gives freedom and continues in it—not forgetting what they have heard but doing it—they will be blessed in what they do. James 1:23-25 (NIV)

I love how James describes our relationship with the word in this first chapter of his letter. We have been gifted with God's word, but do we just hear it, or do we allow it to fill us, to direct us in the ways we should live? Do we hear it and interpret it through the eyes of the world, or do we hear it and seek God's wisdom, as James recommends earlier in the same chapter?[117]

Taking a step back, to help us to understand the context of these verses; we see that the letter starts with James advising the readers to consider it a joy when encountering trials.[118] He gives three reasons for this approach:

1. Because the testing of our faith produces endurance (verse 3).
2. So that we can become mature and complete, not lacking anything (verse 4).
3. We will be blessed with the crown of life (verse 12).

All these are reasons that stand up to scrutiny and are truly desirable for us as Christians. James then goes on to explain what we must do to 'manage' these trials. Again, he is comprehensive in his advice:

i. Ask God for wisdom (verse 5).
ii. Do not doubt what God tells you (verse 6).
iii. Recognise that temptation is not from God (verse 13).
iv. Recognise that temptation itself births sin if it goes unchecked (verse 15).
v. Do not be deceived (verse 16).
vi. Be quick to hear, slow to speak and slow to anger (verse 19)
vii. Get rid of moral filth and evil (verse 21).
viii. Be humble and accept the word planted in us (verse 21).

What James advocates is for us to be 'doers' and not 'hearers' of the word, and this is where the comparison with the man who looks in the mirror comes in to play. Someone who hears the word, but does not allow it to penetrate and therefore does not act on it, is likened to the man looking in a mirror. As soon as he walks away from the mirror, he forgets what he saw. In the same way a Christian, who does not look intently at what God's word says, will not conform to the eight points proposed by James, as ways to manage the trials and tribulations we will experience as inhabitants of the fallen world.

---

[117] James 1:5
[118] James 1:2

The final two verses of this chapter do not leave us in any doubt as to where James stands on those who fail to be doers of the word:

> *Those who consider themselves religious and yet do not*
> *keep a tight rein on their tongues deceive themselves, and*
> *their religion is worthless. Religion that God our Father*
> *accepts as pure and faultless is this: to look after orphans*
> *and widows in their distress and to keep oneself from*
> *being polluted by the world. James 1:26-27 (NIV)*

Whilst many of us may not consider ourselves 'religious,' these verses relate to all those who profess faith in Christ Jesus. If we are failing to adhere to the advice of James, we are deceiving ourselves. If we are failing to keep ourselves from being polluted by the world (or as the NASB version says, 'keep oneself unstained by the world'), then what good is our faith? Is it not as James states here, 'worthless?'

How then, does this all relate to our viewpoint on sexuality? Put simply, it is clear that we need to have more than a passing interest in reading God's word to fully understand what God says about sexuality. We must be committed to our study of the Word, approaching it with humility and a reverent regard for God's holiness, which we find reflected within it. We must keep ourselves unstained by the world, extracting ourselves from any thinking that may have been engrained within us since childhood.

When I first started to study Scripture, some thirty years after I had last been to church, I needed to unlearn some lies that I had believed; lies that told me homosexuality was the worst sin; lies that told me God could not forgive me for my homosexuality; lies that said I was not worthy. I chose to study the Bible and study hard! I came at it with an open mind. I indicate in my first book,[119] where I share my testimony, that I needed to come at it with a childlike faith (as opposed to a childlike mind). I was no Bible scholar, I had no formal qualification, but I did not believe I needed one.

---

[119] Transformed by God's Love – Exploring issues of Sexuality in the Christian Faith

God's word is for all, and I passionately believe that when we come at it with a childlike faith, we do not carry the baggage that causes us to view it through the lens of the world.

Having a counter cultural view about sexuality puts us in the position where, as Christians, we do suffer trials. Earlier this week I met with a Minister who is being maligned for maintaining a strong, Scriptural stance on same sex marriage. How easy it would be for him to admit defeat and bow down to the demands of his congregation. Yet he stands firm, understanding the joy that is before him, recognising that his suffering is simply temporary. He is certainly not alone, and I fear that more Christians will be persecuted in the months and years to come, as they stand on the opposite side of the LGBTQ+ lobby, remaining faithful to the Word of God.

Do not doubt what God tells you so clearly in His Word. Be quick to hear what the Bible says, and do not be deceived by Satan as he whispers lies into your ears. In response to those who say that God made us gay, recognise that temptation is not from God, and it is the temptation itself which births sin, if it goes unchecked. As you read God's word have the advice clearly laid out before you, 'get rid of moral filth and evil,' particularly as you consider what God's holiness requires of us. And finally, read the Word in humility, recognising God as our Sovereign Lord, in direct contrast to us, who are created and sinful beings.

THE REFLECTION OF GOD'S LOVE

We are anointed to reflect God's love. To reflect is defined[120] as, 'to give back or exhibit as an image, likeness, or outline.' Alternatively, it can mean, 'to throw back light or sound.' When we talk about the reflection of God's love, does not this mean that we should exhibit a love that is like the love of God, (of a likeness)? We could also take this to mean that as God loves us, we respond by becoming beacons of light within our own circles of influence; our praise and worship of Him lighting up the space we occupy.

---

[120] https://www.merriam-webster.com/dictionary/reflecting

The greatest testimony of our faith is in how we love. We love because God first loved us.[121] In John's first letter, he talks extensively in chapter 1 about God's love, referencing the perfect love that casts out all fear.

At the start of this chapter, we looked at this concept of God's love as we considered Paul's letter to the church at Corinth. The list of qualities of love was extensive and clearly defined. These qualities are all present in God and as such should be reflected in our lives. But for the purpose of looking at our pursuit of holiness (which is required if we are to reflect God's love), I have picked out a few to explore in more detail:

- Love does not boast, love is not proud.
- Love is not self-seeking.
- Love does not delight in evil but rejoices in the truth.

In seeking to become more like our heavenly Father, we should recognise these traits as ones that should hold no place in our lives. Yet one brief glance at what the LGBTQ+ lobby promotes should immediately sound alarm bells. The word 'pride' and the rainbow symbol of gay pride is to be found in every area of our lives. Product packaging is highjacked during 'Pride' month; popular entertainment shows and events are open to abuse. One example of this was the BBC's coverage of the 2019 Last Night at the Proms, where the guest soloist promoted the LGBTQ+ cause as she waved a 'Pride' flag from the main stage. Other examples include company sponsored staff events where employees are 'expected' to attend 'Pride' events. And one that is difficult to avoid are the cash machine (ATM) screens, where for example, my own bank, Santander, promoted their affiliation and support of the 'Pride' movement. I am not condemning this (although I do find it quite tiresome to be surrounded by so much propaganda), I simply use it as an illustration that many living in this lifestyle and their allies have taken their sexual orientation and turned it into an idol. More than this, they are trying to impose that idol on us and cause us to bow the knee too.

---

[121] 1 John 4:19

I am reminded of King Nebuchadnezzar, who made an image of gold, set it up on the plain of Dura in Babylon, and commanded that all people bow down to it[122]. Those who refused to bow (Shadrach, Meshach, and Abednego), were thrown into the fiery furnace, where God miraculously protected and saved them from death. Whilst the demands of the LGBTQ+ lobby are not that extreme, there is a degree of pressure on us all to fully embrace gay 'Pride' and bow to the LGBTQ+ agenda. Recent reports in the press include those of a bus driver suspended for refusing to drive a bus with rainbow colours on it (because he felt that it promoted homosexuality),[123] and of a Christian mother speaking of how her child was forced to take part in a gay pride event at her primary school, against the mother's will[124]. We also know that small businesses are easy targets, with Ashers Bakery probably the most well-known. Ashers hit the headlines in 2015, as they refused to bake a cake with a slogan promoting same sex marriage on it. The owners were forced to defend their action through the courts, until they finally won their case in the Supreme court in 2018[125]. These stories and many more, illustrate how we are becoming a country where all are increasingly expected to bow the knee to the gay agenda, and those who do not are in danger of being thrown into the furnace of public vitriol and persecution.

This is all indicative of the level of idolatry and pride associated with the gay lifestyle, which sets itself upon a pedestal, seeking much more than affirmation. To be affirmed as valued and equal members of society, living alongside others who may have different or contradictory views, no longer seems to be the goal of the political arm of the LGBTQ+ lobby. The objective seems to have become much more driven towards eliminating a conflicting view and silencing contradictory perspectives in an inflammatory and unbalanced way. Many Christians who dare to speak out are branded bigots and persecuted for their opinion. I have been on the receiving end of

---

[122] Daniel 3:1
[123] Mail Online – 13 August 2019
[124] Christian Today – 21 November 2018
[125] https://www.christian.org.uk/case/ashers-baking-company/

unpleasant comments and accusations of homophobia; sadly, many from within the Christian community.

It is important to note that not all who are same sex attracted are politically motivated. Many do not engage in the activities alluded to above and do not hold to the same values as the more vocal. For example, I know of gay people who disagree with 'Pride' events in schools, and who would not expect a work colleague to be forced to do anything that went against their own convictions to promote homosexuality. But pride, as an attitude, is not just seen in those who try to force Christians to accept a lifestyle that is contrary to God's absolute best for us and contrary to His teaching. Pride is an attitude which is at the heart of the decision by all who read the clear message of God's word on sin (in this case that homosexual activity is sinful,) yet refuse to turn away from their sin. I believe that heterosexual Christians who affirm homosexual sin are also guilty of pride, as they give sexual orientation a higher standing than God. Bowing down in front of the statue of homosexuality, as opposed to standing firm as Shadrach, Meshach and Abednego did, is not standing in God's holiness. Affirming sexual immorality reflects our own inability to trust in God's capacity to save us from sin, showing that we do not trust that God can help us overcome temptation.

Are we denying God's power to transform minds? Too many professing Christians are saying that it is impossible for a gay person to change, but they have missed the point. They need to shift their focus from expecting anyone to change their sexual orientation to one that expects every Christian to pursue holiness. It is the pursuit of holiness that results in us earnestly seeking God's purposes for our lives, and turns our eyes away from our own weaknesses, towards His strengths. When I responded to God's call to repent, I was all in. But in all honesty, for the first few months, it was tough, as I desperately wanted to feel different, to no longer struggle with temptations, and yes, to become 'straight.' It was not until a few months into my Christian walk that I realised that this was going to be a process and that my focus was all wrong. As I started to pursue holiness, to spend more time in the Word, in prayer and in pursuit of an intimate relationship with God, my desire to be closer to Him totally overtook my desire to become straight. And yet the outworking of that, over the past four years, has been that if I had to stick a label on myself, it would be the label of heterosexuality. I have been transformed because God has renewed my mind to recognise His divine purpose for my life.

As we seek holiness let us mirror the Father; God does not boast, God is not proud.

The passage in Corinthians also reminds us that love is not self-seeking. Someone who is self-seeking is someone who puts their own concerns and interests before those of others. The opposite of self-seeking is altruistic[126], 'having or showing an unselfish concern for the welfare of others.' As you read stories of heroes who acted in an altruistic manner, for example war heroes and members of the emergency services who unselfishly place their lives on the line for others, the Bible verse from John 15 comes alive.:

> Greater love has no one than this: to lay down one's life
> for one's friends John 15:13(NIV)

Of course, it is obvious that the greatest act of sacrifice of all time was the death and resurrection of Jesus, as He laid down his life so that we all could have eternal life. The mission of Jesus Christ when here on earth was to overcome Satan once and for all, so that we could have life and life in abundance. That abundant life is a promise from God, available to all of us when we accept and welcome Him into our lives. Satan came along to steal that from us; his mission clearly stated is to steal, kill and destroy.[127]

Satan is the epitome of self-seeking; all that he does is for his own gratification and glory; there is no hint whatsoever of any desire to bring joy or happiness to others through his actions. His lies are whispered into

---

[126] https://www.merriam-webster.com/dictionary/altruistic
[127] John 10:10-11

173

ears, because he wants to pull people into darkness, for no other reason than he wants you to fall; and the harder you fall, the happier that makes him.

How does being self-seeking relate to those who are continuing in sexual sin? Paul helps us to understand this in his letter to the church at Rome:

> *But for those who are self-seeking and who reject the truth*
> *and follow evil, there will be wrath and anger. Romans 2:8*
> *(NIV)*

When we reject the truth and follow evil, we are showing that we only desire to fulfil our own needs and desires. I think of the case of those who hear what God's word says about homosexual acts yet choose to continue to live lives of sexual sin. These are those who do not acknowledge that what God says is true; they either ignore the Bible or find their own interpretation to justify their behaviour. Self-seeking behaviour does not recognise the grace and power of God to change us, so instead we stubbornly continue our path to destruction, seeking to find excuses to justify our behaviour (did God really say that?)

Or it could be that you are one of the many Christians who have rejected truth on behalf of others, through some misguided desire to affirm their same-sex relationship. Your affirmation has the direct effect of encouraging people to continue to live sinful lives. You are guilty of arrogantly ignoring what God's word says, as you fail to mirror the love and truth of God.

As we seek holiness let us mirror the Father; God is not self-seeking. All of us who love, know that true love does not delight in evil but rejoices in the truth[128]. On the contrary, hatred flourishes in evil, and those who are evil hate the truth. Satan does not want the truth of God's word to be known and has twisted the truth of God's plans for men and women as he tries to bury the truth of God's transformative power. Satan's goal is to cause confusion and questioning, both outside and within the church. Within

---

[128] 1 Corinthians 13:6

174

Christian circles, many recognise that SSA came about because of the 'fall.' We recognise, of course, that SSA is a very real temptation, part of a much bigger picture when it comes to sexual temptation and immorality as we know it in the modern world. SSA was never part of God's plan for us, but it is one of many issues that have affected us since the day when Adam and Eve succumbed to the forbidden fruit.

Since the sexual revolution, as we have become much more liberal about sex, mindsets have changed. There was a time, as recent as my grandparent's generation, when most people (not just Christians) interpreted sexuality through the eyes of the Bible. Over the last few decades this has reversed, to the extent that now, most people interpret the Bible through the eyes of their sexuality. Someone who identifies as same sex attracted is seeking affirmational inclusion. Their natural conclusion is that the God of love, who loves us all, has made them this way (same sex attracted) and therefore God must affirm their behaviour and lifestyle. This is in stark contrast to how my grandparent's generation would have addressed this, whereby they recognised God as a God of love who was able to empower any of us to overcome temptations, as we become transformed into His likeness. In direct contrast to Satan, who lies to us, Jesus is full of grace and truth; in direct contrast to Satan who is evil and a liar, God is love and pure truth.

As we seek holiness let us mirror the Father; God does not delight in evil, but rejoices in the truth[129].

MADE IN GOD'S IMAGE

Finally, let us consider the implications of the fact that we are made in God's image, a fact which is mentioned in both the Old and New Testament (both directly and indirectly). References to this are found in Genesis,[130] as well as in both letters to the church at Corinth[131], the book of James[132], Colossians[133] and Romans.[134]

---

[129] John 14:6
[130] Genesis 1:26-27, Genesis 5:1-2, Genesis 9:6

175

When God created Adam and Eve, they were created in His image, and when God saw what He had made, it is recorded as being 'very good'[135]. The 'very good' description is in direct contrast to how each other element of creation is lauded; for everything else is described as good, the 'very good' was reserved for the creation of man, who has been made in the image of God. The image here relates not to a physical appearance, but to the very nature of God. Man had become a vessel to carry a representation of God's own character, and this mirror image was recognised as being more pleasing to God than any other created thing.

When Adam and Eve disobeyed God, their human character (which mirrored God's) became blemished. Through their own pride, Adam and Eve opened the door to Satan's deceit. Their desire to be equal with God was born from a misguided trust in the words of Satan, over and above the words of God. As soon as they ate the forbidden fruit, their disobedience allowed sin to enter their perfect minds. Satan had managed to deceive them and their relationship with God changed in an instant.

Their character was blemished, but the good news for us is that God did not remove His character traits from them. They still had the propensity to recognise right from wrong, to love, to be kind and to show glimpses of God's image. But they were no longer the same, and their sin laid the foundation for all humanity to be sinful and fall short of the glory of God[136]. Yet because God did not remove his DNA from us, once we come back to Him, recognise that we are sinners, and turn our hearts and minds back to God in repentance, we can start to be transformed, to reflect more of His image. Indeed, we know that the fruit of the Spirit is love, joy, peace, patience, kindness, goodness, faithfulness, gentleness, and self-control[137].

---

[131] 1 Corinthians 11:7, 2 Corinthians 3:18
[132] James 3:9
[133] Colossians 3:9-10
[134] Romans 8:29
[135] Genesis 1:31
[136] Romans 3:23
[137] Galatians 5:22

176

And these fruit grow and develop in our lives, as we walk closely with God, as we are connected to the Source. Thus, they are available to all who follow Jesus and walk with Him, and they are effective in helping us to change as we surrender our will to God. Our aim is to be perfect, just as our heavenly Father is perfect[138].

So here we are, humans created with God's DNA running through us on the one side and sin running through us on the other. We will never achieve perfection, but we can achieve wholeness; wholeness being God's original design for us to be well in our mind, will and emotions. Paul emphasised the balance required to obtain wholeness in his letter to the church at Thessalonica, where he talks of the requirement to keep our spirit, soul, and body blameless.

> *May God himself, the God of peace, sanctify you through and through. May your whole spirit, soul and body be kept blameless at the coming of our Lord Jesus Christ 1 Thessalonians 5:23 (NIV)*

Jesus also encourages us to love the Lord our God with all our heart, soul, and mind[139], another indicator of how we will only find wholeness when all three of these vital areas are aligned.

The great John Wesley talked about this as he recognised the importance of holiness and the need for renewal. His words were driven from his despair, as he witnessed many who spoke of having a faith but who did not appear to live out their faith in word and deed. When talking about our gaining our salvation Wesley said[140]:

> *"By salvation I mean not barely according to the vulgar notion deliverance from hell or going to heaven but a*

---

[138] Matthew 5:48

[139] Matthew 22:37

[140] John Wesley (1827). "The Works of the Rev. John Wesley", p.219

present deliverance from sin, a restoration of the soul to its primitive health, its original purity. a recovery of the divine nature the renewal of our souls after the image of God in righteousness and true holiness in justice mercy and truth."

Wesley encourages us to look further in our relationship with God; it is not just about being delivered from hell. He urges us to become whole in the present. Being saved is not just about our eternity, it is about deliverance from the chains of sin in the here and now. This hope and deliverance are essential for the restoration of our soul towards God's intended state for us, as we strive to mirror God's righteousness and holiness. Holiness requires us to experience God in every aspect of, and every moment of our lives.

In the Garden of Eden, before the 'fall,' Adam and Eve were whole; healthy and well in their bodies, pure of mind, with souls that were righteous and holy. This was God's intended state for us all, His design for humanity to live in harmony with Him. That is the good news, because it means that the effect of the 'fall' on our lives is not irreversible. When we accept Jesus into our lives and repent of our sins, God puts His Spirit in us and by His work we start the long journey to wholeness and holiness. This journey is co-dependent on us, as we are called to surrender to God, purify ourselves of the things that taint us, and to hunger and thirst for the truth.

In our perfect state, we mirror God; we reflect His love because we are made in His image.

Which mirror are you looking in? Do you choose the imperfect mirror of distortion, thrown up by Satan, that offers us a cheap imitation of the real thing? Or do you look to the mirror of God, recognising your call to holiness and the resulting sacrificial behaviour that is necessary if you are to become whole and live your life fully inside the will of God?

TESTIMONY, PARESH, INDIA

Paresh did not come from a Christian background and so his understanding of God and His love was extremely limited. Since becoming a Christian, Paresh has been actively involved in supporting the church in India as co leader of True Love, India, who seek to be a support to churches and individuals who have questions over sexuality and faith.

I was bullied as a child by two brothers who abused me, but I was too scared to speak out and tell my parents. When an elderly man started touching me inappropriately, my confusion grew, and my identity became one of worthlessness. Over time, I gave my affections exclusively to men, and as a student this turned to sexual encounters. I had no experience of God; He was a distant deity who meant nothing to me. I threw myself into the culture of alcohol, parties and sex with men, and thought nothing of the choices I was making. My work took me to Dubai, where I had a great life, good friends, and stable job.

Eventually, I was made redundant from the job I loved so much in Dubai and had to return home to India. This was a really low point for me, and I started to question the meaning of life. One night, I was chatting with my friend in Dubai, and I sensed a difference in him; he was not his usual impulsive, cussing self. I asked him about it, and he told me how he had been going to church and was experiencing a peace he had never felt before. He shared a Scripture from 1 Corinthians 13, which speaks profoundly about love, God's love, and I could see from his life this was not just words; this was something he was experiencing for himself. He had changed.

My eyes were suddenly opened; my friend had changed, and it seemed this had happened because of Jesus. That was a revelation to me, and I wanted to know more. I had so many questions. My friend offered to fly me back to Dubai to attend his church, and I jumped at the chance.

I was apprehensive when I attended my first ever worship service with him. But it was there I experienced an overwhelming presence of God and wept uncontrollably. As I was crying, suddenly, I heard a whisper in my ear, I LOVE YOU. I looked around, as I felt the sincerity of the person who said it, but there was no-one there. I realised it must have been Jesus who had spoken to me. That blew me away and changed my life.

As I learned more, I saw that I did not need to do anything to get His love; it was freely given to me. I had a worth; He saw me as valuable, valuable enough to whisper those three words I had yearned to hear for so many years. I started to allow myself to receive this love from Him. As I started to read the Bible, I read so much about Him and His desires for us. I felt strongly that if there was something in my life that made Him unhappy, it had to go. If my sexuality was something He had not given to me, then I was happy to let it go. I now saw God, not as a distant deity, but as a God who genuinely loved me, and had real plans for my life. I saw that the boundaries He has set for us humans, were actually there because He loves us so much, and that was a real eye opener.

Chapter 10 – You shall have no Idols.

You shall have no other gods before me. "You shall not make for yourself an image in the form of anything in heaven above or on the earth beneath or in the waters below. You shall not bow down to them or worship them; for I, the LORD your God, am a jealous God, punishing the children for the sin of the parents to the third and fourth generation of those who hate me, but showing love to a thousand generations of those who love me and keep my commandments. Exodus 20:3-6 (NIV)

You may be thinking, 'What does idolatry have to do with sexuality?' Because after all, sexuality is the main thrust of this book. That is the same thought process that Satan would have you use; wanting you to believe that idolatry is all about bowing down to beautifully formed statues of precious metals, carved stone, or ornate wood. It is probably true for many Christians that our understanding of idols often emanates from our reading of the Bible, where we read of idols which are almost exclusively hand-crafted objects, symbolising some kind of deity. But we also recognise that these physical idols are merely the work of a craftsman;[141]we recognise that they are lifeless[142]and unable to fulfil the place of God in our lives.

We then turn to our alternative understanding of idols; abstract concepts or material objects which start to take the place of God in our lives. In this modern era, this can be as simple as our phones, our addiction to social media and our obsession with Instagram. It is also apparent in our motives for living. We pursue success; we spend hours projecting a false image of the reality of our lives. We are obsessed with materialism, whereby we

---

[141] Isaiah 44:11
[142] Psalm 115:4-8

begin to believe that we need more things to feel fulfilled. In fact, anything that we trust more than God, or that we put our focus on more than we put it on God, could be classed as an idol. There is only one God, and He demands that we give Him our worship. In fact, this commandment is so serious that it is the first of the ten commandments,[143] "You shall have no other gods before me."

Where does sex fall into this category; surely it was designed by God for our pleasure? Yes, that is true, and God's desire is clear on the circumstances where sex is appropriate and encouraged; that is in the marriage of one man to one woman. Unfortunately, man himself has distorted this truth and maligned the purpose of sex to be something a lot different to what God designed it to be. Look around you at advertising, television programmes, social media, and films, and you will see how sexual exploits have become something to be boasted about. Provocative images are now commonplace in advertising (sex sells), and many fictional characters draw their identity from, and pay great attention to, their sexual activity or sexual orientation. When our focus on sex or our sexual identity becomes greater than our focus on God, we have made it into an idol, something we consider more central to our lives than God, and His purposes for us. Jesus warns us that we cannot serve two masters, telling us, "You will hate the one and love the other, or you will be devoted to the one and despise the other[144]." Whilst this direct reference in Matthew was talking about serving God and money, the same principle can be applied to any idol in our lives.

The exclusive worship of God is not solely for His glory, but for our benefit. We are made to worship, and John[145] tells us that the Father is seeking true worshippers to worship Him, and that those worshippers must worship in spirit and truth. Jesus even used this truth to rebuke Satan

---

[143] Exodus 20:3-6
[144] Matthew 6:24
[145] John 4:23-24

when he was tempted in the wilderness saying: "Be gone, Satan! For it is written, you shall worship the Lord your God and Him only shall you serve."[146]

We might belittle idolatry, relegating it to the side-lines because of our blinkered view of what idolatry really means, or because we are in denial that our sexuality, or attitude towards sexuality, is in fact taking our eyes away from God. But I do believe that it is a worthy exercise to ask ourselves this tough question, "Is my view of sexuality idolatrous?" We need to be confident that we have not made this an idol. In being confident of this, we, like Jesus, can rebuke Satan even at our lowest point as he lures us into thoughts of idol worship.

Here are five questions that you can ask yourself as you consider whether your view of sexuality could be idolatrous.

1. Do I accept that my heart is sinful and inclined towards idolatry?

Even those of us who are born again, who have repented of our sins and committed to serve God, possess a sinful nature[147]. Our fleshly desires are in direct contradiction to the desires of the Spirit and so a battle rages within. Idolatry is a by-product of us losing that battle; we want to serve God with all our hearts, minds, and souls, yet if we are honest, there are times that we fail, and our attention is pulled away to thoughts and actions of the flesh. Idolatry was present in the Old Testament, spoken about by Paul in the New Testament (therefore, my dear friends, flee from idolatry[148]) and sadly, continues to be a fact of life today. Twice in Revelation, we see John rebuked for worshipping an angel.[149] This so perfectly illustrates how easy it is for us to mistake something, or someone, as equal to God and deserving of our worship and praise. It is not always a clear-cut defiance of God; sometimes it is simply a misguided, spontaneous bowing down, which could take hold of any of us if we are not on our guard. The answer to the question of whether we have an idolatrous nature, must surely be

---

[146] Matthew 4:10
[147] Galatians 5:16-17, Romans 6:6
[148] 1 Corinthians 10:14
[149] Revelation 19:10; 22:8-9

yes for us all. I recognise my flaws and fallibility; it is only God's grace that has saved me, not my perfection. In recognising this truth, we are put on guard, alerted to the schemes of the devil.

2. Am I acting out of self-interest?

What are my motives for promoting this concept or object to an elevated position within my life? For some material concepts, we can quickly recognise our motives and how these are in our own self-interest. For example, when we make money and wealth our goal, we do this because we yearn for the benefits that having money provides us with; benefits such as security for our future, lack of worry about how we will pay the bills, popularity, and social status. We also seek material benefits, which for some may include having the latest designer gear, luxury house, extravagant holidays, jewellery and top of the range cars. We quickly see that self-interest is demonstrated by those who make an idol of their wealth.

When you are SSA, your focus is on your sexuality (you cannot help that, it is a natural focus to have). Becoming a Christian then asks the question of you, is your sexuality more important to you that God? If you answer this in the affirmative, what is the reason for your yes? For me, the only reason I would have been able to give at that point would be, 'because of my desire to have a sexual relationship with another woman.' That desire, however, is in direct disobedience to God's Word, so there I would be saying, 'I want to follow You Jesus, but not that much.' It would equate to me saying, 'I don't trust that what You have for me is bigger and better and more satisfying than what I already have.' I would be denying God's power and love and acting in my own self-interest, making an idol out of my sexuality and sexual relationship.

What about those who are Christians, who are not SSA attracted, yet continue to defy God's word on homosexuality? I suggest that they too are making an idol out of homosexuality, falling in with the views of the world above those of God. I see their stance also as one of self-interest; let me explain. Standing up to the world is tough. We are seeing Christians come under increasing attack as they hold fast to God's Word, in this country and many others around the world. It is difficult to swim against the tide; let me assure you that being on the side of the debate that says homosexual acts are sinful can be a lonely and difficult place to be in human terms. It is much easier to redefine God's Word, to grasp at the commands to love your neighbour as yourself as your key driver, rather than remaining true to the Scriptures that ask us to gently correct a brother or sister who sins[150]. The compassion these Christians feel towards individuals who experience SSA is being twisted by Satan into a false belief that SSA is OK, that SSA is somehow natural and affirmed in the Bible (yet up to now I have failed to find anyone who can point out where this affirmation is found). They then start to make the sexual identity of others more important than salvation, and as with those who struggle with SSA, they too are saying. 'I don't trust that God has a better plan for your life; I don't believe that God can transform your life,' denying once more God's Word and His power.

And finally, with regards to self-interest, it has been compelling for me personally to hear so many stories of Christians who have turned away from what the Bible says, because they have a child or close friend who identify as LGBTQ+. Self-interest comes into play because they fear that by standing up to God's truth and rejecting Satan's lies about sexual identity, they are somehow rejecting the identity of the person they love. Idolising the lifestyle of the person you love does not give them freedom in Christ.

3. Am I prepared to sacrifice everything to follow Jesus?

I am not sure that any Christian fully recognises the commitment they are making when they say yes to Jesus and ask Him into their life. For many of us it is life shattering; it takes guts, commitment, sacrifice, and hard work. That is not to say it is not worth every second of all we put in, it is just an honest appraisal of what sacrifice looks like. We commit to becoming

---

[150] Matthew 18:15, Galatians 6:1, Titus 3:10-11, 1 Timothy 5:20, James 5:19,

185

disciples, and we understand the terms and conditions of that commitment (or if we do not immediately, over time as we study and immerse ourselves in the Word, we soon do). As soon as we recognise an area of our life that is sinful, we need to address it. Do we, as the Psalmist does in Psalm 139, invite God to search us, know us and see if there is any offensive way in us[151]? If we do this, when He shows us the ways that need correction, are we prepared to work on those areas, to admit that there is need for change and commit to God to try and change? A refusal to respond to God when He highlights sin in our life means that the sin has become more important to us that God. Do you want that to be the case for you? As you read this, do not think that acting on SSA is the only sin I am referring to here. There is sin when we lead others astray, when we cause one of God's children to stumble through false teaching and lies.

> *If anyone causes one of these little ones—those who believe in me—to stumble, it would be better for them to have a large millstone hung around their neck and to be drowned in the depths of the sea. Matthew 18:6 (NIV)*

In Paul's letter to Timothy, he refers to these people as "having the appearance of godliness but denying its power[152]." He also warns us to "avoid such people." If you have made sexuality an idol for yourself or others, remember that we are called to sacrifice, to pick up our cross and follow Jesus. We may not understand where He is taking us as we sacrifice, but from my own experience, He is taking us to a much better place; His ways are higher, His thoughts are higher, and His promise of abundant joy is there for the taking as we lay down our idols.

4. Is my identity primarily in Christ?

This is a simple question and one that does not need much explanation. When I think of myself, where does Christ come into the equation? I explain in my first book,[153]that I took a long time searching for answers as I

---

[151] Psalm 139:23-24
[152] 2 Timothy 3:5

fought to be a "gay Christian." Put simply, I wanted to have my cake and eat it. But over time, through reading God's Word, seeking out Godly teaching and listening to the Holy Spirit, I began to realise that being a gay Christian was an oxymoron. There are many people who would disagree with me, saying that it is not in fact an oxymoron. Some SSA celibate Christians still refer to themselves as a "gay Christian." My concern with this is, why do they feel the need to preface the word Christian with the word gay or even state that I am an SSA Christian? Does a heterosexual feel the need to say, I am a straight Christian? It is not a comment that I have ever heard, so I would suggest not! As a Christian, we must drop any hint of idolatry and ensure our identity is solidly in Christ. My proclamation today, "I am a Christian, a child of God;" no other explanation is required. I believe that continuing to use the label 'gay,' when committed to a celibate life, is a snare that Satan uses to try and keep us partially grounded in an old identity. We are told not to give Satan a foothold[154]; maintaining links with an obsolete identity is just the foothold he needs against which we are warned.

5. What does God's Word teach me?

Firstly, God's Word teaches me the importance of knowing God's Word well; in fact, it goes further than that, it encourages us to delight in doing right and obeying God's law. "Blessed is he who delights in God's law and who meditates on God's word day and night."[155] The Bible also talks about the rewards that are given to those who study hard and seek to obey all that they read:

> *That person is like a tree planted by streams of water,*
> *which yields its fruit in season and whose leaf does not*
> *wither—whatever they do prospers. Psalm 1:3 (NIV)*

---

[153] Transformed by God's Love, Exploring issues of sexuality in the Christian faith – Sarah Sedgwick, Kingdom Publishers 2019

[154] Ephesians 4:27
[155] Psalm 1:2

187

Our walk with God is dependent upon our willingness to trust the inerrancy of His Word and to apply that same Word to our lives. When we do that, we prosper and bear fruit. Reading God's Word requires us to spend time alone, one on one with God, and there is no better place to be, away from the influencing lies of Satan, often delivered through false teachers. Reading God's Word prayerfully helps us to hear from the Holy Spirit and understand the meaning for ourselves. God's Word, when studied, shows us the danger of idolatry. It spells out the consequences for the Israelites, who failed consistently to eradicate idolatry. Their fate clearly shows us the suffering that comes to those who do persist in idol worship. The New Testament also highlights the danger of idolatry as a practice, clearly connected to demons, who seek to undermine our relationship with God and steal God's glory.

> What agreement is there between the temple of God and idols? For we are the temple of the living God. As God has said: I will live with them and walk among them, and I will be their God, and they will be my people. 2 Corinthians 6;16 (NIV)

God's Word teaches us that He desires a relationship with us, and He desires that nothing will come between us and Him (He is a jealous God[156]) . Let us be open in searching our own hearts to ensure we harbour nothing that will come between us and the Lord. I do not see a need to repeat here the Scriptures that so clearly reveal that God designed male and female to be united as husband and wife; nor the ones which clearly condemn homosexuality and sexual immorality, because these have been clearly defined already. But I do urge you to take time to think about how you might be interpreting these verses through idolatrous eyes.

We cannot forget the commandment to love the Lord your God with all your heart, soul, and mind.[157] God demands an intimate relationship with

---

[156] Exodus 34;14
[157] Matthew 22:37

Him. Do not allow yourself to be misled by Satan, thinking it is possible to share your affections or even to give them wholeheartedly to something or someone else. The warning of the outcome of giving your attention to anyone or thing other than God is clearly laid out in the book of Isaiah; they will be of no use to you in times of trouble.

> When you cry out for help, let your collection of idols save
> you! The wind will carry all of them off, a mere breath will
> blow them away. But whoever takes refuge in me will
> inherit the land and possess my holy mountain. Isaiah
> 57:13 (NIV)

Those who are in any sexual relationship, outside of heterosexual marriage are living contrary to the will of God. What they are doing is replacing the inbuilt need that we have for a relationship with God with sexual activity, as they seek to find fulfilment. In looking to another human to fulfil us, we start to worship that person in place of God. Paul spoke about this clearly in Romans,[158] 'They worshipped and served created things other than the Creator.'

If you are in a relationship which is outside of God's best for you, you are being called to face the situation and accept that the relationship you have is idolatrous and will not fulfil you. God calls you to lay this relationship down and to trust that His grace will meet you where you are. My experience is that He does this and remains with you as you navigate the necessary changes in your life. As you take refuge in God, you will find the fulfilment as promised in Isaiah; you will inherit the land and possess God's holy mountain.

---

[158] Romans 1:25

TESTIMONY, HARRY* UK

Harry is married to his beautiful wife, and they have two children together. His marriage is something of a miracle, the result of family prayer for him to leave his homosexual identity and return to the faith of his youth. After a number of years living in a committed relationship with another man, Harry got restless, returned home and his relationship with Jesus was restored.

Harry now mentors others who, like him, have chosen Jesus over their sexual identity but would also say to praying family members – never stop praying!

The idea of Idols in the Bible is one of golden calves and physically bowing down before statues. It appears that in Scripture, people built idols because they did not trust God to come through, or He took longer than they'd have liked to answer them, or they rejected the one true God for a false god.

As we don't tend to build golden idols in our culture, it may seem to not be so prevalent; however, it's far more subtle and widespread. For myself, the idol I bowed down to (not physically but in my heart) was the male form. Growing up, I developed insecurities about myself, particularly my body. I felt small, inadequate, and feared I'd never develop physically. As my peers were going through puberty, I felt like I'd never be like them. I also saw pornography before I hit puberty, which was so shocking to me that I was emotionally and mentally traumatised by the content I saw. This strengthened the lies I had begun to believe as truth. All this was happening in a vacuum of secrecy and isolation. I didn't ask anyone about it, or gain a Godly perspective from an adult.

At the time, I hadn't really put so much value on the male form; I just didn't think I'd ever look like that or would develop in the same way. This was

190

painful and confusing. When I did hit puberty and my emotions connected to the emerging desires and sexual awakening, the inner thoughts and feelings I had about myself connected to the sex drive and turned the thoughts about other men, from envy and longing into a sexual desire. Consciously or not, in that painful and confusing place, I gave the place in my heart where the worship of God should be, to the male form I longed to have but never thought I would have. This went on for years until I saw it for what it was. I had come to put such value on the one thing I felt I did not have. Many of us do this with other things, material things, relationships and status.

Although I cared about what God said about me, it didn't trump the worth I gave to my 'idol' of the particular male form I longed to be like. In time, I have come to see it for the lie that it is. I also started to recognise that the pain I felt, and internal isolation I went through as a young person, distorted my thinking. The pain took me away from the truth of God. Only He is to be worshiped. Once I put God back in His rightful place in my mind and heart, I could begin to work through the issues I had developed, in the light of His truth.

I must keep choosing to put God on the throne and to value His truth, rather than idolising what I may feel or think.

Romans 1, makes so much sense to me. I absolutely exchanged the truth of God (which says I'm fearfully and wonderfully made in Psalms) for a lie (that I'm inadequate; I'll never be like the others boys or like those men I saw in that porn film,) and I began to worship created things (man and the male form).

I thank God that He brought me out of this deception and into the light of His truth. I stand firm in this. At times, under stress and during emotional times, I can sometimes feel old familiar emotions, causing me to feel like that young boy again. But now, rather than reacting to these feelings and thoughts from a mind of a young person without any resources, I can respond to those thoughts and feelings with truth and a rational mind. Praise God.

name changed to protect his identity.

192

Chapter 11 – An Altar of Broken Stones

We are an altar of broken stones, but You delight in the
offering. You have the heavens to call Your home, but
You abide in the song we Sing.[159]

These lyrics from "Hallelujah Here Below," paint a picture of us, members of God's church, worshipping and offering ourselves to God. We are all broken, not one of us can state otherwise, and yet here we are, imperfect and broken people with one thing in common, our desire to draw close to God and live our lives in obedience to Him. Some reading this book will be in total agreement with my interpretation of the Bible, that homosexual activity is wrong. Some reading this book will be in total disagreement with that interpretation, saying that homosexual acts are not sinful. I am sure that some others will be sitting on the fence, wavering from one side of the debate to the other, undecided about what God's word really means. My prayer is that many will have their eyes opened to Satan's deceit as they read this book and begin to recognise the enormity of the battle that we are in. The reason we vary so much is because God has given us freewill; as such we are free to listen to God as much as we are free to listen to Satan. We are at liberty to then make our own decisions as to who or what to believe.

Recognising that Satan's goal is to deceive (and I am sure that no one would dispute that fact), we need to be careful that our response to how we interpret the Bible is not shaped by our own life experiences. Our backgrounds are all a part of life's rich tapestry, part of who we are and where we have come from. Experiences that we have lived through, friendships we have formed, family history, work relationships, attitude to

---

[159] Hallelujah Here Below – by Elevation Worship

sin both past and present, all have a bearing on how we interpret what God is saying to us. God's Church is made up of an altar of broken stones; each stone a person who has been negatively influenced and shaped by their past.

I heard Charlotte Gambill speak at Cherish[160] a few years ago, and she had two photographs that served as a great illustration of the people within the church. The first picture was of a red brick wall with uniform sized bricks, all neatly held together with mortar, creating a solid wall with no gaps; every brick was identical. The second picture, in direct contrast to the first, was of a dry-stone wall. There were rocks of all shapes and sizes, stacked together in a random way, with small ones used to fill gaps, large ones used to create a solid base and smooth ones used to top the wall. Consider which picture best illustrates the Church. Of course, it is the dry-stone wall. Next time you go to church I encourage you to look around you. There you will see all different types of stones; people with diverse backgrounds, stories, and talents, who fit together in an imperfect way to create a solid wall.

The beauty in this is that, although we come from brokenness and are all shaped differently, God makes a way through imperfect people. I just love how God does that; When I hear testimonies from those who were at rock bottom, drug dealers, prostitutes, gang members, alcoholics, all who have turned their lives around, it just screams of God's grace and mercy. My own testimony of freedom from bulimia, self-harm and SSA is testament to God's love for me and fills me with joy, yet also fills me with a yearning to help others to overcome their own temptations and battles.

The precedent for building altars of stone is found in the Old Testament; specifically we read in Exodus that God instructs the Israelites to make an altar of stones for Him. But He specifically states that they are not to build it with dressed stones, 'For you will defile it if you use a tool on it.'[161]

---

[160] Cherish is an annual ladies conference hosted by Life Church, Leeds
[161] Exodus 20:25

Why was this detail of such importance to God; surely an altar to God should be beautiful and ornate? But if we consider God's take on this, altering the stones meant that human effort was required to adorn and cut the stone to shape it into an altar. By making the altar more aesthetically pleasing and adorning it with precious stones and metals, the focus would be taken off God. Our human tendency would be to admire the craftsmanship of the altar, rather than focusing our praise and worship solely on God, and that defiles the purpose of the altar. In Isaiah, we hear what God feels about altars that have been defiled:

> All day long I have held out my hands to an obstinate
> people, who walk in ways not good, pursuing their own
> imaginations— a people who continually provoke me to
> my very face, offering sacrifices in gardens and burning
> incense on altars of brick. Isaiah 65:2-3 (NIV)

The Israelites had ignored God's advice and rejected stone altars in favour of bricks. This was the defiance of a people who wanted to worship God in their own way and on their own terms; a people who did not feel the need to be obedient to God. Perhaps they thought it much nicer to sacrifice in a garden on a brick-built altar, seeing the place of the sacrifice as much more important than the actual sacrifice itself. God merely wants the simplicity of our obedience; our lives are the sacrifice which He desires.

We can learn some lessons from God's requirements, as laid out to the Israelites.

• Our focus is important.

I was impacted by an article which promoted five ways to stay focused on God, specifically point five that stood out for me. Gene S Whitehead[162] shared the importance of starting the day with God, remaining in prayer, limiting our distractions, and serving God, as key activities to retaining our focus. All these are good and valid, but if we do not have the 'Eureka'

---

[162] https://genewhitehead.com/staying-focused-on-god/

moment of his fifth point, they are all worthless. His fifth point stated that to remain focussed on God, we must remove sin from our lives.

In previous chapters, as we have considered deceit, we have looked at smoke from different perspectives and we have looked at mirrors from different perspectives. We now have enough evidence in comparing the smoke and mirrors of Satan with the smoke and mirrors of God, to know that God's ways are higher and better for us all. We have unmistakable evidence of Satan's mission to deceive, as referenced in the Bible, and we have unmistakable evidence that God's laws speak clearly about sexual sin. Jesus himself promoted heterosexual marriage as the one and only place for healthy sexual relationship to take place. We are truly educated in God's Word, but sometimes that just does not cut it. Mark Batterson, author and lead pastor of National Community Church in Washington, D.C, puts it this way:

> "Most Christians are educated way beyond the level of their obedience already! We do not need to know more; we need to do more."[163]

If we are to remove sin from our lives, we can no longer simply read the Word and do nothing about it (so deceiving ourselves); we must do what it says[164]. The Word says, repent of our sins, and that means we show remorse and make a decision to no longer act in the same way. The Bible clearly states what is sinful, and it clearly affirms that homosexual acts are sinful. The time has come to stop reading about it and simply do nothing. We must read it, believe it, and become obedient to it, in our words and actions, our teaching and our pastoring. Our quest for truth and action is not helped by the fact that we belong to a generation who have the tools to find answers to anything at the touch of a button. When we cannot find the answer immediately, we get frustrated and can become obsessed with our search. For those who fit that description, it is important to remind yourself

---

[163] Facebook post by Mark Batterson from Oct 26, 2014
[164] James 1:22

196

that God does not always require your understanding, but He does always require your obedience.

One of my first life group leaders talked of having a metaphorical shelf, where she shelves the difficult things of God that she just does not understand. Sometimes she can come back to that shelf having gained more insight. Other times the question remains on the shelf for an undetermined time in the future, when she will find the answer, or it may remain unanswered until she meets God in eternity, and she can ask Him herself! But the message is clear, if we do not understand something God asks of us, it does not mean we can totally ignore it. It may be that our spiritual maturity is not yet where it needs to be to fully grasp the concept, yet rather than interpreting this for ourselves, it is fine to give it to God, to be answered when He feels that we are ready. The point is, not understanding something God asks us to do, does not mean we should ignore Him. Of course, that is counter-cultural; we like to have all the answers, but let us not forget that part of our faith calls us to trust God, in all things.

Obedience means that we must remove sin from our lives. Matthew speaks about this by telling us that if our right hand causes us to stumble, we cut it off and throw it away[165]. This is not a literal command, but he is telling us to remove ourselves as far from our sin as possible. Those coming to freedom in Christ, having distanced themselves from a love of sinning, are then able to maintain their focus, through developing their relationship with God (which includes the four other elements spoken of above), free from the sin that so easily entangles them. Whatever our personal battle with sin, how we choose to respond to it, and live our lives, is because of what our heart is set on.

I do not believe that SSA is something that we freely choose, but I do believe that it is a real and imposing enemy which seeks to usurp the Lordship of God in the lives of those who have fallen prey to its sting.

---

[165] Matthew 5:30

When we focus on a symptom of the 'fall' such as SSA, the danger is that we will seek our own solutions or excuses for our wayward behaviour. When we allow the symptoms of the 'fall' to push us into seeking God, we come to know Him better and our yearning and longing for relationship starts to become fulfilled. This in turn allows us to pull our focus away from our sins. We stop looking for excuses and gladly start to put the past behind us, as the Lordship of God starts to overwhelm us in a powerful way.

- We come as we are; God does not seek perfection.

When we come to faith, we come as we are, imperfect humans with a past. But that is OK; God does not mind that, in fact He uses it. There are many examples of how God uses imperfect people in the Bible, including some of the great names of the faith: Moses, Abraham, and Peter. But more than our past, God also recognises that we will never be perfect this side of eternity. He recognises that we will continue to have flaws and make mistakes, because that is the nature of the fallen human race.

There is a certain weight associated with seeking perfection. Perfectionists often lack peace because of their quest for something that is unattainable. Often, they are people who have the mentality of 'it's all or nothing;' they are driven towards achieving their goal and they see non achievement of perfection as failure. This drive can be all consuming, which results in a failure to enjoy tasks because of such a blinkered approach. Perfectionists may not appreciate the path to success, the learning curves, the difficulties that shape us.

In an article which originally appeared on 'The Conversation'[166], Marianne Etherson and Martin Smith concluded that there is evidence to show that perfectionism has skyrocketed among university students in the past three decades. Their findings showed that: "Perfectionism generated depressive symptoms in the undergraduates because it caused students to feel like

---

[166] https://theconversation.com/how-perfectionism-can-lead-to-depression-in-students-97719

they were falling short of other peoples' expectations[167]." Perfectionism is understandably linked to depression and often the pressure emanates not only from the individual themselves, but from their perception of elevated levels of pressure put on them from peers, parents, lecturers etc. to perform well.

Approaching God does not require perfection, no matter what anyone else or Satan tries to tell you. We do not have to change the rules so that we feel adequate to approach Him, which is what many Christians are doing today. Neither do we need to set our sights so high that we put ourselves under too much pressure to be successful. Our relationship is with God alone; what other people think is irrelevant; how other people interpret the Bible is extraneous. The relationship needs to be solely between you and God. Allow the Holy Spirit to convict you of the way to live.

Satan is instrumental in trying to take away our peace as we commit to God. As we pursue a relationship with God, Satan points towards the perfectionist version of what we think our discipleship should look like, telling us that it is so hard to achieve we may as well give up now. For one who has SSA, this can manifest itself as a series of taunts which include lies such as: 'you can never be heterosexual; you can't get rid of lustful thoughts towards the same sex; you cannot change your orientation; you will never be married or in a significant relationship; your past cannot be redeemed.' And the new convert risks becoming overwhelmed, thinking that they have failed at the first hurdle.

Compare this with a recovering alcoholic for example. When they think about having a drink, yet do not act on those thoughts, they are applauded for their strength of mind in standing up to temptation. In the same way, those who find freedom in Christ from SSA should not feel a failure if their mind wonders off track for a few moments. The danger lies in the perceived need to rid yourself of all sin and failings if you are to become

---

[167] https://www.bbc.com/worklife/article/20180626-how-perfectionism-leads-to-depression

the perfect Christian (as if there was such a thing!). If the SSA Christian thinks that immediately after they come to faith they will be attracted to the opposite sex and married within a few months, they are aiming for holy perfection instead of wholeness. The reality is that change can and does come, but there are many factors which contribute to our change as Christians, not least of which is time. Some who have struggled with SSA are now happily married to a member of the opposite sex and have families of their own; some are living productive and happy lives in singleness and no longer class themselves as experiencing SSA, and others continue to struggle with temptation and fall from time to time. Change is a reality, but when it happens, and how far we progress, is in both ours and God's hands.

The perfectionist view of, 'it's all or nothing,' is twisted by Satan to say, 'if you are not one hundred per cent changed, you are not changed at all.' This could not be further from the truth; we are all on a journey of faith and change is a process. We are changed by God's grace and to receive this, we simply approach Him in truth and humility. That means we do not try and hide our failings and our slip ups; Jesus died so that we do not have to hide or live in shame any longer. It is good for us to be strengthened as we receive God's grace.

> Do not be carried away by all kinds of strange teachings.
> It is good for our hearts to be strengthened by grace,
> Hebrews 13:9. (NIV)

When I first became a Christian, I could never imagine being in a heterosexual relationship; that was an alien concept for me, having only ever been in relationships with women. Now, a few years later, I am in a different place; God has shaped me and opened my eyes to my identity and the possibilities that offers for my future. Had I been told as a young Christian that my goal was to find a man and marry, so that I could be fully heterosexual, I would have seen that as unattainable. But through seeking wholeness in Christ, the change in me has been so gradual that I am unrecognisable now from that new, young Christian, and I believe that everything is possible in Christ.

God sees our hearts[168] and knows our intentions. As we journey towards wholeness, not perfection, our destination is accessible, and we see the progress which we are making. Whereas a perfectionist's ambitions are all consuming, the seeker of wholeness can appreciate the journey as they learn from their mistakes and as God shapes them through prayer, Bible study and nurture.

- It is in the detail.

Have you ever marvelled at the level of instruction God provides within the Bible? Exodus chapters 25 to 31 lay out strict instructions from God for the building of the Tabernacle and all that would be in it; including what garments the priests would wear, the design of the altars and detailed instruction on how the priests should be consecrated. Six chapters all dedicated to intricate detail from God for how the task was to be conducted. Whilst there are times that we question the detail in the Old Testament books, we must remember that all Scripture is useful to us.[169] Finding the usefulness can sometimes be the challenge, but does not negate the instruction to be obedient to God's requirements. When God was instructing the Israelites about building an altar of unhewn stones, He was extremely specific, no tools were to be used on the stones. God does not give instruction lightly and when He does, the detail must be observed, and His requirements adhered to. This is the same God who struck down Uzzah for touching the ark in direct opposition to His instruction; we would do well to pay attention to His words.

The Holy Spirit has inspired the Bible, and it is all to be used by us to learn and grow in our faith. Instructions within it are there to be obeyed; that is what makes us stand out from the rest of the world. So, when we look at the Bible as we seek an answer to questions on SSA, let us remember that

---

[168] 1 Kings 8:39
[169] 2 Timothy 3:16

the answer is in the detail. That detail must not be taken out of context, but must be taken as part of the whole picture of God's Word and intentions for us. Let us look at the evidence contained within, all the pointers that lead towards an unmistakeable instruction for us to flee sexual immorality and offer ourselves unblemished and faultless before the throne of God.

- Details of the creation of Eve as a suitable 'helper' for Adam (Genesis 2).
- God's command that a man leave his father and mother to be united to his wife (Genesis 2).
- The ten commandments reinforce traditional family structure as we are told to honour our father and mother (Exodus 20).
- Detailed moral laws found in Leviticus which prohibit homosexual practice (Leviticus 18).
- Jesus reinforces the teaching of Genesis chapter 2 (Matthew 19).
- Paul writes to the Church at Rome with an explanation of how God has given us over to shameful lusts and he clearly references men lying with men and women lying with women, showing this to be engaging in sexual immorality (Romans 1).
- Paul writes to the church at Corinth and whilst condemning homosexual practice also acknowledges that 'that is what some of you once were.' A clear reference to God's transforming love for those who struggle with this temptation (1 Corinthians 6). There are other references on sexual immorality, also made by Paul, which allude to the same message, gay people will not inherit the Kingdom of God.[170]
- Paul writes of the importance of honouring marriage and for the marriage bed to be kept pure (Hebrews 13).
- Both Peter and Paul offer advice to those in marriages, clearly referencing husbands to honour and love their wives and wives to submit to their husbands (1 Corinthians 7, 1 Peter 3, Ephesians 5). The reference in Ephesians 5 in the NIV version is entitled,

---

[170] 1 Corinthians 7:2, 1 Timothy 1:8-11
202

'Instructions for Christian Households', the purpose of this passage could not be clearer.

- Revelation 19 recounts John's vision and we hear within this how the return of Jesus is likened to marriage – *"Let us rejoice and be glad and give him glory! For the wedding of the Lamb has come, and his bride has made herself ready[171]."* The Bride of Christ will be the church; this picture of marriage a beautiful reflection of God's perfect purpose for us to be married, the same institution that we read about right at the start of the Bible in Genesis 2.

In the same way, when reading the Bible, we also see the level of detailed warnings pertaining to false teaching; warnings that the church has been slow to notice and, in many cases, guilty of ignoring. These warnings started with the prophets of Old Testament times; we considered Isaiah and Jeremiah earlier, but we also have Micah[172] and Ezekiel[173] who warned their people of impending falsehood. As we move into the New Testament, it is littered with references and warnings, many of which have been discussed earlier in this book. Coupled with clear references to Satan as 'the deceiver,' we have ample evidence of how the Bible builds up the picture of our need to be cautious of all that we see and hear. It is in the detail; we just need to open our eyes and hearts to that detail and allow the truth of Satan's consistent and forceful attack on the church to sink in, until we sit up and finally take notice of what is going on before our own eyes.

Through opening our eyes to the fact that we, and others around us in our church, are indeed just broken stones, can we cut ourselves a bit more slack? I know that initially I put a lot of pressure on myself to be perfect, to change quickly, to be 'holy,' This self-imposed pressure was too much for me to keep up with and threatened to drag me down on more than one occasion. It was only when I took a step back, having recognised through relationships with other Christians that I was no different from them, that I

---

[171] Revelations 19:6-7
[172] Micah 3:5
[173] Ezekiel 13:9

embraced my brokenness, recognising that it was contributing to who I was becoming in Christ.

The altar of broken stones should serve as a permanent reminder that we must continue to focus on God and on Him alone. We do not need to strive for perfection; God receives us as we are. And finally, God is interested in the detail. All our days are ordained and written in His book[174], nothing is wasted and all we have been, all we are, and all we are becoming, can be used for His Kingdom.

---

[174] Psalm 139:16

TESTIMONY, MICHELE, JAMAICA

Michele was an active lesbian throughout her twenty's and thirty's, until at the age of forty-two she met with Jesus and recognised how she had rejected His truth and turned from His ways. She is now in her sixties and has a testimony of the faithfulness of God, not only speaking into her SSA, but other burdens she carried from her life experiences. Here she talks about how God has helped her to overcome perfectionism.

"Gentle Jesus, meek and mild" was the start of my learned childhood prayer on my knees every night. For, as far back as I can remember, I had been "reared in the fear and admonition of the Lord." I had been disciplined and trained to know a Heavenly Father to the point where I felt specially privileged to be the only one of my tender peers to have a mother who went to be with Him after she died of cancer when I was 5 years old. But as I grew up and was exposed to other influences – a perfectionist nature became a rigid and admired added element of my identity, in what became more of an albeit religious experience of God over time.

How did I get there? Maybe it had something to do with falling into the hands of successive strict and demanding guardians, who took the place of my parents, as I was also estranged from my father when I relocated to another island during my formative years. For their idea of love came with some exceedingly exacting standards and expectations of excellence, as I happened to be a naturally bright and then exceptional child. This, coupled with the fact that, although I lived in a household of faith, none of the adults attended church any longer (I was just sent with an overseer or dropped off and picked up at the required confirmation classes of my traditional Anglican upbringing) added to my woes. Thus, the poor example of 'do as I say' rather than 'as I do' was set, and thereafter became my legalistic role model.

Fast forward to age 42 when I had a personal epiphany and divine intervention. I was living a life that was wrought with wrong choices, way out in the left field of a wilderness where I still believed in God, but was unknowingly far away from His way, will and word. Now set on a newfound "born again" path and relationship, I discovered that I had to unlearn and reject a whole host of erroneous beliefs and practices. For I had come to believe some deeply embedded lies about the character and nature of both God and me, which included this little dreaded stronghold of perfectionism, that continued to plague me in matters big and small.

But for the grace of a loving, patient, and longsuffering God, who walked and talked with me as I worked though this fear of my salvation. For, while I still prided myself in a few good qualities of an obsessive-compulsive personality, He slowly but surely started to deal with the pressures and stress of its demands. He did this by immersing me in circumstances where both I, and things, fell far short of the high-performance grades, weights, and measures that I sought. At first, and for a long while, the below par comparisons with others and perceived failures in situations, sorely grieved a competitive Michele who was accustomed to being and/or having and doing the best. However, I began to gradually submit to the Lord's authority and sovereignty, as I came to understand that what He allowed or initiated under His control, and apart from my plans and designs, was best for me. Furthermore, thank God that His acceptance, unlike us judgmental and usurious human beings, was not dependent on, nor driven by, my earning His affection and attention through works.

Likewise, I came to see the blessing in disguise of finally being freed from a self-imposed responsibility that was too hard to bear, for both me and the victims of my controlling nature. As I write, I am maturing in a godly wisdom and revelation; that is teaching me to respect the lower outcomes and limited boundaries of a fallen and broken world. For, this is the same beloved world that "very God" loved and died for amid our human transgressions and foreknown imperfections. Consequently, this prodigal and rebel, now turned servant and child of God, is not, and can never be, greater than her Master. Indeed, may I continue to live and learn as I "let go and let God."

Chapter 12 – Discipleship and SSA disciples

As followers of Jesus, we are all targets for Satan; in fact the more on fire for God we are, the more dangerous we become (don't you just love that?!) That is why it is so important that we all recognise our vulnerabilities and are equipped to denounce Satan's lies, as he seeks to demoralise us and strip us of our faith. All are at risk, but there are some specific areas of attack adopted by Satan to target the Achilles heel of those who have been saved out of homosexual sin. This chapter will look at each of the most common deceptions, with a view to exposing his lies and equipping us to overcome them. Whatever your experiences, this chapter is important to read, so that we are all equipped for battle. Whether the battle is personal, or whether you are battling on behalf of others who have found freedom in Christ, we must be ready and able to fight the enemy to move forwards as disciples of Jesus.

By definition, a disciple is a follower; a person who accepts the doctrine of God and who is instrumental in spreading the Good News to others. Christian discipleship is a process; from the time we repent and offer our lives to Jesus we start to grow, to lay down roots in preparation for our role as disciples. Paul's prayer in Ephesians is a great illustration of what we need to succeed as Christians, to be strengthened, faith filled, rooted, and established in love; filled with God's fullness:

> *I pray that out of his glorious riches he may strengthen*
> *you with power through his Spirit in your inner being, so*
> *that Christ may dwell in your hearts through faith. And I*
> *pray that you, being rooted and established in love, may*
> *have power, together with all the Lord's holy people, to*
> *grasp how wide and long and high and deep is the love of*

Christ, and to know this love that surpasses knowledge—
that you may be filled to the measure of all the fullness of
God. Ephesians 3:16-19 (NIV)

As we put down strong roots, we become more able to rebuke Satan. We start to see through the lies and recognise his tactics. That does not mean that as disciples we will never be caught out by Satan, so it is essential that we equip ourselves as best we can for the fight. Eddie Smith, in Making sense of Spiritual Warfare[175] says –

> *"Being saved does not mean freedom from temptation, it*
> *means being equipped for victory over it."*

I asked members of an online community of believers, who have all chosen to renounce the gay identity to follow Jesus, what were the most common lies that Satan used to try and disrupt their discipleship. The experiences they reported were all similar in varying degrees to my own. I have shared these because being forewarned is to be forearmed, both for the one fighting SSA and the ones supporting and nurturing them. Below I have listed eight common lies, that we as a group felt, that Satan uses most to pull us back into his clutches and derail our transformation process.

Lie #1 - You do not need to give up sex; the Bible does not condemn homosexual sex if it's in a loving and committed relationship.

Lie #2 – Singleness is a lonely life; you will not be able to do it.

Lie #3 – You do not fit in to church; people still think about you as gay.

Lie #4 – No one loves you.

Lie #5 – You are under scrutiny; you must be perfect.

Lie #6 – You will only find satisfaction in a same sex relationship; you will never be able to marry and settle down.

---

[175] Making Sense of Spiritual Warfare by Eddie Smith, published by Bethany House Publishers, 2008

Lie #7 – A lot of Christians say it is OK, so why don't you listen to them?

Lie #8 – You were born gay; you cannot change nature.

Put yourself in the shoes of someone who has become a Christian and because of that commitment, recognises that their previous lifestyle was sinful. They may have had a few years living in the LGBTQ+ community, or they may have been in it for a considerable proportion of their life (for me it was thirty years). Overnight their position changes, yet there is history, and there are experiences that cannot be undone; there are mind-sets that need to change. There is an immense pressure on them as they seek the way forward, to change patterns of behaviour that are deeply engrained into their lives. They require everything mentioned in the prayer from Ephesians above; strength, power through the Holy Spirit, faith and to be fully rooted and established in God's love. Until they reach a point of maturity in their faith, there will always be a danger of them being tossed and turned in the waves, and I can vouch for this from a personal perspective. Consequently, when you read these eight lies, do not think they are trivial or easily overcome. Our fight is not against flesh and blood[176], it is the attack of demons, as they taunt and jibe, that is relentless. Our defence against them is the inspired Word of God, and sometimes it can take a while for us to understand it, to learn it and to use it in our defence.

Lie #1 - You do not need to give up sex; the Bible does not condemn homosexual sex in a loving and committed relationship.

This lie is becoming more successful for Satan, as the Church is divided on the authority of Scripture. If Satan can sow a seed of doubt into your mind to think that the Bible is unclear on this matter, or even that there is no condemnation of this sin, the temptation to continue to live in a same-sex relationship gains momentum. With some of the major denominations now championing same sex marriage and ordination of gay Ministers, there is an alternative 'Christian' response being modelled that can seem an

---

[176] Ephesians 6:12

attractive substitute for repentance and celibacy. Earlier chapters in this book have given full evidence of how the Scripture refutes this lie.

Response #1 – Our response to Satan is that there is nowhere in the Bible where homosexuality is affirmed, yet it is condemned in both the Old and New Testaments. The Bible also clearly teaches that that all sex outside of marriage, between a man and a woman is immoral. The Bible is our authority on these matters, as Paul himself wrote:

> ALL Scripture is God-breathed and is useful for teaching, rebuking, correcting and training in righteousness. 2 Timothy 3:16 (NIV)

We are also reminded in Hebrews about the power of God's Word:

> The word of God is alive and active. Sharper than any double-edged sword, it penetrates even to dividing soul and spirit, joints, and marrow; it judges the thoughts and attitudes of the heart. Hebrews 4:12 (NIV)

We are confident in the power and authority of God's Word and harness that power to rebuke Satan's lies.

Lie #2 – Singleness is a lonely life; you will not be able to do it.

This lie is powerful; it is one that feeds our insecurities and can become more noticeable the longer we are walking in freedom. Satan's goal is for us to feel isolated and lonely; he wants those who are single to crave companionship and return to old relationships or to seek inappropriate liaisons. Satan plays with the mind, seeking to make singleness feel more like alienation or seclusion, rather than a relationship status which offers a healthy and attractive alternative to marriage.

Jesus was single; Paul in the Bible and many single Christians of all ages, celebrate singleness and are happily serving the Lord. This may not be an immediate comfort, but it does show that there is a Biblical model for single people being happy and fulfilled in their lives. We also recognise that God

211

will be with us in every situation and has provided us with a book full of advice for how to live our lives. The Bible includes verses that encourage us not to focus inwardly on our feelings (in this case our loneliness,) but to take control for ourselves.

- Rather than focussing on yourself, direct your thinking to others;[177] do things for other people. You can be sure that through directing your focus and energies away from your own circumstance, God will strengthen you and satisfy your soul through your acts of compassion and kindness.[178] This is Biblical; we are called to respond to the needs of those around us.

- Choose your attitude; we have the ability, and a choice, to control how we approach every situation. If you are struggling with loneliness, ask God for His help. You can pray for the fruit of the Spirit to fill you; two that spring to mind are love and joy[179].

- Choose your friends wisely[180]. Do to them as you would have them do to you,[181]without expectations of them returning the favour! Invite people over, arrange to meet up, have people in your life who you can be honest and open with about how you are feeling, and who will hold you accountable if you withdraw or stop meeting together (as the Bible instructs us)[182].

- Be a regular attendee at church and weekly activities (such as small groups), and become an active part of a community of believers. Be aware of the need to encourage and support others in your group, recognising their vulnerabilities and weaknesses too.

---

[177] Philippians 2:4
[178] Isaiah 58:10-11
[179] Galatians 5:22
[180] Proverbs 12:26
[181] Luke 6:31
[182] Hebrews 10:24-25

Response #2 - Our response to Satan is that singleness is a gift from God, which allows us to serve God without distraction. We also respond that God has given us a gift of joy and we intend to use it; we are part of a new community of believers and are constantly uplifted and encouraged by those who surround us.

Lie #3 – You do not fit in to Church; people still think about you as gay.

Oh, how Satan likes to play the same card. However strong we are in our faith, we all succumb to Satan's lies from time to time, and don't we just tend to beat ourselves up as we see our own weaknesses and our struggles? Romans 8 was written to show us that despite being Christians, God knows that we are not yet perfect and that we will continue to battle with sin. But we are not condemned, because Jesus has freed us from the law once and for all. We are set free, not in our own strength, but because Jesus functioned as a sin offering for us; we are free, period.

Until we recognise this, the guilt we feel about our past actions fuels our feelings of unworthiness and can lead to anxiety, stress, worry and shame. If you are living in condemnation, whether with something from long ago, or something that happened this morning, know that this is not God's plan for you. That condemnation comes from Satan; God is not your accuser. Satan may look in his book and see our sins, calling me a failure, someone who succumbed to homosexual temptation and who lived apart from God for many years. But the truth is that God has not even got a record of my sins[183] and my past decisions; they were blotted out when I repented and asked Him into my life. God calls me His precious daughter; redeemed and forgiven. God does not guilt trip us, not now, not ever.

Response #3 - This is our powerful message for Satan; condemnation is not from God. He no longer remembers our sins; we are forgiven, we are acquitted as though we had never sinned, and we are not going to be captivated again by fear, guilt, bondage, or shame.

---

[183] Psalm 130:3-4

Lie #4 – No one loves you.

Experiences of becoming a Christian vary for us all and will always require changes to our lifestyle. My position is typical of many, but not all Christians, who have left the LGBTQ+ community behind them. I was in a committed, loving relationship, and overnight that relationship was turned upside down. It was not just about the fact that it was no longer a sexual relationship, it was so much more. The emotional connection was shattered, the closeness of being in a loving relationship broken, the love for the one I had committed to as a lifelong partner was in disarray, and I was struggling to see how to move forward.

Over time, as the truth of what my new faith meant, I lost the confidence and love of some friends; my family were surprised and did not immediately agree with the theology of my choice, and I started to feel increasingly isolated. The love that had anchored me to my partner, my family and my friends was disintegrating, and yes, Satan popped up with his usual tact and diplomacy and said, 'See no one loves you now; you're all alone.'

When you are at that kind of low point, you do not immediately appreciate that Satan's desire is to isolate you (divide and conquer), to push you to crave the love that you are missing, and to seek closeness in the wrong places. This is the time when you need to know the love of the Father and trust that His love is enough.

One of the Bible verses that is most precious to me is from the prophet Zephaniah:

> The LORD your God is with you, the Mighty Warrior who
> saves. He will take great delight in you; in his love he will
> no longer rebuke you but will rejoice over you with singing
> Zephaniah 3:17 (NIV)

My God delights over me with singing (that is more than any human has ever done for me!!) There are so many more verses that express God's love for me, from Psalm 23 to John 3:16; I have a wealth and depth of promises from my God.

One other favourite verse which I love to refer to when rebuking this lie is:

> *See what great love the Father has lavished on us, that we should be called children of God! And that is what we are! 1 John 3:1 (NIV)*

Response #4 – God loves all his children and His love for us is sufficient to meet all our needs. His Word is abundantly clear on this, and we can all use our own favourite, 'go to' Scriptures to tell Satan, 'Get behind me; don't you know who my Papa is!'

Lie #5 – You are under scrutiny; you must be perfect.

Perfection, as I have written earlier, is impossible for us to attain. Yet, I think that those who have walked away from homosexuality, or gender identity issues, feel an intense pressure to be perfect, to be seen as beyond reproach. It is related to lie #3, where we desire that people do not think we are lying or living a double life. When I gave my life to the Lord, He made a way for myself and my ex-partner to remain friends. We continued sharing a house for a few years before we finally went our separate ways. For a long time, and even on occasions now, I feel judged for that decision and am convinced that I must explain my circumstances to others, putting undue pressure on myself. Satan's desire is for us to fail; if he tells us perfection is what we must achieve, we will always fail. If he continues to attack us when we feel vulnerable, cracks in our resolve may begin to show.

In 2018, I was feeling particularly vulnerable after my living circumstances were likened to: 'an ex-smoker who keeps a packet of cigarettes in the drawer in case they fancied a sneaky smoke'. What made this worse, was that the comment was made by a Christian lady who I was supporting as she struggled with her daughter's relationship with another woman. This comment rocked me; I was horrified by what she had said and started to believe that this was something others thought of me too. It was so significant to me, that after two years of being clean of self-harm, I slipped up once more.

That weekend I had offered to run the sound desk for a prophetic conference to be held at my church. I was not in a good place and showed up, ready to do my job and disappear, yet God had other ideas. Immediately after the first session, one of the conference leaders came up to me with a prophetic word. He had no idea of who I was or what I was going through, and he said (taken directly from my journal):

"I believe God is saying to you, listen to the Word of God and not the word of man. Isaiah 41:10 says, so do not fear for I am with you, do not be dismayed for I am your God, I will strengthen you and help you, I will uphold you with my righteous right hand, all who rage against you will be shamed and dishonoured, those who contend with you will be as nothing and perish."

I was stoked; God knew me, recognised the hurt and despair this comment had caused me and wanted to speak this truth into my life, 'Listen to what I have to say, not what everyone else has to say.'

Response #5 – Satan, you will be shamed and dishonoured; you are as nothing and you will perish. I listen only to the Word of God and have no interest in what you, or man, has to say about me and my circumstances.

Lie #6 – You will only find satisfaction in a same sex relationship; you will never be able to marry and settle down.

We all yearn for connection and many of us yearn to be in a relationship with a significant other. We often see this amongst young Christian singles who are so desperate to find a partner, they become deceived by the urgency of this desire and marry outside of the faith, rather than trusting God's plans for their lives. For one coming out of a same sex relationship, there is often no immediate change in their sexual orientation. The

216

temptations that come will still be towards the same sex, and it is tough for them to believe that this could change.

Satan loves this; he will combine this lie with lie #2, urging us of the need to have a permanent partner, expressing how difficult it will be to remain single and then ridiculing us if any thoughts of ever having a heterosexual relationship enter our minds.

Response #6 – Given time God will change me; my God is a God of transformation.

> *Therefore, if anyone is in Christ, the new creation has come: The old has gone, the new is here! 2 Corinthians 5:17 (NIV).*

This change may not be a permanent transformation to heterosexuality, although there are many instances of this happening. One of my missional supporters has recently celebrated twenty-six years of marriage after leaving homosexuality behind. He is happy and fulfilled and living the life God has always planned for him. Others that I know are living celibate lives, not having experienced a change in orientation, yet persevering in obedience to the Lord. Still others experience partial or significant change in their orientation. There is a website[184] called 'Two Prisms,' which features many who have walked out of the LGBTQ+ community. Each profile has a statement of their experience of changed sexual orientation which are defined as, 'no change, some change, significant change or full change.' At the time of writing,[185]there are 180 people featured on the website and the ratios of change were:

- No change 0.6% (1 person)
- Some change 5.6% (10 people)
- Significant change 43.3% (78 people)
- Full change 50.5% (91 people)

---

[184] https://www.twoprisms.com
[185] December 2023

Over half of those who have chosen to follow Jesus have experienced full change. Combine this with those who have found significant change, we see that 93.8% have experienced the transformative love of Jesus in their sexual orientation.

These statistics are testament to God's transformative love, but also to His faithfulness in supporting us to keep running the race with perseverance.[186] Our final response to Satan on this one – I can do all things through Christ who strengthens me[187], whether that's remaining single and celibate, or experiencing newfound attraction to the opposite sex.

Lie #7 – A lot of Christians say it is OK, so why don't you listen to them?

We are back to smoke and mirrors. The level of deceit that has infiltrated the established church is quite shocking. Charles H Spurgeon is quoted as saying:[188]

> "Brethren, we shall not adjust our Bible to the age; but before we have done with it, by God' grace, we shall adjust the age to the Bible."

Our calling is to listen to God and God alone. When Satan uses other Christians to cause us to stumble it is more confusing for us than when the obstacles come from the outside world. But as Spurgeon says, we should be looking to adjust the age to the Bible and if that means standing up to misguided Christians, then so be it.

In the build up to the vote on same sex marriage in the Methodist church, I read a Facebook post calling on Methodists to approve same sex marriage. One lady's response to those who want to uphold Biblical authority on this point said, and I quote, 'the world totally ignores Leviticus now anyway.' She missed the point totally; the world is not the one to tell

---

186 Hebrews 12:1
187 Philippians 4:13
188 Charles Spurgeon, An All-Round Ministry: Addresses to Ministry and Students (London: Passmore & Alabaster, 1906), 230

218

us how to gain eternal life, nor how to live in obedience to God. It is God who tells us what the requirements are for our salvation.

Response #7 – Whoever is of God, hears the Word of God.[189] As a child of the living God, I have heard God's Word, responded to His Word, and am living in obedience to His Word. God has made His paths known to me;[190], He leads me in His truth.

Lie #8 – You were born gay; you cannot change nature.

If Satan can convince us that we were born this way, then it makes sense that we will think that it is God's fault that we have this struggle. Satan's purpose is to get us to blame God, and in our anger to reject Him, or to believe that SSA is of God and as such believe that it is acceptable to Him.

It is my belief that we are not born gay (and no gay gene has been discovered), but that it is a combination of factors that leads to us experiencing SSA. SSA was not part of God's plan for our lives before the 'fall'. It was because of the 'fall' that sexual immorality became a factor in humanity, and that can be solely attributable to Satan. But our role as Christians is not to debate the whys and wherefores of homosexuality, rather to accept that SSA is a fact and show grace and concern for those who struggle with it (including showing grace towards ourselves if it is our own struggle).

Response #8 – My response to this lie of Satan is firstly to tell him that I am fearfully and wonderfully made,[191]and that God's plans for me were perfect before Satan's deceit changed the course of history. I serve a God who loves and cherishes me, and He is a God who understands my struggles. It does not matter how I got this thorn in my side, for God is at work within me to use this for His glory. As Paul so eloquently wrote, God's grace is all I need.

---

[189] John 8:47
[190] Psalm 25:4-5
[191] Psalm 139:14

219

His grace is sufficient for you, for my power is made perfect in weakness." Therefore, I will boast more gladly about my weaknesses, so that Christ's power may rest on me. That is why, for Christ's sake, I delight in weaknesses, in insults, in hardships, in persecutions, in difficulties. For when I am weak, then I am strong. 2 Corinthians 12:9-10 (NIV)

Recognising the tactics Satan uses is important in our defensive battle; understanding how to rebuke his lies is essential, but we now need to understand how we can go on the offensive as Christians with a history of SSA, to bring revival to a community who need God's truth and God's love.

TESTIMONY, KAY*, UK

Kay endeavoured to honour God with her sexuality, but peer pressure eventually saw her resolve crumble, and she endured the most difficult of circumstances being raped by a male friend. Turning to a female for comfort, Kay also discovered masturbation and self-harm as a form of soothing the pain that she carried.

These addictive behaviours plagued Kay for many years, but through love and support from other Christians, she became equipped for victory over temptation, tackling the root cause and developing a relationship with God where she could be vulnerable and honest, opening the door to her receiving His love, as she stopped condemning herself and started to accept His forgiveness.

Kay is now offering support to other Christian women who have been the victims of rape.

I was brought up in a Christian family; church was central to family life, not just on a Sunday, but throughout the week. Encouraged by Mum, I started reading the Bible regularly on my own before the age of ten and gave my life to Jesus when I was fourteen. My mid-teens were a time of drawing closer to God and learning about prayer, listening, and obeying Him.

My sister, brother, and I, were sheltered from the world, especially in the realm of sexuality. I do not remember my parents talking about sex; I simply had the overriding impression that you should not have sex before you are married. To be honest I was more interested in lads for playing football with as opposed to anything else anyway!

When I went to University, I entered a different world, one where sex was the primary factor within relationships. I did try to stick with the ideals I had been brought up with; I continued to go to church, though was not as fully involved as I had been. I had a few relationships with men, but I refused to have sex; these relationships did not last long. One man really hurt me because he slept with someone else while still in a relationship with me, just because I would not have sex with him.

That changed something in me, and relationships became sexual. I had somehow mixed-up love and sex, and thought it meant the same thing; and I did so crave to be loved.

I was saying I was a Christian, acting as if I was, by going to church, but I was not living as a Christian. I had several sexual relationships, one of which became abusive and ended in rape. There followed many months of trying to get completely free of him.

I then had a sexual relationship with a woman, and throughout all this time I was learning how to satisfy myself sexually through masturbation. This was a way of satisfying my sexual urges without the need to connect deeply or put myself in a position where I could be hurt again. The temptation to sexually sin was now deeply ingrained within me.

When I had a bad relapse of a chronic illness, masturbation became my go to when I desired comfort. I also began to self-harm, another temptation, one where I could control the pain I was in. The two were soon linked, as the pain I inflicted on myself heightened my sexual satisfaction. This became a daily occurrence, whenever I should have been resting. My thoughts were constantly thinking about sexual desires, how to make those few moments of blessed relief more intense.

While all this was going on, I was also growing in my Christian faith, beginning to really grasp that God loved me as an individual, and I began praying and reading my Bible more. But so much emotional baggage had built up over the years that I got to the point where I felt a really intense anger towards God. It was at this point that I sought help and God brought an amazing woman into my life who began listening and journeying with me. After a few months, I began to open up about the self-harm and masturbation, and she was able to help me. God was still working in me, tackling my thoughts about sex. I began to realise that what I was doing to myself was wrong, even though several friends tried to tell me that masturbation was not wrong, but God was telling me otherwise.

This is when my struggles with temptation really set in; the devil really did not like the fact I was trying to live a more holy life. When I tried to resist temptation, it just seemed to build and build, till I lost the battle, and I was left in a mess of tears, shame, and self-condemnation. I struggled with the thought that God was not condemning me; on the contrary I felt Him close, just loving me after I sinned. It did not make sense.

I did not have much resistance to start with, but over time, and with God's help, I got stronger and the temptation to self-harm, reduced. God began to unpick all the emotional baggage I had been carrying. I was able to release my intense anger to God, all the anger over illness, rape, and grief that I had been carrying.

God helped me to work on the connection between love and sex, and my desire for sex began to lessen. The temptation and failure were still a regular event; I tried all sorts of things to help me: prayers, imagining Jesus with me, getting up from my rest, texting friends for prayer.

I began to see small victories, but I regularly fell back into temptation, especially during more stressful times. I started to recognise that this signalled an issue between me and God. So, I tried to bring things before God more, being real with Him about how I was feeling.

It was really when I connected with Transformed Ministries that I started to speak openly about how I was feeling sexually, and my desire to live without the need to masturbate. I wanted to be free from this. I committed my body to God and prayed for strength to not sexually sin. I ended up praying that prayer several times after I fell into temptation. I was blatantly honest and when I sinned, I brought it into the light and told someone, confessed the sin to God and then tried to work out what had triggered the desire to sexually sin.

Thankfully, I always had someone there who would not condemn, would pray with me, and would encourage me to get up, dust myself off and start again.

I think the Bible verse that helped me most was Psalm 32v7, 'You are my hiding place; you will protect me from trouble and surround me with songs of deliverance.' Whenever temptation started to rear its head, I would pray this verse and there were times when I would be lying on the bed and imagining God surrounding me with songs of deliverance and would feel His embrace around me.

I finally got to a day where I had sinned, yet again, and I cried out to God, 'I have had enough, please help me God to stop this sin! I hate myself for it, I do not even know where it came from!' Two days later I got my answer. I had sinned again, but in the time of bringing that before God I realised how the sexual sin had started. I confessed that original sin to God and wow! How much easier it became to go for a rest in the days after; I could actually lie down and rest and not worry of falling into sin!

Yes, the temptation still happened; I could still feel sexual desire at times, but the thoughts became so much easier to bat away. I had a quite simple method now for when temptation came: text friends for prayer, repeat Psalm 32v7, imagining God with me, and if it persisted, then it was a warning signal that there is a problem between me and God, so I would bring that before Him.

Life is so much easier now; it is like a huge burden has been lifted. I continue to sense sexual temptation from time to time, but I can walk away from it now and there is not this massive conflict going on in my life, which means there's peace in my mind.

Looking back, it feels that I was not just in a battle, but in a war, one that lasted over 10 years. A war of many battles, some lost and some won, the battles became fewer and further apart, and that war is now won through the grace of God.

*name changed to protect her identity.

Chapter 13 – The Art of Distraction

The most exciting message we have is that Jesus has already overcome Satan. This was accomplished when Jesus conquered sin and grave, and rose triumphant on the third day. There is nothing that Satan can do about this; he cannot gain power. But one tool he does have is the art of distraction. He has become expert at distracting humans from hearing and living in the Good News. This now a key strategy he uses in his mission to prevent us from being obedient to God. For those who do not yet know Christ, distracting them from hearing the Good News is Satan's goal. For those who do know Christ, Satan's game plan is to distract them from achieving their goals, challenging them through their relationships and working hard to undermine their faith.

Nehemiah was no stranger to these tactics as he worked with the many families in Jerusalem to rebuild the walls. Satan used Sanballat, Tobiah and Geshem the Arab,[192] in an attempt to disrupt the work and undermine his determination, yet Nehemiah stood firm. Satan will not stop after his first attempt; with Nehemiah he tried four times, and it was only because Nehemiah was so grounded in his faith that he saw the distraction for what it was. Yet his response was a splendid example to us all; when we are convicted that the project or mission we are working on is for the Lord, our obedience to Him will come above all other things; distractions will be more easily ignored.

One of Satan's tactics is to separate us from our source of power. If he can cause a disconnect, then you can be sure he will. And if you are anything like me, easily distracted, you need to guard against this to stay connected to God. God is our source of truth and power; we need to remain

---

[192] Nehemiah 6:1-4

connected to Him through prayer, reading His Word, and communing with other Christians.

One of the most common distractions Satan uses is relationships, whether that be with a partner, parent, family member or with work colleagues. As soon as we get involved in a relationship, our focus can shift from God to the people we are relating with. Our relationship with others can affect how we think and how we act, and if they are not connected to God in the same way that we are, the danger is apparent. The relationships that are most likely to get in the way of our relationship with God, are those that are sexual in nature. These relationships take up most of our time and, if not centred on God, can pull us away from time spent in God's company. They also have the capability to take our mind and focus off God's plans for our lives and onto our own desires, which can easily undermine our system of belief. For example, the teenager who is following Jesus but then meets a non-Christian and starts a relationship with him, soon finds her commitment to prayer, her time spent reading the Bible and the time she spends in church diminishes. She may encounter ridicule or even misunderstanding about her faith, and as such she may struggle with which relationship to follow. For this teenager, the result may be that she embarks on a sexual relationship with her boyfriend, which causes her to move outside of God's will for her life. This is the battle spoken about by Paul in Romans 8, flesh versus the Spirit. Compare this with the teenager who meets another Christian and can share her love of the Lord with him, pray together, attend church together, and discuss their faith openly. Her focus can then remain firmly on God, with no external pressure or distraction; she is much more likely to walk into God's plans for her life.

These distractions can also take place within a marriage, as is clearly demonstrated in the Old Testament. We read of many instances where the Israelites married outside of the faith and were drawn into idol worship. Solomon, though wise, had many wives from foreign countries, and Satan used their beliefs to distract Solomon from total devotion to God as he sought to appease their desires.

As Solomon grew old, his wives turned his heart after
other gods, and his heart was not fully devoted to the
LORD his God, as the heart of David his father had been.
1 Kings 11:4 (NIV)

Satan was able to distract Solomon because his heart was not fully devoted to God; he had divided loyalties. His situation illustrates the important of the relationships that we commit ourselves to. If Satan can deceive us into believing that we will never find a relationship inside the faith, we will lower our sights, and compromise through marrying a non-believer, to satisfy our desire for connection. If Satan can convict us that relationships outside of marriage or with someone of the same sex are no different than marrying within our faith, then he will have achieved his goal of taking our eyes of Jesus.

I wrote earlier about how Satan desires to mirror God, and by doing this, he is mocking God. Everything that Satan does is the opposite of what God wants for us; everything he says should be considered in light of that fact. If we go back to Genesis 2, we see quite clearly that God's desire for us is marriage, male with female. Satan's desire is clearly the opposite; he desires for us to live confused and unfulfilled lives, in relationships which are unhealthy and ungodly, and which take our focus away from all that is holy.

One of the biggest distractions of the modern era for Christians is the debate that rages within churches over homosexuality. As we are arguing about this, rifts are forming, confusion reigns and division exists. It is becoming increasingly difficult to find clear teaching and direction for anyone who experiences SSA. It is becoming increasingly difficult to find church leaders who are prepared to dive into the sea of confusion to bring clarity. Satan has mastered the art of befuddling our churches, and whilst we spend more time in-fighting, this sin is becoming something that is celebrated and endorsed by many Christians. This endorsement is coming from deceived Christians, who have been distracted from the main thrust of the argument to an argument that revolves around compassion and God's

228

love for all. Frustratingly, all this bickering over what God's Word means, has also distracted us from our main purpose, to know Jesus and to make Jesus known.

Increasingly, I am hearing stories of parents who were once staunchly committed to the authority of God's Word, changing their mind-set as they focus on their child who struggles with SSA or gender dysphoria. Satan knows the Bible inside out; he knows that we are called to love our neighbour as ourselves; he knows that love is an essential element of every Christian's walk. He uses this knowledge to get us to question what love is and how that love needs to be shown to our children. He therefore questions us; is not love about accepting everything your child does, is not love about supporting your child's choices, is not love about showing compassion as they struggle with their new-found identity? This relentless questioning is without doubt distracting, as is any form of dogged badgering. With the added emotional pull of parental love and loyalty, the cracks can quickly appear.

I refer to my earlier point; we must not lose sight of the fact that relationships are extremely important to us in our human way of thinking. We must therefore protect ourselves, changing our pattern of thought to one that is more like God's, because pursuing human relationship beyond all God teaches us, is not healthy. Love without truth is of no help, in the same way that truth without love is of no help. The only way to help and support those around us is through demonstrating a compassionate combination of love, tempered with truth. To do this, we must be blinkered, keeping our eyes fixed firmly on Jesus, blocking our ears to the lies of the enemy, and standing resolutely on the Word of God.

We must be aware of the voices around us and what their source is. Satan is quick to use other people as his voice piece to try and distract us from our calling. The most famous of these times certainly being when Satan tried to use Peter to distract Jesus. Jesus' words will be familiar to us all, as he responded, 'get behind me Satan.'[193] In fact, the fullness of what

Jesus said to Peter was that he was being a stumbling block and that Peter was not thinking with the mind of God. His mind was looking at what Jesus had told him, without the lens of God. Peter was merely considering his own human concerns, putting himself first. We know that Jesus himself warned against being an obstacle, so it is important that we do not put ourselves in a situation where we may unwittingly cause another to stumble. I urge those who may not personally be affected by SSA, yet do not believe it to be sinful, to consider how their endorsement of gay behaviours within a faith setting, may be the cause of many a stumble.

We have already focused on the common distraction that Satan uses, the old tactic, 'Did God really say that?' He then uses this in combination, with him encouraging us to look at things from our own perspective, 'How does this affect me?' We are by nature selfish beings; our first thought very often will be about the consequences for ourselves. Spending time with God in His Word, praying and listening to God, testing what we hear through His Word, is the only way to avoid Satan's tactics of distraction, as we equip ourselves to differentiate truth from lies.

Distractions come in all shapes and sizes; we may kid ourselves that we will not be taken in by a distraction. Let us think about the example in Mark's gospel, of the disciples stuck in their boat in the storm[194]. The disciples were so distracted by the storm, they missed the miracle of Jesus walking on water. They saw Jesus walking on the lake, yet thought that he was a ghost. Talk about a major distraction taking our eyes off the real deal! Are there times of storm in our lives, where Satan has managed to draw our eyes off Jesus and His ability to do miracles, drawing us into the middle of the storm, thereby distracting us from the reality of what our Saviour can do?

That storm might be the day your child tells you they are gay; it may be the day that you first realise that you have SSA. The storm may come because

---

[193] Matthew 16:21-23
[194] Mark 6:49

230

of a marital breakdown, or the storm may come as you despair of ever finding a Christian spouse. The storm may come when you change churches and find your beliefs are at odds with most of the congregation. The storm may come when the denomination you have been a member of all your life, decides to change its theology. When that storm comes, where are your eyes fixed?

David Wells in his book, God in the Whirlwind: How the Holy Love of God Reorients our World[195], identified two challenges which face the modern Christian. Firstly, Wells discusses the pressure we are under to conform to the world, yet emphasises that we should allow God's Word to conform us, rather than allowing the narrative of the world to shape us. Wells writes:

> *"The shaping of our life is to come from Scripture and not from the culture. We are to be those in whom truth is the internal driver and worldly horizons and habits are not."* [196]

Let us not kid ourselves, to ignore the ways of the world will be exceptionally difficult for us to achieve in all we do in our daily lives. We are under intense pressure from the world around us; for us to be successful, to achieve remarkable things, and to value ourselves above all others. We need to turn to God to help us cope with all the pressure, as well as remaining focussed on Scripture. However, if we fail, and surrender to the mind-set of the world, it means that Satan has accomplished what he set out to do, to confuse our mission and undermine our testimony.

Wells goes on to identify another significant challenge, and he writes:

---

[195] God in the Whirlwind: How the Holy-Love of God Reorients Our World, David F Wells, Published by Crossways Books (2014)

"The second challenge I am going to mention is the extraordinary bombardment on our mind that goes on every day from a thousand different sources that leave us distracted, with our minds going simultaneously in multiple directions. How, then, can we receive from Scripture the truth God has for us if we cannot focus long enough, linger long enough, to receive the truth? Every age has its own challenges. This one is ours. It is the affliction of distraction."[197]

If we think solely about the topic of homosexuality, we recognise that we are being bombarded from many different angles. We receive messages through education, our workplace, politics, media, television, social media, advertising and the legal system, as well as from our churches and our own personal interpretation of the Bible (I am sure there are many other influences which I have missed). We can no longer have a healthy debate about topics as divisive as homosexuality. Disagreement often leads to accusations of hate speech or homophobia, and as the debates rage, our minds are filled with information, conflicting arguments, emotions, and questions. Add to that, all the other things that are thrown at our minds daily, and you can see how easily we can become distracted as we strive to fully understand God's intention for our lives.

Jesus talks about this in the parable of the sower, where He speaks about the seeds that fall among the thorns and likens this to how the worries of this life come in and choke the word,[198] making it unfruitful. Our worries and our distractions all emanate from Satan and these distractions are just one further form of deceit which he uses to pull us away from God and into

---

[197] God in the Whirlwind: How the Holy-Love of God Reorients Our World, David F Wells, Published by Crossways Books (2014)

[198] Mark 4:19

232

a sinful life. Distraction is very real, but if we resolve to recognise it, we can become equipped to fight against it. As David Wells wrote, we need to take the time to linger in God's Word, to be still and know that He is God. The most important thing we can do is to invest our time in waiting on God, and as we devote our time to hear from Him, the myriad of voices clamouring for our attention will soon be silenced as we tune in directly to our Shepherd's voice.

TESTIMONY, MARK, UK

Mark became a Christian in his teenage years, before the many distractions of the world lured him into a lifestyle that drew him away from God. Lured by the promise of a good life, fuelled by sex and alcohol, then falling into a gambling habit, Mark could not find satisfaction until he finally surrendered and turned away from the distractions, fixing his thoughts and mind back on Jesus.

My name is Mark and at the time of writing this I am 57. I became a Christian as a 13-year-old, but was lured away from following my faith by the world on several occasions. Looking back, I can see that I wasn't totally devoted to God; I'd not fully surrendered my life to Him and was easily distracted and tempted to live in the ways of the world.

I realised that I had SSA when I was eleven and this was a big struggle for me. I wanted to follow God, but struggled to overcome the physical attraction I had for other men. For a while I managed to pursue a relationship with God, but later in my adult life my pursuit of same sex relationships caused me to leave the church. I didn't return for 15 years because I couldn't overcome the thoughts that distracted me; I didn't trust God to help me overcome them, and didn't see a way of living with them.

I yo-yoed in and out of church and relationships; nothing lasted very long. At one point I had a three-year relationship with another guy, even while I was attending church and calling myself a Christian. It was an exceedingly difficult period in my life, and I struggled with feelings of guilt and shame. It wasn't just the SSA that caused me to stumble; I have an addictive nature, mainly alcohol and nicotine, both of which have led me away from God on many occasions. In fact, there are many things which distract the believer, the pursuit of money and good jobs can be as debilitating as the fleshly struggles.

It took God to shout into my life and get my attention. I was living in Amsterdam, with all the fleshly temptations available to me. But God had not abandoned me, and He called me to a wonderful church where I started to get to really know Him and pursue Him with all my heart. My faith was deeply buried at that point, but I passionately believe that a seed once sown does not die in the soul, and the prayers of my family and friends led me back to Jesus.

Now life is good. I still have daily struggles, but I do not face them alone. The Lord has blessed me with friends who are strong believers, and I am involved in church and ministry which are vital to my continued walk with God. Going into a new season in my life, I am excited to see what the Lord has in store and believe we will see great advances for the Kingdom. Of course, we all must be wary of our weaknesses and the devil's schemes to distract us, but greater is He who is in us than he who is in the world.

I am extremely glad that I have recognised the distractions of the devil and do not pursue them these days. I recognise that there is not room for sinful relationships in the life of a believer. I see that our God is a jealous God and pursues us down, but also that He is full of grace and whatever our personal struggles He empowers us to overcome them every single day. He has done that for me and can do it for you.

Chapter 14 – The Battle belongs to the Lord – Revival

*In heavenly armour we'll enter the land, the battle belongs
to the Lord, No weapon that's fashioned against us shall
stand, the battle belongs to The Lord, We sing glory and
honour, Power, and strength to the Lord[199.]*

What a wonderful reminder in this song, that no matter what we go through in this life, the battle does indeed belong to the Lord. All that you have read in previous chapters, highlights that Satan's weapon is one of deceit and lies. In direct comparison, the weapon we have is God's truth, His trustworthiness, and His justice, which will prevail. As such, I am encouraged to give God all the glory and honour as I sit here in awe and wonder, recognising God's power which is already at work within the LGBTQ+ community.

I honestly believe that God is planning for revival, as He prepares the ground with a wave of new Christians coming out of the LGBTQ+ community. It seems that over the past couple of decades, whilst the world and the church has become more deceived, God has been raising up an army of men and women who have found freedom from Satan's deceit; men and women who are prepared to put their lives on the line and share their testimony. As Revelation proclaims:

*They triumphed over him by the blood of the Lamb and by
the word of their testimony; they did not love their lives so
much as to shrink from death. Revelation 12:11*

---

[199] The Battle Belongs to the Lord - Words and music by Jamie Owens-Collins

It only takes an internet search to find story after story of freedom from same-sex relationships and transgenderism. Some of these stories are from those who now head up their own ministries, but many are from ordinary men and women who want the world to know that Satan is a liar. They are testament to the fact that whilst SSA and gender dysphoria are real, so is our God, who silences the lies of the enemy as he tries to tell us that change is not possible. For every testimony that you hear from those who are courageous enough to speak out, putting themselves in the line of fire, there are many more testimonies from men and women who are walking in new-found freedom, yet are reticent to speak out publicly for fear of a backlash from friends and family. But things are about to change; the smoke and mirrors that Satan uses will be revealed as an outrageous fraud, and Christians will rediscover God's holiness. How will this happen? Simply this, by the power of our testimony.

Take a long, hard look at society and see how vehemently Satan has attacked the LGBTQ+ community. He has perpetually sought to bring confusion to their understanding of identity. In fact, many might query why I have simply used the acronym LGBTQ+ in this book, when many now refer to this community as LGBTQIA+.[200] The honest answer is that I had to draw the line somewhere. Personally, I see the further extension of this acronym simply as an additional indicator of the confusion surrounding many people's understanding of their own identity. In September 2019, the BBC came under attack for releasing a short film[201] for use in schools which clearly stated that there are over one hundred gender identities. Just a couple of examples which are spoken of in the film by a teacher are:

1. Bi-gender - a person whose sense of personal identity encompasses two genders.

---

[200] LGBTQ+IA+ refers to Lesbians, Gay, Bisexual, Trans, Queer, Intersex, Asexuality and the "+" symbol simply stands for all of the other sexualities, sexes, and genders that aren't included in these few letters.

[201] Understanding Sexual and Gender Identities – released by BBC Teach to support the PSHE curriculum in schools.

2. Gender-queer - 'one who does not consider gender as a binary of two exclusive options (male and female) and who identifies as neither male nor female, or as a combination of genders.'[202]

It is incredible to me how quickly the confusion continues to grow; the identities multiplying every year, with scant resistance from any quarter. I work with parents whose children are transgender, but also identifying as gay; two biological girls now identifying as boys, in a sexual relationship together. The confusion out there is mind-blowing.

Sadly, there is still scant resistance, and I am not sure whether it is apathy, a genuine lack of interest, or a fear of standing up to those who peddle the lies, which stops us from saying enough is enough. What I can say is that Satan is behind this; his attack is provoked, prolonged, and targeted at people who hold immense potential, people who have a tremendous destiny.

I do not think it a coincidence that so many of those who are coming out of the homosexual lifestyle come from a Christian background. Similarly, I do not think it is a coincidence that so many children of Christian parents are struggling with homosexuality and gender dysphoria. Satan's attack is targeted; he is attacking those who have a destiny and a future doing Kingdom work, he is attacking those whom he is worried about, and worried is what he should be. Revival is so often instigated by the most improbable people; people who have been discounted by others within their faith. There are so many prodigals who have wandered from the truth because they were tempted into a same-sex relationship and did not know how to reconcile their faith with their feelings. But God is calling them back, and as they encounter the Holy Spirit, they are being convicted of the truth; their eyes are opened to the deceit that they have believed for so long. We

[202] Oxford Dictionary

238

are going to see mass revival within the LGBTQ+ community as God works within their hearts over time, to bring them full freedom.

Just so we are clear, revival is described in its most simplistic form as, 'a period of renewed religious interest.'[203] Revival is much more than that, and I suppose if I am honest, it is going to mean something different to different people, depending upon their own life experiences and relationship with God. But revival amongst the LGBTQ+ community will be reflected by significant increases in those who recognise that freedom is available to them, who understand that Satan has lied to them for too long, and who accept the offer of joy and salvation, which each one of us can experience when we respond to God.

And this is exactly why we are not hearing enough about those who have walked out of the homosexual lifestyle. Our message is countercultural; our message is a difficult message for churches who have preached that homosexual acts are not forbidden, nor sinful, to reconcile. How can they then explain away the message of freedom being spoken of by people who once agreed, as they did, that sexual identity and sexual orientation were innate and unchangeable? Where does the "ex gay[204]" congregant fit into their community? Where does the message that says, Satan has lied to me, but God has set me free, fit into a church that has followed the path of false teaching for so long?

Even more difficult, is the conversation with those outside of the church, who are convinced that homosexuality and feelings of SSA could not be something that people would want to overcome. Particularly in the States, we read of many court cases trying to ban any form of counselling for those with unwanted SSA. The story here is that where any young person may feel confused over their sexuality and seek help with transitioning, if

---

[203] https://www.merriam-webster.com/dictionary/revival
[204] Ex-gay – I don't like this term, but it is used simply to illustrate that some people no longer identify as gay.

239

that same young person is confused, yet expresses a desire to challenge their feelings (perhaps wishing to remain faithful to God's Word, or even as a non-Christian desiring to marry and have a family), the help they are seeking may soon be illegal.

In both situations, whether with Christians or non-Christians, Satan's fighting hard to silence the good news of our testimony. He is fully aware that it is by the word of our testimony that he will be defeated; is it any wonder that the battle is on? Many who report on those who have found freedom are now questioning their transformation and accusing it as being the outcome of 'conversion therapy.' This is a clear attempt to undermine our testimony and to deflect attention away from the power of the Holy Spirit. When we as Christians talk to the press and say, I've not been to counselling, I've not been to therapy, no one has 'prayed the gay away', my change has come because I encountered the Holy Spirit who changed me, they are unable to understand (the truth of God's Word is hidden from those who don't believe). Using the misnomer, 'conversion therapy,' to explain what they see as a temporary change in us, helps keep the myth alive that change is not possible. From a church perspective, it is not necessarily how people have changed, or encountered the Lord, which is in question, it is the need for change itself which is so often questioned. But God is changing things; the more I have opportunities to bring my testimony to a Christian audience, the more I feel that He is on the move, changing hearts and minds.

As Christians, whatever our background, we hold a significant role in helping to share the good news and testimony of those who have found freedom. For as long as we are deceived by Satan's smoke and mirror illusions, we do our Christian brothers and sisters a disservice. If we, as Christians, discount their testimony, we not only contribute to hurt and division within our churches, but we also contribute to Satan's master plan; that is to confuse and befuddle, to distract and misinform, to unsettle and demoralise, to cause utter confusion and chaos within the church.

240

I do not know what your personal circumstances are, but if you have changed your theology because a friend or family member came out to you, what will you do when they tell you they were wrong, that they have repented and no longer live in homosexual sin? Do not allow misguided family loyalty to cause you to stumble and turn your back on the Word of God. This is the very Word that cuts through joints and marrow, through spirit and soul, the Word that judges the thoughts and attitude of the heart.

If you yourself struggle with SSA, was your approach to reading the Bible one that started with the premise; God's Word is truth, God's Word is without flaw, God's Word is perfect in every way? Were you open enough to pray before seeking an answer to what God's Word said about SSA? Ask yourself honestly, did I ask God to open me up so that I could receive His truth, and did I commit to obeying whatever He said through His Word with joy, knowing that God's ways are always the best? Or did I read His Word through a lens that said God created me gay, therefore that must be His will for me, and His Word will show me how I can live within His will?

The second question I have for anyone struggling with SSA is this, 'Where in the Bible is it clearly stated, or shown that homosexuality is not sinful? Or where in the Bible is it stated or shown that it is fully acceptable in the eyes of God?' That is the challenge I put out there, and I have never found anyone able to meet the challenge without fudging their answer, using inference or innuendo, or seeking to re-interpret words that are already clear in their meaning. I think this question is one that we could all go back to, bearing in mind the clarity with which the Bible does declare that we should flee sexual immorality.

Rather than embracing smoke and mirrors, let me encourage you that the time has come to fully embrace our brothers and sisters who have found freedom from the LGBTQ+ lifestyle. Let us shout about their testimony of freedom from the rooftops, being secure in God's Word as we understand that He is holy. Revival is coming have no doubt; God is calling His children home. How great it would be if the church stood united, equipped, and prepared to stand together in prayer as this battle is fought, and victory is won; as lives are set free, families reunited, and disciples are made.

> *How good and pleasant it is when God's people live together in unity! It is like precious oil poured on the head, running down on the beard, running down on Aaron's beard, down on the collar of his robe. It is as if the dew of Hermon were falling on Mount Zion. For there the LORD bestows his blessing, even life for evermore. Psalm 133 (NIV)*

TESTIMONY, THE REV12 PROJECT

Revival is coming and we believe that the time is already here when many are actively seeking answers. People are no longer satisfied with lukewarm teaching and platitudes from Christians who have no idea of the depth of unhappiness and pain that there is within the LGBTQ+ community. People want truth and sincerity; they want to know that there is something more, to hear people's testimony and make their own minds up. The Rev12 Project provides an insight into the pain, the reality of the life experienced by many members of the gay community, and then the freedom when they finally meet Jesus. Here is a testimony from one of the co-founders of the Rev12 Project (www.rev12project.com)

I grew up in church. I loved Jesus and enjoyed serving Him. I always felt a bit different (sportier) than most girls but never thought much about it. I was emotionally dependent on my same-sex friends. Upon experiencing my first sexual encounter with a woman, my world radically transformed for the worse. I lost all sense of who I was in Christ.

Although the relationship had ended for years, I could not help but think about the "what ifs" of being in a romantic relationship with a woman. I started watching all kinds of lesbian films/TV shows, music, and began hanging out with gay-affirming friends. I sought 'truth' about who I was and why I felt so different. I suffered in silence, as I did not feel comfortable speaking of how I was feeling with anyone, especially anyone from the church.

I eventually gave in to my curiosity and left the church completely, because I did not want to be a hypocrite. I began to do things I told myself I would never do, such as pre-marital sex, drugs, parties, alcohol etc. I hated the person I was becoming. I was very depressed, and just wanted to self-isolate. I would smoke a lot of marijuana to numb my feelings until, one day, I could not take it anymore and prayed for God to help take me out of the mess I had made for myself.

God met me exactly where I was and, shortly thereafter, I started dating a guy I met at Bible camp a few years prior. Since I was dating a man, I thought I was healed and was officially "normal"! I never truly fully surrendered to God, and I still carried a lot of emotional baggage/sin from my backslidden days. A year later, I fell again with a woman. And that is when I really realized that I had a problem and needed God's help.

I repented and immediately got plugged into a Christian group for persons struggling with unwanted SSA. For the first time in my life, I was putting in the work and admitted that I had these types of feelings. It was weird at first, because I had been taught not to disclose these kinds of thoughts with others. By confessing my sin, establishing accountability, and diving into God's Word daily, I am no longer ashamed or shackled by my previous bondage. I openly share my testimony now with others and I only care about what Christ thinks of me. I am free in Jesus Christ and more in love with Him than ever.

> *"Now the Lord is the Spirit, and where the Spirit of the Lord is, there is freedom. And we all, who with unveiled faces contemplate the Lord's glory, are being transformed into His image with ever-increasing glory, which comes from the Lord, who is the Spirit." 2 CORINTHIANS 3:17-18*

Chapter 15 – An Overview, Questions and Challenges

Smoke and mirrors - an elaborate, yet effective tool that Satan has been using to attack the church throughout the centuries, can be quickly dispersed by those who recognise the holiness of our God; those who know that we can reflect that holiness in our own lives. This last chapter is a recap of what has gone before, to remind us of God's presence at the centre of every smokescreen thrown up by Satan. The plan is to equip us to fight back with the holy form of smoke and mirrors, no longer to be conned, duped, or snared. In fact, just the opposite, being fully aware of Satan's battle plan, we can laugh in the face of his schemes, trusting in the truth of God's Word and the power of His anointing upon us.

Please dip in and dip out of this chapter as you see fit, considering the questions posed, and taking the challenges with an open and receiving heart.

Chapter 1

In the introductory chapter, we established that Satan lies to us all and there are times when all of us will listen and be taken in by him. We need to break his hold over us and can do this by putting ourselves in places and situations where God can talk to us either directly, or through the ministry of others.

I do not feel that it is up for debate as to whether Christianity is under significant attack by Satan; it seems clear that we are all in agreement on that. Can we also agree that the family is a clear target, and homosexuality/gender dysphoria a preferred tool used by Satan to cause disruption and to break up traditional family units, and cause division within the family of God? The attack is threefold:

1. Persecution of individuals and churches.
2. An attack on strong moral teaching, which comes from our biblical roots.
3. False teaching.

We need to recognise the three points of attack to equip ourselves and fight back. As soon as we determine that there are many who are trying to silence or discredit those who speak out about sexual immorality, we can battle against their words.

Challenge. Can you see the three points of attack for yourself and thereby equip yourself to reverse the impact of persecution, attacks on our moral teaching and the prevalence of false teaching?

Within this first chapter, we were reminded of Paul's exhortation to not be conformed to the patterns of this world. This is a challenge to us all, regardless of whether we are new Christians or have been Christians for many years (for even those who have longevity in their faith are susceptible to attack).

Question. Are you set apart, prepared for the day when we will all stand before God's judgement seat, a day where the truth will no longer be negotiable or open to human interpretation?

This question is not one we can take lightly, for we will be answerable to God for everything we say and do in this life.

Chapter 2

In chapter 2 we were also challenged, understanding that Satan's intention was always to suck us into his lies.

Question: Are we humble enough to recognise that deception is possible?

246

If we are too proud to admit that we could fall prey to this deception, we are the most likely to be deceived. Let us remember that it was Eve, who had an intimate relationship with God, who first fell foul to deception, and Satan continues to use those five little words to this day, 'Did God really say that?' Satan is relentless, and like Eve we may not cave immediately, but we do need to get to the stage in our faith where we can stand tall, extend our backbone, and rebuke his lies. It is so important to trust God because He does know what is best for us.

Question: Are you at the point where you know God's Word inside out and you can confidently rebuke Satan's lies?

Like Jesus when he was tempted in the wilderness, we need to use the Word of God as our weapon of choice.

There was also a reminder in this chapter to pick up your cross and follow Jesus. There are some people who continue to shape Christianity into everything they want it to be, rather than everything God designed it to be. Our challenge is to no longer follow the crowd, but to get ourselves in the best possible position to live a holy life.

Question: Are you immersing yourself in all that is holy so that you can discern the spirits and remain securely rooted in the faith?

Chapter 3

Chapter 3 explored whether the writing really is on the wall and if so, asked the question, "Where are the Daniels who can interpret it?" Is it fair to say that we are a generation who are wavering in our belief of the Bible? Maybe there are more people around us who are religious, as opposed to people who are full of faith in Jesus. We might be seeing more people in our churches who are talking the talk, as opposed to those walking the walk. Knowing that God expects a sacrifice from us we ask the question:

Question: What kind of sacrifice do I bring, an empty one, or the sacrifice of a broken and contrite heart?

247

And then there was the further question of how we approach the Bible, are we open and desiring?

Question: *When I read the Bible, do I come with a simple heart and a teachable spirit?*

Challenge. *If the answer is no, are you prepared to revisit the Bible with the mind of a child, learning from it with childlike enthusiasm and trust?*

As we looked at Jeremiah there came some stark warnings for leaders. If you are a leader, and bear in mind that whatever your position within the Christian faith others will be looking up to you, then you are challenged:

Challenge. *What are you teaching others about what God says when it comes to homosexual acts? If you are teaching that homosexual acts are not sinful, then ask yourself whether you are:*

    i.   Encouraging people to live in a sinful lifestyle.
    ii.   Shutting down hope for those who want to repent.
    iii.   Marginalising those who follow God's Word.

Let us not forget that God has elevated expectations of those who shepherd his flocks.

The warning here is also aimed at those who recognise the sin of homosexuality but misuse their position as leaders; those who condemn, without thought of the pain and suffering their condemnation causes; those who do not practice the commandment to love your neighbour as yourself; those who in their pride see this sin as worse than their own and who may cause even just one of God's children to turn away.

Question: *If you agree that the Bible is in fact clear about homosexual acts being sinful, are you confident that you are not judging others, perceiving their sins as worse than your own?*

It is easy sometimes to have a holier than thou attitude; the gentle reminder is to let him who is without sin cast the first stone. However, it is also true to say, as Jesus did, when we are presented with situations

248

where people are seeking a relationship with God, 'repent and go and sin no more.'

Jeremiah spoke about lying and false prophets.

Question: Do you know who the lying and false prophets may be in your community? Is there any chance that you could fall into this category?

Beware of teaching free grace; beware of watering down God's word in a compassionate attempt to be politically correct or fully inclusive. We must all come out of the deception into God's light.

Chapter 4

In chapter 4 we started to look at the various smokescreens that Satan uses, recognising these as part of the spiritual warfare that we were clearly warned about.

Challenge. Pray the prayer from Psalm 118, 'Open my eyes that I may see wonderful things in your law.' In praying this with a sincere and open heart, we are inviting God to mess up all our preconceived ideas and reveal His truth to us.

In this chapter, we also considered sexual temptation, the clouding of our understanding of sexual desire and sexual design.

Challenge. What do you personally feel about singleness? Think about your attitude towards those who have not married; do you consider them second class citizens? If so, how might you change your attitude towards singleness?

Question: Do you think of sex as a right, a self-serving pleasure, or do you see sex as a gift from God reserved for marriage?

You may have strong opinions on this; often our opinions have been shaped by our families and our peer group.

Question: How might your opinions change if you took some time to study the Bible afresh, with no external influences?

We also considered pride, and we know that the Bible teaches humility over pride, so therefore it is not an attitude that we should harbour. Transformation is only possible when we ditch our pride, humbly asking God to forgive and transform us.

Question: *Have you relinquished your old identities?*

Giving our lives to Jesus necessitates a total surrender of who we once were. Conduct a self-audit, who do you say you are, as opposed to who God says you are?

Our thoughts and actions are often shaped by cynicism and bitterness. Sometimes we carry this for many years before we finally see the light.

Question: *Are you carrying bitterness? Do you feel that it is unfair that to follow Jesus your sexuality or the sexuality of others is called into question?*

Talk to Jesus about this; He is not unable to sympathise with our struggles and will offer us the answers and the strength we need to remain faithful to His commands.

And finally, in this chapter we talked about our faith, and the importance of having a strong and unwavering Faith in God and His Word.

Challenge. *How strong is your faith, are you confident in your understanding of God's Word, or are you occasionally or maybe often, tossed and turned like the waves of the sea? How can you strengthen your own faith to ensure that you remain firm in your understanding of God's intentions for how we live our lives?*

Chapter 5

Having spoken about smoke in all its negative forms, this chapter turned to the sheer beauty of God's holy smoke.

Challenge. *Prayerfully re-read Revelation 15: 3-4, consciously thinking about the holiness of God, consciously drawing close to His power. Do* *this, not in the familiar way which we may have gotten too used to, but in a reverent and awe filled manner, recognising the enormity of blessing we receive as we are able to approach our Creator, God. How does this change your perspective of God's Word?*

Question: *Is your church or church denomination growing? If yes, can you see how God's glory is being managed correctly? Sadly, if you answered no, can you see where compromise, and liberal theology has undermined the holy Word of God?*

Church is to be led by strong and committed leaders, who take everything to God in prayer. It may be time for you to do a health check on your leaders, or on yourself if you are a leader.

Challenge. *Is the heart of your leadership team to see the glory of God manifested within your church family and communities? Do they see and do life through God's eyes? And finally, do they preach the gospel, standing on the authority of God's Word?*

There are some church leaders today, who do not like to talk about the wrath of God, but I have sought to show in this chapter that God does experience the emotion of anger. Indeed, we are made in His image, and we all have things that stir up a righteous anger within us.

Question: *Do you believe in the wrath of God; what does it look like to you? How might it affect your approach to those struggling with habitual sin?*

To answer that question, you might like to take the challenge:

Challenge. *Prayerfully consider each of the ten commandments and what they say to you about sexual immorality and God's design for marriage.*

Considering your own position and the position of those who struggle with SSA, the final question posed in this chapter talks about trust.

Question: *Do you trust God to do what is right for you? Do you trust God to do what is right for your SSA friends or family members?*

251

Chapter 6

Don't you just love the fact that Jesus took time to warn us about the devil and his schemes? He did not leave us ignorant or in the dark; He was up front and direct.

Challenge. Think about the ways you are tempted; how good are you at resisting temptation? Consider in what ways remaining celibate, in the light of SSA, can be used by God to build that person into a stronger disciple.

Recognising that coming to faith is not all about "what will God do for me?" but rather, "what am I going to do for God?" we start to see that there will be an element of sacrifice as we commit to living our lives differently.

Challenge. As with those who live with SSA, our experience of how we manage temptations varies from person to person. Think about the things that you struggled with before you became a Christian. Have you totally overcome those temptations or are you still tempted from time to time? Has changing your attitude towards those temptations involved an element of sacrifice in your life?

If you are not someone who has struggled with SSA, I trust that this challenge will give you a greater insight into the difference between temptation and sin.

There were several warnings in this chapter, one that was key, was warning #2, have we recognised sin as sin, and therefore have we repented of our sin?

Question: If homosexual acts are sinful (as the Bible tells us), does it make sense that those who have struggled with SSA no longer identify with those sins as they repent of their past behaviours?

I asked this question because there are still many Christians who identify as "gay" Christians, albeit celibate gay Christians. This shows that their identity is still partially rooted in their past behaviours, and I believe that we can hope for so much more than partial change, from our God of transformation.

There have been some challenges to people like me who are open about the freedom we have found from SSA, where we have been questioned, accused of lying or of suppressing our feelings. I referenced those people who look like Christians, yet peddle a false doctrine, how important it is to see the fruit of our faith?

Question: Are you inquisitive; do you look for the fruit from those in your Christian walk? What does that fruit look like in those who proclaim freedom from SSA? Compare and contrast their fruit with those who preach a false gospel.

This next question is it difficult one to ask; it saddens me to think that there are those who will answer this question in the affirmative, yet when they arrive in heaven will realise that they have got it wrong.

Question: Will God recognise you when you stand before Him?

We should be sure of our eternal Salvation; we need to be walking in the will of God. We also need to recognise that sometimes that means conflict within our own families. But we do know that those who repent and turn to God do receive eternal life.

Challenge. Are there conversations that you need to have with others in your family? Are you equipped to have these conversations, confident to share your interpretation of God's Word in a loving yet uncompromising way?

Finally, in this chapter, we talked about the crux of our calling, to pick up our cross and follow Jesus.

Question: What is Jesus calling you to address as you follow Him?

For some of you this may be your sexuality; for others this may be your attitude towards those who are different from you. Or it may be that your challenge is to review your interpretation of Scripture, so that you are better placed to teach God's truth and support Christians or non-Christians who   experience   some   degree   of   SSA.

Chapter 7

False teaching has been going on since the time of the early church; it is no surprise to us that it still goes on today. I suspect that we are more open to the obvious false teaching of some church cults, but less aware of the subtle false teaching which occurs in some of our pulpits on a Sunday morning.

Challenge. When you next listen to a sermon, take notes. Go home and challenge the teachings that you heard by re-reading any Bible passages and praying for discernment. Ensure that you do not blindly accept any message you hear without reading it for yourself, so that you are well placed to know if the message is true to God's Word or not.

Paul wrote widely in his letters about sexual immorality, and about the relationship between the desires of the flesh and the desires of the Spirit.

Challenge. Take some time yourself to re-read Paul's letters, with a particular desire to fully understand what he is trying to teach the early church. How does this change your perception of sexual sin?

It would not say very much about God if Christians did not stand out as different from the world. That is why we must be salt and light; if not, we just merge into the melting pot of humanity.

Question: Are you different from those around you; do you stand out from the crowd? Are you confident enough to ask a non-Christian friend, "What is different about me?"

In asking that question of a non-Christian friend, could you then put yourself in the position to talk about sexuality and what the Bible teaches us, asking them how they see your Christian position? This understanding may be a platform from which you can build your testimony or witness, so that you can help others see God's perfect love and plans for their lives.

As well as being different from the world, Christians are asked to live by faith, not by sight.

Question: *Do you have faith in God even for the things you cannot see or understand?*
It sometimes takes that step of faith for us to feel God's power and strength at work within us, as He champions our cause and helps us to overcome our fears.

The last topic from this chapter is that of pride. As we know, God calls us to be a people of humility.

Challenge. *Think about the concept of gay pride. What do you feel about it personally; do you think it is right to celebrate a particular lifestyle in this way? Then ask yourself the same question as a Christian; do you feel it is right to celebrate the LGBTQ+ agenda when you recognise that in effect you are celebrating sin?*

At the end of this chapter, we presented the following question, which I am sure you have already considered:

Question: *As a Christian, does my stance on homosexuality make me different from the world?*

I believe the answer to this question should be yes, but I leave it up to you to consider what you think and whether your beliefs make you stand out from society or not.

Chapter 8

Reflections in mirrors can often distort the truth and that is what this chapter sought to remind us.

Challenge. Reflect again on the names used to describe Satan; consider how these names may reflect any ways in which you have been taken in. I ask the question first posed in chapter 8 again:

Question: Do you take the threat of Satan and his lies seriously?

Taking his threats and lies seriously is important, firstly because we recognise that we need to be on our guard, and secondly, we are then fully equipped to resist and rebuke his lies, because of our faith and our trust in God.

Unless we recognise the diverse ways, people and practices, Satan uses to distort the truth, we are helpless to respond.

Challenge. Consider the seven types of false teacher that Tim Challies identified. Can you identify any of these types of teachers who are around today?

There are many arguments and debates over the interpretation of Scripture and the fallibility of the humans who wrote it. Each of us need to spend time with God and the Holy Spirit in prayer, searching our own heart and conscience, as to whether we believe that all Scripture is God breathed.

Question: What is your attitude towards 2 Timothy 3:16? How does that sit with your understanding of the Bible teaching on sexual immorality?

Challenge. Which sits better with you? Looking at the world and its morality through the eyes of God, or looking at God and His morality through the eyes of the world?

Chapter 9

The way we love, reflects God's holiness; isn't that a beautiful picture? As we were reminded in this chapter, children are vastly different from us adults. Isn't it time that we reverted to viewing life through the lens of a child?

Question: We have been gifted with God's Word. Do you just hear it and move on, or do you soak it up as a child and allow it to direct you in the ways you should live?

It is pertinent to consider whether we are simply seeking to be religious, or whether we have a living faith, where we seek above all things to be obedient.

Question: Are there any lies you are holding onto that you need to unhear or unlearn?

Sometimes lies are so deeply ingrained in our minds that we no longer recognise them as lies, particularly where teaching has been received as a child and we know no different. With topics as immense as sexuality and faith, we may need to go back and challenge a long-established viewpoint, as we seek to honour God in getting this right.

The greatest reflection of our faith is demonstrated in how we love.

Challenge. How do you feel about the saying "You have to be cruel to be kind?" When you see somebody struggling, living outside of God's plan for their life, yet happy, what is your mind-set? Consider whether you should speak or stay silent, how you could speak and the compassion that would be required for your words to be received as those from somebody who is not judging, somebody who genuinely wants that person to live in God's best for their life.

What are our motives for loving those around us; is our love proud, self-seeking or delighting in evil, or are we humble, selfless and searching for righteousness? Regardless of our own interpretation of Scripture, particularly when it comes to interpretations that can cause personal hurt, let all that we do, all that we say, and all that we post on social media be done with the right motivations and purely in love.

Question: If you are heterosexual, what are your motivations for becoming involved in the debate around SSA (whether you are an advocate for same sex relationships being accepted in a faith setting, or conversely, you are a

Christian who remains faithful to biblical teaching on marriage as being between one man and one woman)?

Depending upon your answers to this question, you might find that you are denying God's transformative power. Your motivation may be to bring a false type of hope or compassion to those who struggle, preaching a gospel that says they can continue in their sin. This misplaced compassion could be the downfall of those you are trying to save. There are many positive testimonies of freedom that you can watch or listen to online, which reinforce God's grace and mercy, and display Him as the God of transformation, without the need to compromise and share false hope.

Challenge. Think about the sexual revolution and how life has changed since that time. What effect do you think the sexual revolution has had on Christianity; is this for good or is this detrimental to the good news of the gospel?

We must be careful that we are not being led by the ways of the world; yet sadly, increasingly that is what we see.

Chapter 10

It is so difficult in the society that we live in not to allow things to become idols in our lives. One of the most challenging areas is around relationships. How often we put someone on a pedestal and idolise them, when we are called to have no idols, no other gods.

Challenge. Consider your own attitude to your loved ones or partner. Is it a healthy relationship; do you ever put them before the Lord your God?

Within this chapter there were five specific questions. It may be worth reviewing these again, now you have read the whole book. These questions specifically target the question of idolatry.

Question: Do I accept that my heart is sinful and inclined towards idolatry?

Question: Am I acting in self-interest?

Question: Am I prepared to sacrifice everything to follow Jesus?

Question: Is my identity primarily in Christ?

Question: What does God's Word teach me?

Considering your answers to these questions, you may need to review your own relationships to address any areas of idolatry. You may also use these questions as you support others who struggle with SSA. Asking these questions should help them to see any areas where they may be putting other people or things ahead of the Lord.

Chapter 11

Obviously, our interpretation of the Bible is affected by our life experiences. This is important, but not when we allow ourselves to be deceived into thinking that sinful activity is harmless. We learnt that our focus is important; we recognise that as humans, our focus often drifts. But we also recognise that we come as we are; God does not seek perfection.

Challenge. We will never be perfect. Considering that truth, do you think that you worry too much about what other people think about your relationship with God, and lose sight of the fact that it is what God thinks that is most important?

Question: Do you listen to Satan's lies when he tells you that your temptations define you and that you will never be good enough?

Keeping our focus on God and recognising that He does not require perfection is essential. When we can come to God with a willing heart and a sincere desire to change, that is enough to show Satan that we will not be deceived.

Being open to God's power and presence in our lives results in transformation. The level of transformation varies between individuals, yet it is undeniable that many Christians are not only able to live celibate lives whilst managing their SSA, but there are also countless others who have experienced considerable change.

Challenge. Look at some of the stories on websites such as www.twoprisms.com, www.changedmovement.com, www.rev12project.com, and familiarise yourself with stories of real transformation.

Recognising that the Holy Spirit inspired the writing of the Bible, we see much evidence within it of the need to flee sexual immorality. Many Scriptures are referenced in this chapter.

Challenge. Prayerfully review the list of Bible references from Genesis to Revelation. Consider how important it is to see the bigger picture, rather than to pick out verses in isolation.

Chapter 12

Whilst this chapter may seem most relevant to those who struggle with SSA, those in pastoral positions or even those who want to support family members, may find it worth reviewing in more detail.

Challenge. Look again at each of the eight lies and consider which ones hook you in. As you identify the lies that you have believed or are still believing, take time to pray into each one, asking God for His help in seeing the truth.

This exercise will take some time, and should necessitate reading God's Word, identifying God's promises, and claiming them for ourselves. It has helped me to learn certain Scriptures for each lie that I was believing, Scriptures that I can now use as a positive response to Satan's negativity and attack.

Chapter 13

If Satan cannot lie successfully or deceive us, his next tactic is to distract us.

Question: How easily distracted are you?

I know that if I am not careful, I can be easily distracted. It does not take much today, with all the electronic devices and instant communication encouraging us, to take our eyes off what is important. Recognising that we may tend to be easily distracted is the first step in the right direction towards remaining focused.

Question: *Are there any relationships in your life that are distracting you from your walk with God?*

It is worth bearing in mind that if you are single, it may be the desire for a relationship that is the distraction, that lure of "the grass is always greener on the other side!"

I talked a lot in this chapter about the confusion within the church over homosexuality. It saddens me that this debate so often takes our focus away from evangelism and from important Kingdom work.

Challenge. *Imagine yourself in a vacuum. You are not influenced by your church denomination, you are not influenced by your church leaders, you are not influenced by your family members, you are not influenced by society, theologians, bloggers, or activists. You are in a bubble. You pick up your Bible and you start to read it, with one question in mind, "What does this book teach me about sexual morality?" I then ask you the question, "Are homosexual acts sinful?" What is your answer?*

Distraction often occurs because of disruption in our own lives, things that happened to us or around us which affect our thinking.

Question: *Are you reading this book because a child, grandson or granddaughter or other family member has told you they are gay or transgender? Has their story influenced your interpretation of the Bible?*

It might be difficult to place yourself in that bubble if that is the case, but I do encourage you to re-evaluate your thoughts from a place of neutrality.

It has been difficult in recent years to have healthy debate over this topic, sadly from both sides of the debate there has been little tolerance, and mud has been flung far too frequently.

Challenge. Whatever your stance, can you take time to listen to those who oppose your views? Are you happy to take time to explain your views clearly, concisely and in a way that continues to portray God's heart for us all as His beloved children?

It would be so lovely if we were able to have open and lively discussions, instead of debates that are closed down quickly with accusations of homophobia or liberalism being used as weapons. Let us seek to be people who keep God at the centre of every discussion we have.

Chapter 14

Talking about revival, what a suitable place to finish this book. But the closer we come to revival, the harder Satan will be fighting, as we see with all their gender identity issues that are currently hitting the headlines.

Challenge. Think about your Christian friends who are personally affected by SSA, whether themselves or their family members. Take some time to pray for them; pray for revival to come from the heart of the prodigal community.

Challenge. As you have read earlier, there are many stories of Christians who have found freedom from SSA and transgenderism. Pray that their voices will be heard, the power of their testimony will bring freedom and hope to many generations.

Challenge. Can your church become a church that embraces your brothers and sisters who found freedom from SSA and transgenderism, giving them a platform to spread God's Word? Can you support a ministry of this nature through prayer?

Praying for revival is an exciting prayer to pray. Please continue to support this community in prayer long after you put this book down.

I hope that through reading this book, you now fully appreciate the battle which we are in for the lives of all those affected by SSA and gender dysphoria. I pray if you started reading this book as someone unsure, or even as someone who had mistakenly been taken in by Satan's smoke and mirrors tactics, that you now stand convicted that God's holy Word is clear. I pray that you clearly recognise God as a compassionate and loving God, who has set out His absolute best for His children. I pray that you have the courage to review God's Word, free of preconceived ideas and prejudices, recognising that what God requires of us is for our best; and that is so much more than our best intentions could ever be.

I encourage you to ask yourself this one final question:

Question: *What actions can I take to overcome the smoke and mirrors of Satan, and promote the holiness and transformational reflective powers of God?*

Transformed Ministries offers support to individuals and churches impacted by questions of sexuality and faith. We believe in the transforming love of Jesus to help individuals to overcome temptation and to live transformed lives. We believe that Christ empowers each of us to bring His message of freedom and transformation to others and we want to help church leaders and members to do this with compassion, while not compromising God's word.

For more information on the work of Transformed Ministries please visit our website

www.transformedbygodslove.com or you can email us tbglministry@gmail.com

Also available from Transformed Ministries

Transformed by God's Love – Exploring Issues of Sexuality in the Christian Faith – A Personal Testimony by Sarah Sedgwick

Made in United States
Troutdale, OR
12/28/2024

27354254R20149